Amazin' Avenue Annual 2011

The Writers of Amazin' Avenue
Edited by Eric Simon

WWW.AMAZINAVENUE.COM

ACTA SPORTS

SB★NATION.

AMAZIN' AVENUE

AN SB NATION BLOG

Front cover photo © Nick Laham/Getty Images

Cover and book design by Brad Lappin

First edition March 2011

Distributed exclusively by
ACTA Sports
4848 N. Clark Street
Chicago, IL 60640
(800) 397-2282
www.actasports.com

ISBN-13: 978-0-87946-460-8
ISNB-10: 0-8794-6460-7

To Oscar, who stood by me,
Riley, who always stood by him,
And Kim, who fed us all.

CONTENTS

AMAZIN' AVENUE ANNUAL 2011

FOREWORD

KEN DAVIDOFF

If sports fandom represents a marriage of sorts, then is rooting for the Mets comparable to how Paul Rudd described the institution in *Knocked Up*?

"Marriage is like a tense, unfunny version of *Everybody Loves Raymond*. Only it doesn't last 22 minutes. It lasts forever."

In the age of the Internet, no fans have suffered quite like those who cheer on the Mets. Whether your measure is volume, variety, or just the visceral, the Mets stand out for their ability to break hearts.

If Al Gore hadn't invented the Internet, then some enterprising Mets fan surely would have. Good Lord, do these folks need a community. A support group. The knowledge that they're far from alone in their despondence and frustration.

But the coolest thing happened on the way to some sort of *Heaven's Gate: Flushing* incident (for which the Wilpons, let's note, surely would have blamed Carlos Beltran). Among a fan culture that often seems consumed by emotion, on a medium that can scrutinize every pitch in a Steinbrennerian fashion, reason and logic found a home.

Amazin' Avenue is hardly the only blog to examine the Mets through a statistical lens, but, well... it's the only one that asked me to write a foreword to their annual book. So here we are.

2011 will mark my 17th season around the Mets, in varying levels of frequency; I'd like to think I generally know my stuff. Yet sometimes you're so close to such a situation that you fail to grasp greater truths.

I remember watching Oliver Perez defeat the Nationals on August 14, 2008, at Nationals Park—three runs, six hits, three walks, and eight strikeouts over six and two-thirds innings—and I immediately saw Omar Minaya in the visitors clubhouse.

"Man, Ollie is really figuring things out, isn't he?" I said to Minaya, and the Mets' general manager smiled and agreed, noting, "We've fixed his mechanics."

I know that start was in my mind, more than Perez's overall mediocre statistics, when I (gulp) publicly supported the Mets' three-year, $36-million investment in the daffy left-hander.

"The guy is 27 years old," I wrote, shortly before the two sides agreed to terms. "Mensa is probably never going to recruit him, but he's a decent kid who clearly tries to work with his pitching coaches—Rick Peterson pushed him forward, and then, after the entire team tired of Peterson, Dan Warthen picked up the baton and advanced Perez some more—and has so much talent. He's worth the risk."

Yeesh.

What was Amazin' Avenue's take? Upon the completion of the deal, founder Eric Simon wrote: "From where I'm sitting, Omar Minaya looks like an absolute chump."

Eric and his gang helped me appreciate the value in taking that step away as a baseball analyst. That, yeah, while there's real journalistic value in getting to know folks, whether it's Jeff Francoeur, Jeff Wilpon, Jerry Manuel, or Barry Manuel, sometimes you've got to prioritize the numbers accessible to everyone over the people accessible only to accredited media.

It's part of a greater movement, of course. The induction of Bert Blyleven into the Hall of Fame validated the greatness of Blyleven's actual numbers, trumping the notion that he didn't "look" like an all-time great. Felix Hernandez received the American League Cy Young Award despite tying for the 18th most wins in the junior circuit.

At times, the Mets' universe has felt like one of those remote Amazon tribes that not only shuns modern advancements but also appears willfully oblivious to industry developments. Mets baseball operations under Minaya didn't exhibit knowledge of important concepts like player value, roster depth, payroll distribution, market assessment, and player performance volatility. That ignorance turned Minaya's Mets from a dynamic, promising franchise into a laughingstock in just a few years.

In line with that, many of the team's fans blamed the continuous disappointments on the likes of Carlos Beltran, Jose Reyes, and David Wright, rather than understanding the team's real problem was a lack of quality players to complement that strong core.

Times have changed for the better. Sandy Alderson is one of the most innovative front-office people in baseball history. Paul DePodesta and J.P. Ricciardi are considered disappointments in their respective runs as GMs, the former with the Dodgers and the latter with Toronto, but Alderson has hired them in positions where they can better deploy their clear strengths as talent evaluators.

That's not to say that Alderson won't make some mistakes; I'm extremely skeptical of the Terry Collins hiring, for starters. Overall, however, we can look at the new Mets GM and know that he's using every tool in the proverbial box to improve the Mets.

Alas, life is never so simple and easy for the Mets. Just as they get their baseball operations in order, their ownership is in disarray. As of this writing, the Wilpons are publicly searching for someone to purchase a minority stake in the Mets, which could prove to be an impossible task. Their ownership is in serious jeopardy. At this point, it's hard to know how everything will resolve itself, and how much of that will flow downward to Alderson and company.

Hey, if there weren't angst, these wouldn't be the Mets, right? You're used to this. It's why the two championship clubs, 1969 and 1986 (for those of you old enough to remember one or both, at least), are so revered. You had to walk through fire to get to those parades.

Most of you trudge forward, hoping that Alderson's leadership and intelligence can neutralize whatever ownership-fueled chaos lies ahead. Because you can't help yourselves.

Go with your gut. The Mets may seem at times like some logic-defying force of ineptitude. By reading this book, you can remind yourself that the Mets are, ultimately, just a baseball team. They aren't cursed by bad luck, even if it sometimes feels that way. They aren't "losers" who lack "toughness."

No, when you take a step back and look at things, you'll realize this is a marriage worth saving.

INTRODUCTION

ERIC SIMON

T his book is going to change your life.
Not in the way having children changes your life, or even in the way hearing Pink Floyd—or the Beatles or, I don't know, Rick Astley—for the first time changed your life. But if we did our job, then you will walk away from this book a more knowledgeable Mets fan than you were going in, and that's good for all of us.

As a Mets fan in 2010, you bore witness to a second consecutive losing season and a fourth straight disappointing one from a team whose superstar core appeared to be on the cusp of greatness as recently as 2006. It hasn't unfolded as we all hoped, and the architect of our most recent misery, Omar Minaya, has been shown the door. In his place is Sandy Alderson, an accomplished baseball man who is well-spoken and media savvy in ways Minaya never was, and who consumes information from all sources with a voracity unseen in a Mets executive since Frank Cashen. Alderson has stocked his front office with his old comrades, Paul DePodesta and J.P. Ricciardi, a pair of former GMs who share Alderson's zeal for baseball innovation as well as his skepticism for outdated baseball axioms, a vast body of which has yielded—and will continue to yield—its authority to the unbiased scrutiny of objective analysis.

If 2010 truly represents the death throes of baseball's old guard in Queens, we've done our best to give it a proper send-off. Whether it deserves one remains open to debate. We begin with a comprehensive recapitulation of last season, leaving few stones unturned and discovering many surprises—some shiny baubles, some poisonous slugs—on our way. If you simply can't bear to relive the insufferable dreariness of it all, I'll summarize for you: R.A. Dickey: Yay! Jeff Francoeur: Hiss!

On the subject of Dickey, we spent much of the past year lionizing the knuckleballer-cum-literati on Amazin' Avenue, the culmination of which was the grandest of possible tributes: the "R.A. Dickey Face" Photoshop Contest. Pop culture met Dickey's gaping craw, cast upon a continuum of digital artistry ranging from the charmingly inept to the technically magnificent. You'll find the results of that sociological experiment on our website,[1] but if you want to get to know the man behind the face, look no further than Sam Page's exclusive interview with Dickey contained herein. Both interviewer and interviewee are alumni of the same esteemed Nashville high school, so it was the fulfillment of a lifelong dream for Sam to visit R.A. Dickey at his Nashville home. In the interview, Dickey opens up about books, the fraternity of knuckleballers, and his breakout 2010 season.

We can't put a bow on 2010 without a bit of in-depth analysis, so to that end you'll find a PITCHf/x evaluation of Mike Pelfrey with a particular emphasis on his performance against left-handed batters. As we always strive to criticize constructively, should Big Pelf happen upon his own copy of this book, he'll find within it a tip or two that might just help to even out his platoon splits.

As we move past 2010 and into 2011, you'll notice some things have changed, mainly for the better. The Alderson team is still feeling its way around, but there's much to be excited about, even if the Mets didn't drop as much coin at the free-agency craps table this offseason as they had previously. We start with Ted Berg's primer on the new front office, which serves to introduce Mets fans to Sandy Alderson's management philosophies—and the important ways in which they diverge from Omar Minaya's—as only Ted can: by way of keg-party analogy.

While you relax and acclimate yourself to your new surroundings, Jeff Sullivan will help make sense of the brave new world around you, where gut-thinking has been displaced by mental acuity and intellectual curiosity. You see, two years ago Jeff's favorite team, the Mariners, underwent a similar enlightenment when Jack Zduriencik replaced Bill Bavasi as general manager. From Bavasi's ashes emerged a newfound organizational respect and a rekindled love affair with the franchise.

I know, you're probably thinking that all this talk about intellect and enlightenment points to one indisputable conclusion: The Mets are run by nerds. In a manner of speaking I suppose they are, and Sam will explain why nerdishness is not merely a good thing for the Mets, but why it's a good thing for baseball. He'll also dispel the myth that these are the Moneyball Mets, explaining that they're far more concerned with information—of all kinds—than they are with on-base percentage or market inefficiencies, though both of those things are important, too.

And if you're worried that these emboldened nerds might not have

---

1. amazinavenue.com/pages/amazin-avenue-r-a-dickey-face (http://sbn.to/d5qOdO)

done enough this offseason to compete with the Phillies and the Braves in the National League East, Grant Brisbee will explain why that's no reason to mail it in for 2011. A Giants fan his whole life, Grant watched with delight as a mediocre collection of talent—plus a couple of well-placed superstars—defied all probability by winning the World Series last year. The salient piece of advice: Have hope, Mets fans.

If the Mets are going to make a run in 2011, they'll have plenty of competition from the aforementioned Phils and Bravos, while revamped Marlins and Nationals teams will similarly look to wrest control of the division. We'll bring you up to speed with a bifurcated approach. The first prong takes the form of a text-based adventure game (think *Zork*) which will help restore your proper bearing. The second is a more traditional preview that will flesh out the details and keep you informed through another MLB-sanctioned unbalanced schedule.

Then it's on to the Mets, where we'll introduce you to new manager Terry Collins and his field staff, a group which includes incumbents Chip Hale and Dan Warthen, plus hitting guru Dave Hudgens, loyal organizational soldier Ken Oberkfell, and the return of fan-favorite Mookie Wilson. We'll also preview three dozen players in camp this spring, many of whom you'll already know (David Wright, Jose Reyes) and some of whom you'll know little or nothing about (Chin-lung Hu, Brad Emaus). You'll find textual profiles and illuminating stats to stimulate the mind along with visually stunning charts to please the eyes. And while we can't predict the future (yet), we have 2011 projections to give you an idea of what a really smart computer expects from the Mets.

Maybe you've already written off the big league team and anxiously await a youth movement in Queens, in which case we've got you—and the entire Mets farm system—covered. To properly understand why a farm system looks the way it does, you have to start with the person most responsible for its composition: the scouting director. In one of his first acts as general manager, Sandy Alderson dismissed Rudy Terrasas, the architect of the last five drafts under Omar Minaya. Alex Nelson deconstructed those drafts and, in so doing, marshaled a comprehensive legacy for Terrasas—some of it good, most of it not. To make sense of what Terrasas left behind, we locked Rob Castellano, savant of the Mets' minor leagues, in my mother's basement and refused to release him until his prospect coverage was complete. Haggard and emaciated, he emerged with a meticulously organized list of the top 50 Mets prospects. I'll admit to feeling a mild pang of remorse when we cut the list to 30, but, hey, that's publishing for you. In addition to full prospect profiles, Rob also covers the organization from top to bottom with 2010 reviews of every minor league affiliate.

Not impressed? You want some star power? Here you go: We asked two-time sports columnist of the year Joe Posnanski to set the record straight on Carlos Beltran's greatness, and he happily (and a little surprisingly) obliged with his brilliant rebuttal to the stubborn myopia of the small-minded "Blame Beltran" faction. We also have three-time "Youngest Writer On Amazin' Avenue" nominee Sam Page, who evocatively revisits the seminal moment of his emerging Mets fandom which occurred one night in Levittown. Our second and final interview slots in nicely here, as I had the occasion to grill Andy McCullough of *The Star-Ledger* on his experiences as a rookie beat writer and his unique— among reporters, anyway—penchant for advanced baseball statistics.

McCullough wasn't alive when the Mets won their last World Series in 1986, but plenty of Mets fans were. Many of them are puzzled by the team's aversion to celebrating its history, a fact which was never more apparent as when Citi Field opened in 2009 and one could scarcely tell that the stadium was the home of the Mets. Fear not: Greg Prince and Jason Fry have brought a plan for preserving the Mets' storied—yes, storied—legacy. Jon Matlack is a small part of that legacy, and Alex Nelson ensures that we remember him as the great pitcher he was.

Meanwhile, back in the 21st century, Will Leitch unravels the diaspora of the Mets' most recent playoff team—the 2006 club that came within a Yadier Molina home run of going to the World Series—to determine the current whereabouts of that impressive roster of players. The year after that playoff appearance, the Mets blew a huge lead to the Phillies down the stretch and missed the postseason by one game. That one game was a total stinker by Tom Glavine on the last day of the season, and James Kannengieser wonders if there is a conspiracy afoot. Stepping back even further, Matthew Callan compares the 1999 and 2000 playoff clubs and decides that they were both pretty great.

Well, that oughta do it. If you've made it this far, then I can only assume one of two things: I still haven't convinced you to buy the book, in which case shame on both of us; or you know me personally, in which case, "Hi, Mom!" Either way, I thank you for bearing with me this long, and I likewise thank you for reading our book. I hope it changes your life, at least a little bit. When you've finished, we have plenty more for you at AmazinAvenue.com.

CHAPTER ONE

Ten For '10

Eric Simon

In some ways, the 2010 Mets were a muffled version of the 2009 team that lost 92 games on the field and many more to the disabled list. Last year's club dropped just 84 games and suffered fewer physical setbacks, but it would be disingenuous, and perhaps delusional, to say it was an improvement in any meaningful sense. The Mets still finished 18 games behind the Phillies and they spent an awful lot of money doing so. For a franchise whose history has so often been steeped in disappointment, 2010 was just a slightly different arrangement of the same sad song.

But that's not to say it wasn't without its stories. Shakespeare, after all, wrote 10 (or 11, as some argue) tragedies, some of which are among the greatest stories ever told. You may never see a Summer Stock performance of the 2010 Mets season, but it may nevertheless be instructive to see what value we can glean from its triumphs and travesties. There were dark clouds aplenty, but enough silver linings to warrant a final look back before we shift our gaze to 2011.

Rather than opting for a chronological review which might force us to tediously slog through 2010 one month at a time, this retrospective will capsulize the season in ten distinct parts, each presenting two tales of opposing polarity: one recounting a positive outcome for the Mets and the other a less favorable offering. The good with the bad and vice versa, which is surely nothing new to Mets fans.

Good
David Wright's first half of the season

Bad
David Wright's second half of the season

This could just as easily be a comparison of David Wright's performance against pitchers of differing handedness: He clobbered lefties and was merely decent against righties. Wright's pre- and post-All-Star break offensive disparity is more interesting if only because most batters hit better when they have the platoon advantage—in other words, when left-handed batters face righties and right-handed batters face lefties.

Throughout his career Wright has actually been a slightly better hitter in the second half than in the first, but he didn't hold to that pattern in 2010, hitting quite well prior to his fifth All-Star appearance and struggling—along with the rest of the Mets offense—after the break.

David Wright's Two Halves										
	PA	2B	HR	BB	K	AVG	OBP	SLG	OPS	BABIP
First Half	378	25	14	45	97	.314	.392	.532	.924	.398
Second Half	292	11	15	24	64	.244	.305	.466	.770	.261

While the All-Star break is a traditional point at which to cleave the season, there's nothing magical about that July intermission. Wright's midseason decline actually began a couple of weeks before the break, but we'll use the All-Star Game as the dividing line for reasons of convenience.

In the early part of the season, Wright appeared to have laid to rest the concerns about his lack of home runs in 2009 by hitting for average and power through the opening months of 2010. He was also striking out at an alarming rate, but that was mitigated by excellence in most other areas. Things started to unravel a bit near the midway point of the season when his rate stats—batting average, on-base percentage, and slugging percentage—began to gradually decline. As the schedule wore on, Wright was far less patient at the plate, swinging earlier in the count and drawing fewer walks as a result. The lone positive from this aggressive approach was that Wright struck out less frequently.

Worth noting are Wright's discrepant Batting Average on Balls in Play (BABIP) marks in the early going—when he was prosperous—and in the later months when things went awry. Batted balls were falling in for hits more often when things were going well for Wright than when they were not. This point may seem elementary, but one of the fundamental underpinnings of BABIP is the role that luck often plays in determining whether a ball winds up in a fielder's glove or beyond it (or in front of it). While certain aspects of Wright's plate approach may have changed from month to month, it seems quite likely that he had luck on his side in the first half of the season and, as if to balance things out, found himself without that same luck in the second half.

BAD
Carlos Beltran was injured and mostly ineffective.

GOOD
Angel Pagan was healthy and incredibly productive.

After missing half of the 2009 season with a knee contusion, Carlos Beltran had offseason arthroscopic surgery without first notifying the Mets, the revelation of which led to yet another public relations black eye for the Omar Minaya administration. Beltran would miss the first three months of the 2010 season before returning after the All-Star break to ostensibly provide a boost to a surging Mets team that was eight games over .500 and just four games behind the first-place Braves.

The Mets began the second half with a west-coast swing that saw them drop seven of their first eight games to the Giants, Diamondbacks, and Dodgers as they quickly fell seven-and-a-half games back in the NL East. The protracted skid effectively sucked the life out of a team that, just two weeks earlier, was surging toward the top of the standings. Some unscrupulous writers seized this opportunity to ignorantly indict Beltran for the sins of the team, going so far as to blame the stoic outfielder for allowing his negative energy to pervade and, ultimately subvert the Mets' otherwise indomitable offensive attack.

The misplaced condemnation of a few confused scribes notwithstanding, Beltran did indeed struggle after returning from his months-long stay on the disabled list and was hitting just .214/.324/.324 at the end of August. He looked like his old self in September, but that could hardly make up for a half-season on the shelf and six weeks of subpar performance.

Thankfully for the Mets, Angel Pagan stepped in during Beltran's absence and was not only the best player on the team during the first half of the season, but also ranked among the best players in all of baseball over that stretch. At the All-Star break, Pagan was batting .315, had smacked 29 extra-base hits, and had been successful in 19 of 24 stolen base attempts. He also put on a defensive show, displaying Beltran-like grace in center at Citi Field as well as on the road.

He didn't get, but probably deserved, an All-Star nod for his performance over the first three months of the season, helping to keep the Mets in the race while Beltran's knee was on the mend. Pagan also filled in admirably at leadoff when Jose Reyes missed the first week recovering from an overactive thyroid, as well as when Reyes was inexplicably moved to the three-hole in late April in a classic Jerry Manuel managerial brain fart. Though Pagan tailed off in the latter part of the season—perhaps due to fatigue, natural regression, or both—he did everything that was asked of him in the first half and roundly excelled in all areas. If Beltran leaves as a free agent after 2011, the Mets may not have to look very far to find their next center fielder.

GOOD
Rod Barajas's first six weeks with the Mets

BAD
Rod Barajas's last eight weeks with the Mets

After giving 306 plate appearances to Omir Santos in 2009, the Mets handed out modest offseason contracts to Rod Barajas and Henry Blanco to shore up the catching position for 2010. Never much for the walk, Barajas carried a good defensive reputation and had decent pop at a position that is typically short on it. It wasn't long before he had endeared himself to Mets fans, going 2-for-4 with an RBI double on Opening Day. Four days later he smacked two home runs against the Nationals, and readers of Amazin' Avenue were proclaiming, "In Rod We Trust."

Barajas led the Mets with five home runs when the curtain fell on April, and despite drawing just one unintentional walk all month, his gaudy-for-a-catcher .485 slugging percentage made it easy to overlook his other offensive deficiencies. By May 20 Barajas was slugging .586, easily the best on the Mets, and his 10 homers, two more than David Wright, led the team. He still had just two unintentional walks in 125 plate appearances to that point, but he was hitting for more power than Joey Votto, Albert Pujols, and Adam Dunn, so nobody cared—or wanted—to notice that his on-base skills left a bit to be desired.

BARAJAS: LEAVING ON A DOWN NOTE										
	PA	2B	HR	BB	K	AVG	OBP	SLG	OPS	BABIP
April 5 – May 20	124	6	10	4	17	.276	.306	.586	.893	.242
May 21 – August 19	143	5	2	4	22	.180	.225	.263	.489	.200

Barajas began play on May 21 with a .306 on-base percentage—already terrible, even by catcher standards—and it would be the last time in 2010 he could claim an OBP that high. His performance dropped off precipitously as he displayed zero patience at the plate and flailed away uselessly at pitches he had crushed earlier in the season. In the three months that passed from his offensive zenith until he was mercifully claimed by the Dodgers on August 22, Barajas hit just .180/.225/.263, an unthinkably bad composite batting line that was worse than any Mets performance over the same span, save that of 20-year-old shortstop Ruben Tejada.

Nothing obvious had changed in Barajas's swing or his approach; he was merely the victim of what statisticians call "regression to the mean," the natural—and largely predictable—decline of a player who was performing far better than his talent level. Barajas was a career .239 hitter with a .412 slugging percentage; through May 20 he was hitting .269 while slugging nearly .175 points higher than his career norm.

BAD
Japanese import Ryota Igarashi

GOOD
Japanese import Hisanori Takahashi

In December 2009, while the Phillies were trading for Roy Halladay and the Red Sox were spending big money on John Lackey, the Mets went out and signed Ryota Igarashi, formerly a reliever for the Tokyo Yakult Swallows of the Japanese Central League, to a two-year, $3 million deal. Igarashi had missed all of 2007 after undergoing Tommy John surgery, but he was still just 30 years old and brought with him a reputation as a high-strikeout reliever with mid-90s heat. The talent level in Japan is generally considered better than at Triple-A but not quite as good as the major leagues. As a result, projecting Japanese league performances to MLB can be tricky, so it was tough to know exactly how Igarashi's "stuff" would translate.

Igarashi looked good early on, allowing just one run in his initial seven appearances spanning the season's first two weeks. Then a strained left hamstring landed him on the disabled list. When he returned from a successful minor league rehab stint he was about as bad as a reliever can be, pitching to an 11.37 ERA and allowing 28 base runners in just 12.2 innings. Opposing hitters were embarrassing him to the tune of a .932 OPS. For perspective, that's like saying every batter he faced was the offensive equivalent of Cardinals slugger Matt Holliday.

In early July Igarashi was sent down to High-A St. Lucie to work on his command. He rejoined the team in late August and pitched better. Not great, mind you, but when you perform as badly as Igarashi did before his demotion, it would take quite an effort to pitch worse. All told, his first season stateside was forgettable, and one can only hope—given that his 2011 contract is guaranteed at $1.75 million, even if he pitches in the minors—that Igarashi finds a way to get big league hitters out in his second year with the Mets organization.

Two months after signing Igarashi—and just a few days before pitchers and catchers reported to spring training—the Mets came to terms on a one-year deal with Hisanori Takahashi, who had spent his entire career to that point with the Yomiuri Giants of Nippon Professional Baseball. In contrast to Igarashi, Takahashi was a finesse lefty who had primarily been a starting pitcher in Japan.

For the first six weeks of the season Takahashi was used out of the bullpen, compiling a solid 3.12 ERA and striking out 33 batters in 26 innings, an impressive ratio. As it became increasingly obvious that Oliver Perez had no business starting games for the Mets (or anyone, for that matter), Takahashi took Perez's spot in the rotation and shut down the Yankees and the Phillies in his first two starts.

The rest of Takahashi's stint in the rotation was less impressive, though hardly awful, and he returned to the bullpen for good at the beginning of August. From that point through the end of the season, Takahashi appeared in 24 games, striking out 23 and walking just seven as he pitched to a 1.32 ERA In 27.1 innings. He made many of those appearances as the de facto closer once Francisco Rodriguez had been suspended for inexplicably assaulting his girlfriend's father following a loss to the Rockies at Citi Field on August 11.

Takahashi finished the season with a 3.61 ERA and 3.65 FIP, to go along with good peripheral numbers—lots of strikeouts (8.41 K/9), a reasonable amount of walks (3.17 BB/9), and a manageable home run rate (0.96 HR/9). His impressive performance, coupled with his ability to start or relieve, made him an attractive free agent target this winter. The unorthodox contract he signed with the Mets precluded them from offering him arbitration—a privilege they'd normally be entitled to with any would-be free agent—so when the two sides failed to agree on terms for a return engagement, Takahashi hit the open market and signed a two-year, $8 million deal with the Los Angeles Angels.

BAD
Veteran pitchers Oliver Perez and John Maine were terrible.

GOOD
Rookie hitters Ike Davis and Josh Thole were pleasant surprises.

Prior to the 2006 season, the Mets traded disappointing starter Kris Benson and his meddlesome sexpot wife, Anna, to the Baltimore Orioles for a hard-throwing young righty named John Maine and erratic reliever Jorge Julio. Maine spent the second half of 2006 with the Mets, pitching reasonably well and starting three games in the postseason that year, the last a masterpiece in Game 6 of the NLCS against the Cardinals. The 2007 season was even better for Maine, who stuck with the big club all year and led the team in strikeouts with 180, 14 of which came in a one-hit, seven-plus-inning effort against the Marlins on the season's penultimate day that drew the Mets even with the Phillies for first in the NL East. The following day, Tom Glavine pitched one of the most forgettable games in franchise history, and the Mets fell a game short of the playoffs. (For more on that game, see Chapter 22, "Glavotage.")

The past three seasons have been fraught with disappointment for Maine, Mets fans, and everyone else involved. Injuries to his hip, shoulder, forearm, and elbow have robbed Maine of playing time. His innings-pitched totals dropped from 191 in 2007 to 140 in 2008, and down once more to just 81.1 in 2009. Each season began with great promise and ended with the taint of unmet expectations. This past year brought more of the same, as Maine missed the bulk of 2010 with a right-shoulder injury. His pitiful 6.13 ERA was of secondary importance to the scant 39.2 innings he spent on the mound. When the time came for the Mets to tender a contract to Maine for 2011, the decision to cut ties was swift, practical, and decidedly unsentimental.

From the time he was acquired from the Pirates at the trade deadline in 2006, Oliver Perez's career with the Mets has been inextricably tied to Maine's. Though Maine came to the Mets a half-year earlier than Perez, he initially spent some time in the minors, so both pitchers wound up joining the team for the stretch run that season. Like Maine, Perez also pitched well in 2007, striking out nearly a batter per inning without letting his walk rate spiral out of control. Despite a team-best strikeout rate in 2008, Perez's command began to betray him in a manner that was reminiscent of prior failings and a portent of his future collapse.

Perez was just 27 when he became an unrestricted free agent after the 2008 season, but his history was checkered enough to keep most suitors at bay. The Mets were undeterred, though, and signed up for three more seasons of baseball's version of *Press Your Luck*, a 1980s game show whose antagonists were "Whammies," a pack of crotchety little gremlins who sought to steal your hard-won money and laugh in your face while doing it. For the next two seasons, few could be surprised when, every five days, the Mets rotation would circle around and come up square on a Whammy. Over 21 starts and four relief appearances since signing his contract, Perez has averaged eight walks every nine innings. The Phillies' Roy Halladay, one of the league's stingiest pitchers where walks are concerned, has averaged barely one base on balls every nine innings over the same period.

While Maine and Perez brought little but disappointment and frustration, two rookie position players emerged who made 2010 far easier on the eyes, and whose performance suggests that brighter days may lie ahead for the Mets' offense. Ike Davis, the son of former Yankees All-Star reliever Ron Davis, was selected 18th overall by the Mets in the 2008 draft, a compensation pick awarded when Glavine shuffled back to Atlanta after pitching the Mets out of the 2007 playoff hunt on the last day of the season. Davis hit .298/.381/.524 between High-A St. Lucie and Double-A Binghamton in 2009, and laid waste to Triple-A pitching through the first ten games of 2010 before he was called up to the Mets to replace the recently dispatched Mike Jacobs.

Davis made his big league debut on April 19 against the Cubs and went 2-for-4 with an RBI in a 6–1 Mets win. He continued to dominate major league pitching for the next three weeks, hitting .311/.427/.525 through his first 19 games and looking every bit the pro. His early excellence was hardly limited to the batter's box, as Davis made three highlight-reel catches that sent him tumbling over the fence in front of the Mets' home dugout. The defensive acrobatics became so routine for Davis that the Brooklyn Cyclones held a giveaway promotion featuring an upside-down bobblehead of his likeness.

But it wasn't all good for Davis in his rookie season, as a woeful three-month stretch from mid-May to late August led many to question his ability to adapt to pitchers who had themselves adapted to his initial stretch of dominance. Davis rediscovered his stroke as August drew to a close, though, hitting .329/.435/.514 over his final 41 games and picking up a couple of Rookie of the Year votes for good measure. If you start and end well enough, most folks will probably forget about the middle bit altogether. Davis ended the season on an upswing, and his impressive performance at the age of 23 augurs well for his future.

Davis had a two-month head start on catcher Josh Thole, who was called up to the Mets in late June as a hedge against Rod Barajas's wonky back. Thole wound up sticking with the team for the duration of the season and hit well enough to be considered the favorite to take the starting catcher spot in 2011.

Thole doesn't hit for much power, but his compact swing leads to plenty of line drive base hits and a fair share of hard outs. He also has a mature command of the strike zone that hitters many years his senior should envy—I'm looking at you, Mr. Francoeur—and what he may lack in punch he makes up for with discipline and preparedness. Even if he never becomes any kind of slugger—he doesn't exactly have superstar upside—he should find his way on base often enough to be useful. He's also still figuring things out as a catcher, having taken up the position full-time just three years ago.

GOOD
Jeff Francoeur through the season's first ten games

BAD
Jeff Francoeur the rest of the way

Baseball success, both in the short and long terms, is largely a matter of probability. Even the most hopelessly inept "major leaguers" can appear positively dominant for reasonably short stretches of time. Exhibit A in the case of Random Variation vs. Small Sample Size should be Jeff Francoeur, an affable, strong-armed Georgian with scarcely enough power to make up for a thoroughgoing lack of strike zone judgment.

After nearly three full years without contributing much of value to the Braves, the Mets traded for Francoeur midway through the 2009 season and must have been elated to the point of openly weeping at his surprisingly decent production down the stretch. So insatiable is our thirst for redemption stories that many of us quickly bought in to the fairy tale of the still-young Francoeur rediscovering his once-enviable promise of superstardom.

We were convinced all the more when, through the first ten games of 2010, Francoeur had three home runs, seven walks, and was hitting .457/.535/.857. That remarkable 1.392 OPS has been topped just once over a full season—Barry Bonds had a 1.422 OPS in 2004—but is routinely matched or bested by ballplayers of all stripes over assorted week-and-a-half stretches each year. During his hot streak, many were quick to proclaim Francoeur a changed man, suggesting that he finally took ownership of his shoddy plate discipline and, if you can believe it, had literally reinvented himself overnight.

Like a student after cramming for a final exam, Francoeur must have quickly forgotten everything he learned, because the very next day he went 0-for-8 in the Mets' 2–1, 20-inning win over the Cardinals, and thus began his unsurprising fall from glory that was as precipitous as it was predictable. Francoeur spent much of the next four months reminding everyone why the Braves had been so eager to divest themselves of the replacement-level outfielder less than a year prior. He hit just .216/.267/.322 over the next 114 games, failing stupendously at the plate in every way imaginable. So utterly complete were Francoeur's struggles that one could only marvel at Jerry Manuel's stubborn insistence on penciling him into the lineup day after day after day.

By the time Francoeur was mercifully dealt to the World Series-bound Rangers for nonentity Joaquin Arias, those ten glorious days of early April were just a vague memory, fuzzy enough that with a little effort we could quite easily forget they had even happened. The statistical record confirms two things about Francoeur's hot start: it did, in fact, happen, and like so many other out-of-character moments in our lives, it was fleeting and unsustainable.

BAD
Kelvim Escobar was guaranteed more than a million bucks and didn't throw a pitch.

GOOD
R.A. Dickey was guaranteed nothing. He won the hearts and minds of Mets fans.

Desperate for bullpen help last offseason, the Mets sought out former Angels starter Kelvim Escobar and signed him to a major league deal worth $1.5 million guaranteed, plus the potential for millions more in playing-time bonuses. This despite Escobar having made just one start in 2009 and missing all of 2008 recovering from labrum surgery. But the Mets had their man, and their man couldn't even make it out of spring training before suffering another shoulder injury that would require season-ending anterior capsule surgery.

While Escobar wasn't exactly a big-ticket signing, the Mets gave him a respectable deal with expectations commensurate with the money they committed. Instead they got nothing, which can't be too surprising from someone who had hardly pitched in two seasons. However, the paltry return on investment the Mets got out of Escobar was more than made up for by another right-handed offseason pickup, of whom the Mets had little reason to expect anything at all.

R.A. Dickey was born in 1974 in Nashville with an unwavering determination to succeed but, as the Texas Rangers found out after drafting him in 1996, no ulnar collateral ligament in his right elbow. Either that or, as some doctors have supposed, Dickey was born with the ligament only to have it fall away and dissolve over time. Dickey spent much of the next decade floundering in the Rangers organization with a repertoire that was barely distinguishable from any other low-upside minor league starter, save for a curious forkball-like pitch that had been dubbed "the thing." "The thing" turned out to be a hard knuckleball, and with the help of Charlie Hough he was able to turn it into a more conventional knuckler with a repeatable delivery that still resulted in a faster-than-usual time to the plate.

There was no miraculous turnaround for Dickey, though, as he struggled through his first four years as a full-time knuckleballer with the Rangers, Mariners, and Twins. All that time he was working on what other knuckleballers will tell you is the key to throwing the pitch: consistency. Dickey signed a minor league deal with the Mets last winter and began the season with Triple-A Buffalo with little fanfare and no real expectations of him. After dominating the International League for the first six weeks of the season—including a one-hitter in which he retired the final 27 batters—Dickey was called up at the end of May when Oliver Perez was ousted from the Mets' starting rotation.

For the next four months Dickey put on a play in three parts: "How to embrace the knuckleball," "How to win over New York fans," and, the stirring climax, "How to be a big league pitcher." He dazzled and confounded opposing hitters with two different knuckleballs that kept them off-balance and, above all else, off the base paths. His walk rate was impressive throughout the season, an uncommon trait for knuckleballers whose predominant offering has notoriously capricious movement.

Dickey made 26 starts for the Mets from May through September and pitched at least six innings in all but three of them. He allowed three runs or less in 19 of those starts and walked more than three batters just twice. He pitched into the ninth inning four times and completed two of those games, including a 1–0 shutout of the Phillies on August 13. He hit a little, too, batting .255 in 61 plate appearances. Oh, and the faces he made! With every pitch, Dickey bore the gaping scowl of a surprised cheetah or maybe a perplexed ocelot. Iconic and inescapable, it was the face that launched a thousand Photoshop creations.

BAD
Jason Bay on the road

GOOD
Jason Bay at Citi Field

Last offseason the Mets handed Jason Bay a four-year, $66 million free-agent deal and told him to go out and do what he does best: hit the ball hard. For the most part that didn't happen, as Bay turned in an injury-shortened season in which he hit far worse than anyone could reasonably have expected. Even if you grant that Bay was moving from a good ballpark for righty power hitters (Fenway) to an especially bad one, his .749 OPS in 2010 was still well below his .882 career mark. He also missed the last two months of the season following a whiplash-induced concussion after running into the left field wall at Dodger Stadium.

Before he got hurt, Bay generally struggled with the bat in all situations, but he was particularly stymied in Mets road games. In just over 200 trips to the plate, he hit an extortionately disappointing .243/.326/.354 away from Citi last year, or roughly what the charmingly inept Jeff Francoeur hit for the whole season. The numbers tell a different story when the venue shifted to Queens, though. Despite Citi Field's well-earned reputation for depressing the power stats of subsequently emasculated home run hitters, Bay found considerably more success there than on the road last season, hitting a respectable .277/.371/.459 at Citi. It's tempting to paint a picture of Bay having figured out the dimensions of Citi Field in a way that has eluded other hitters, but the disparity can probably be explained in other terms.

1. Players are more comfortable playing at home and usually perform better there. This shouldn't be surprising. In the National League last year, players had a home OPS of .747 and a road OPS of .700.

2. Bay struck out a lot more often on the road than at home, and while it's not entirely clear why that would be, not putting the ball in play is a terrific way to grind your production to a halt. Approximately three of every ten batted balls put into play become base hits, and that doesn't even include home runs, which are not technically considered to be in play, since, with very few exceptions, no defender has an opportunity to turn them into outs.

3. Funny things can happen in a small number of plate appearances. It's hardly unusual for performance to fluctuate, even wildly, from season to season, and there's a much greater likelihood that this kind of sta-

tistical "noise" will factor into a player's production when we're talking about as few as 200 at-bats. That's the equivalent of a rough two-month stretch, and even some of the best hitters go through extended slumps of that sort.

The vagaries of home and road splits notwithstanding, the Mets and Bay will both expect bigger and better things in 2011.

GOOD
Jose Reyes spent most of 2010 on the field.

BAD
Jose Reyes stopped drawing walks.

The 2010 season began inauspiciously for Jose Reyes, who was diagnosed with an overactive thyroid in spring training and was prescribed rest while Mets fans resorted to finger-crossing and nail-biting until, some three weeks later, their franchise shortstop was declared fit for action. Reyes also missed a few weeks here and there with a nagging oblique injury, but after a 2009 season in which he played a scant 36 games, the Mets were thrilled to have him for huge swaths of the 2010 schedule.

Though progress at the beginning of his career was regularly impeded by a laundry list of leg injuries, Reyes averaged 158 games per season from 2005 through 2008 before missing most of 2009. Notwithstanding the thyroid-related concerns, the fact that Reyes spent the majority of 2010 on the field surely came as a relief to the Mets.

Another early-career problem which Reyes eventually outgrew was an aversion to walks. From 2003 through 2005, his first three seasons with the Mets, Reyes coaxed a walk in just 3.6% of his plate appearances, a figure which was among the lowest in the league. About that time, someone must have tapped him on the shoulder and made the point that leadoff men were expected, above all else, to get on base, not just flail away up there like an old man swatting at flies. Reyes showed a marked improvement from that point on, walking in 8.9% of his plate appearances from 2006 through 2009. The evolution of Reyes from free-swinging out machine to keen-eyed table-setter was swift and glorious, and the Mets were the beneficiaries of a young dynamo who quickly earned a spot among the most valuable players in the game.

But in 2010, either as runoff from his spring training thyroid scare, something lingering from his lost season in 2009, or a different reason altogether, Reyes's plate discipline backslid dramatically and his walk rate dipped to 5.1%, his lowest since he walked just 3.7% of the time as a 22-year-old in his first full season. His overall value dipped in turn, and for the first time there was debate about whether the Mets would—or should—retain Reyes when his contract expires after the 2011 season.

It may be fair to consider 2010 the exception to an otherwise encouraging progression in Reyes's career approach at the plate, and in interviews he was quick to acknowledge his lack of patience in the batter's box, even as he was frustrated by his own inability to explain it. Mets fans can reasonably hope that, with a healthy offseason and a full spring training to kick things into gear, Reyes will be able to piece things back together for 2011. If he doesn't, then the Mets will have a very difficult decision to make next offseason when Reyes becomes a free agent for the first time.

BAD
Mike Pelfrey in July

GOOD
Mike Pelfrey in all the other months

While Mets fans mill about waiting for Mike Pelfrey to become the next Brandon Webb, it's easy to overlook the fact that in the meantime he has turned into a very nice, albeit unspectacular, pitcher. His 204 innings pitched in 2010 were the most on the staff, and he was the only Mets starter to take the hill for his full complement of 35 starts. Consistency is key, they say, and for most of 2010 Pelfrey was just that. He took the ball when asked to and usually pitched well enough to win. Far too often, however, the Mets arrived at the ballpark with something less than a passable offense, so Pelfrey may not have been rewarded in the otherwise meaningless win column as regularly as he probably deserved.

Culpability for losses didn't always rest at the feet of poor run support, however, as Pelfrey spent all of July treating fans to his one-man show, "How Not To Be A Big League Pitcher." His 10.02 ERA was just the beginning of the story. Pelfrey walked more batters (13) than he struck out (10) that month, and he averaged just over four innings per start. Here is how he fared in his five July outings:

PELFREY'S ROUGH JULY				
	OPPONENT	IP	R	ER
July 5	Cincinnati	4.2	7	7
July 10	Atlanta	4.0	4	4
July 19	at Arizona	1.1	6	6
July 24	at Los Angeles (NL)	5	2	2
July 30	Arizona	5.2	5	4

Outside of July, Pelfrey was another pitcher altogether. His ERA by month shows just how awful the month was for him:

PELFREY'S MONTHLY ERA	
April	0.69
May	3.82
June	3.52
July	10.02
August	1.82
September	3.86

If you squint a little and hold the page at just the right angle you can blur the July line enough so that its hideous ERA can no longer be discerned, which is really how Pelfrey's 2010 should be viewed: five very nice months and one that you wish weren't there. So miserable was Pelfrey's July that without it his 2010 ERA would have been 2.95 instead of 3.66. That mark would have nearly cracked the top ten in the National League, and while Pelfrey's not really a "top ten in the National League" kind of guy, if he pitches as well in 2011 as he did for five-sixths of 2010, the Mets could wind up with a pretty good starting rotation, particularly once Johan Santana returns from offseason shoulder surgery.

CHAPTER TWO

PELFREY, PITCH TYPES & PLATOON SPLITS

ENO SARRIS AND JOSH SMOLOW

He's 6 feet 7 inches tall and was selected in the first round of the 2005 draft with the ninth overall pick. He's from Wichita, home of the Double-A Wingnuts. He's averaged just short of 200 innings over his first three major league seasons for the team that drafted him. He owns a 92-mph sinking fastball that has accrued over 20 runs above average according to pitch-type values based on linear weights. He gets grounders. He's managed 7.5 WAR in his first three seasons despite earning just $4.7 million in salary. He's even had flashes of excellence.

And yet, the consensus on Mike Pelfrey is that more is expected of him.

Countless articles on Amazin' Avenue and elsewhere have debated whether or not he will actually reach his potential. We've even penned some of them ourselves. Coauthor Josh Smolow took a PITCHf/x-based look at his entire arsenal to try to determine his potential,[1] and my less PITCHf/x-filled Bloomberg Sports piece came to the same conclusion early in the season: Pelfrey needs to work on his secondary stuff to get anywhere.[2]

We've looked at dead-arm phases and parsed his pitches. We've debated if he's actually got upside or if this is all we can expect. Now it's time for yet another attempt to 'figure out' Mike Pelfrey, but this time we're working together and focusing on one particular question: Why does Mike Pelfrey struggle against left-handers?

In his career to date, Pelfrey has a strong 3.51 FIP against righties, built on an excellent 56.7% ground ball percentage and a passable 5.59 K/9 and 2.53 BB/9. Compare those numbers to Derek Lowe's career

---

1. amazinavenue.com/2010/9/21/1699166/mike-pelfrey-a-potential-star-or (http://sbn.to/d2G9Hb)
2. bloombergsports.mlblogs.com/archives/2010/04/big-mike-pelfrey-and-his-soft-stuff.html (http://bit.ly/d1lull)

numbers—a 3.80 FIP, 5.88 K/9, 2.59 BB/9, and 62.9% ground ball rate—
and you see Pelfrey has something good going... when facing righties.

Flip to his work against lefties, and you can cue the whammy sound.
His strikeouts drop to 4.65 per nine, his walks soar to 4.02 per nine, his
ground ball percentage disappears (42.8%), and the resulting FIP, well,
at 4.83 it isn't pretty (the league average was 4.08 last year). What happens to Pelfrey's stuff against left-handed batters?

The table below shows the 2009–10 splits for each of Pelfrey's pitches. Keep in mind that he throws the four- and two-seam fastballs a combined 70% of the time and you quickly see where the problem is.

PLATOON SPLITS BY PITCH TYPE					
YEAR	PITCH TYPE	NUMBER THROWN	BATTER HANDEDNESS	Swinging Strike %	GB%
2009	Changeup	123	LHP	8.9%	43.8%
2009	Changeup	11	RHP	0.0%	33.3%
2009	Curveball	107	LHP	13.1%	57.9%
2009	Curveball	30	RHP	6.7%	100%
2009	Four-Seam FB	560	LHP	5.5%	32.2%
2009	Four-Seam FB	484	RHP	6.2%	47.3%
2009	Two-Seam FB	820	LHP	5.2%	53.8%
2009	Two-Seam FB	569	RHP	6.9%	64.5%
2009	Slider	154	LHP	5.8%	22.2%
2009	Slider	261	RHP	7.7%	47.1%
2010	Curveball	157	LHP	10.8%	33.3%
2010	Curveball	28	RHP	7.1%	33.3%
2010	Four-Seam FB	681	LHP	6.5%	33.9%
2010	Four-Seam FB	571	RHP	5.6%	43.5%
2010	Split-Finger FB	387	LHP	9.0%	50.0%
2010	Split-Finger FB	216	RHP	11.1%	51.7%
2010	Two-Seam FB	543	LHP	6.3%	38.6%
2010	Two-Seam FB	513	RHP	5.5%	61.9%
2010	Slider	70	LHP	2.9%	50.0%
2010	Slider	217	RHP	7.4%	61.8%

Look at the ground ball rates for the two fastballs. His two-seam fastball gets 61.9% ground balls against righties, compared to only 38.6%
ground balls against lefties. That's a huge split—he's a ground ball pitcher against one, a fly ball pitcher against the other.

At this point in his career, it's probably not going to be about whiff rates for Pelfrey, and the table shows that. The average swinging strike rate across baseball is usually around 8.5%, and only Pelfrey's split-finger managed that number against batters of both hands. From the amount that he uses the curve, and the fact that he uses it mostly as a first-pitch attempt at a surprise strike, we can assume it's just a show-me pitch.

So we are left with a split-finger that gets whiffs and ground balls against batters of both hands, and two fastballs that have poor platoon splits. It can be tricky to advise a pitcher to throw a secondary pitch more often since it may cease to be effective as batters see it more often and learn to anticipate it. But the split-finger gets whiffs and ground balls and works against lefties. Should Pelfrey use it more often against opposite-handed hitters? The answer: probably.

If you look at Pelfrey's 2010 month-by-month splits for his splitter, you might wonder why its usage seems to be going in the wrong direction.

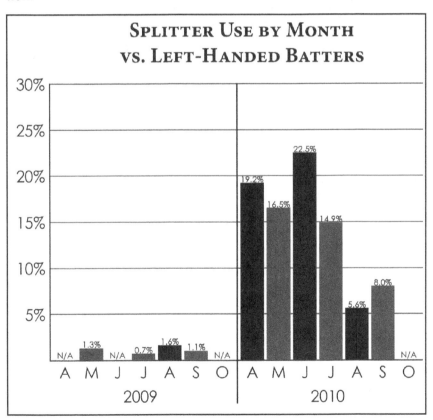

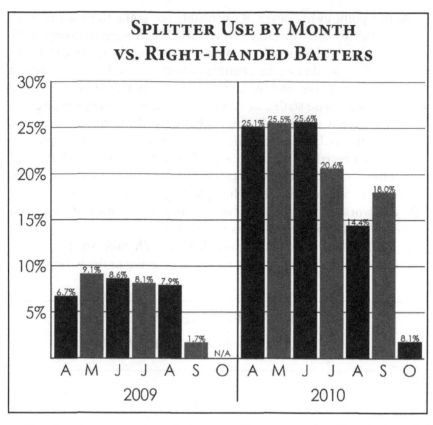

Despite a less pronounced platoon split compared to his other pitches, Pelfrey never used the splitter as often against lefties as righties. He didn't even use it 10% of the time against lefties in the second half of '09.

Other than a dip in late-season ground balls against lefties, there's little in the pitch splits to suggest that it had lost effectiveness. And since that sample size was a mere 110 pitches or so, perhaps Pelfrey should use it more often when facing left-handers.

That still leaves the troubling platoon split with the two-seam fastball. The 20% difference in ground ball percentages seems daunting, but the pitch is otherwise too good and too fundamental to his approach to advise scrapping it against lefties entirely.

Perhaps there is something about the pitch—or how he uses it—that leads to this split. Keeping in mind that the strike zone starts a foot and a half above the ground, look at the distribution of Pelfrey's two-seam fastballs. We can see that he throws most of the two-seamers around eight-to-ten inches off the bottom of the strike zone.

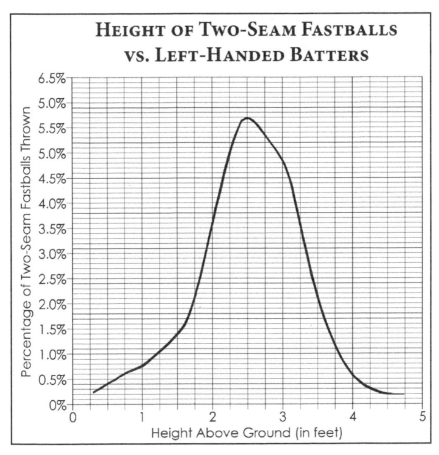

Almost any pitch benefits from being kept away from the middle of the zone, but it looks like Pelfrey's two-seamer, in particular, should also be kept down in the zone.

The next graph shows how Pelfrey's ground ball rates on two- and four-seam fastballs correspond to the height of the pitches as they cross the plate. The ground ball rates against left- and right-handed batters are informative, though the discrepancies between the results are striking, too.

GROUNDBALL RATE
BASED ON FASTBALL HEIGHT

- - -Two-Seam Fastball
——Four-Seam Fastball

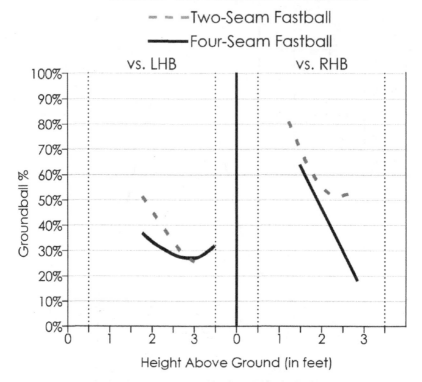

Clearly, his two-seamer should be thrown about six inches off the bottom of the plate if ground balls are the goal. It's also interesting to see the platoon split inherent in the pitch—all pitchers get a lower ground ball rate, on average, from their two-seamer when going against left-handers—so Pelfrey may gain from getting the pitch farther down.

It looks like he stands to gain significantly—as much as ten percentage points in ground balls—by locating his two-seamer six inches lower. Add some added confidence in, and reliance on, his split-finger, and Pelfrey might be able to iron out some of his platoon issues in the upcoming season. Since his FIP (3.82) was higher than his ERA (3.66) in 2010, such an improvement may not mean a lower ERA, though.

Certainly, smoothing out the platoon splits would help Pelfrey be more consistent from start to start.

CHAPTER THREE

A Conversation With R.A. Dickey

Sam Page

"Southern hospitality isn't some myth. The people down here are more cordial than you might find up north or on the East Coast."
—*Barry Trotz, Nashville Predators Head Coach*

The first 500 times I walked past R.A. Dickey's corner of my high school's trophy case, I didn't think much of it. People stopped to notice trophies at my school like New Yorkers notice yellow cabs and crosswalk signals. After all, I knew Dickey's story, at least in general terms. He was another flame-thrower who burned out in the minor leagues, an electric arm that couldn't keep the power on, another chapter in the Texas Rangers' quixotic quest to replace Nolan Ryan. I knew there was something wrong with his arm, but didn't know what. Most pitching prospects lose their careers to arm injuries in the minors, anyway. Nothing to write home about.

I thought I knew all this, because I had googled the name on those trophies once. And when you read my other chapters in this book, you'll realize I still believe in the deductive power of googling a player's name and looking at his stats. Around 2006, R.A. Dickey's stats typified the young-power-arm-falls-apart pattern. When you start sorting through the numbers, you realize this unfortunate career path is the norm for young pitching prospects, not the exception. Dickey seemed like the perfect player to have a shrine to his greatness in a dark corner of his former high school—the young athlete whose star slowly faded with age. I half-expected him to show up any day and be the full-time pitching coach for our varsity squad.

Dickey ultimately did return to Nashville in 2007, but coaching was probably the last thing on his mind. He had no time to teach. He was still learning the knuckleball, and the Triple-A Nashville Sounds were a fitting team for his rebirth. To truly master the unusual pitch is to discover baseball's fountain of youth. The knuckleball knows nothing of typical career trajectories, age, or missing ulnar collateral ligaments.

Dickey returned to Nashville exactly as he had left it ten years earlier: as a prospect.

From that summer on, I predicted big things for R.A. Dickey. The only story I ever wrote for my high school paper was a celebration of his return to the majors in Seattle. His story became as triumphant and extraordinary as it had once seemed common and tragic. People like to say about some players that "you have to root for that guy," and R.A. Dickey certainly qualifies. But his continued success took on extra meaning to me, as Dickey embodied the best qualities I saw in the community where I grew up—humble, hard-working, and gentlemanly. Besides, there's something quintessentially Music City about someone chasing his dreams, failing, refusing to give up, and reinventing himself.

At a certain age, you think you're beyond viewing athletes as heroes. There's too much out there to jade you. Meeting R.A. Dickey this past Thanksgiving, however, I felt like my wide-eyed, nervous, ten-year-old self approaching Mike Piazza for his autograph. Over the holiday weekend, and on the day of a University of Tennessee football game no less, R.A. responded to my request for an interview by graciously inviting me into his home. He patiently responded to every question I could stammer out. The results of that interview are below, and I think they're pretty interesting. To me, however, the gesture meant as much as any specific answer he gave. It was a rare, rewarding culmination to years of rooting. R.A. Dickey really is as great as he seems.

❖   ❖   ❖

Sam Page: What's your impression of the new front office?

R.A. Dickey: My impression, which a lot of times is very different then the reality of things, is good. I think it's a good bunch, a thoughtful bunch, that's going to take us in a direction where you might not see immediate results, but you're going to see very deliberate, intentional moves with purpose behind them, instead of just taking fliers on guys and hoping it works out. I think that's a good place to start—having a very prepared, plan-oriented front office and I think that's what we have.

I read your comments in the *New York Post* about Terry Collins and intensity being good or bad. Who are some managers you played under that you liked?

I played under Buck Showalter. He's intense, but at the same time, he lets the players police themselves to a certain degree. I think the best managers that I've played for have struck a very good balance between knowing when to get in your face and what for, and treating you like a man and letting you do your work and letting you be a professional, letting you take care of the business. When you neglect to take care of business, they get after you. But when you take care of business, they leave you alone. I think what our team needs is a guy that Terry seems to bring to the table. It doesn't matter who's on the team, doesn't matter the contract status, doesn't matter the superstar persona. He's going to tell you what he thinks, and he's going to motivate you to be better. I think that's something that we all need.

Can you talk a little more about why he would be good for the Mets specifically? I asked the readers for questions, and people want to know about the clubhouse dynamic, as we don't have any insight into that.

This past year we had a lot of good guys in the clubhouse. When you're in the clubhouse, you can't ever pick your friends. For seven months of the year, you've got to get along and find the best way to do that, find the best way to have the common ground that you need to succeed, where guys are pulling for one another, where guys don't have hidden agendas, guys aren't selfish. They put each other in a good position to win and do their job well. I think that's what we need. I think we're going to have a little bit better leadership from top to bottom this year, which is going to be great. And then, of course, they've been pretty public about not being able to make a lot of moves, because of their financial situation. So you're going to be looking at a lot of the same faces, which isn't all bad either. Guys will start to really be familiar with other guys and how they act, respond, what they need, what they don't need. From my point of view, there's not a lot you can do from a leadership standpoint, outside of just play your butt off. That's all I can do.

As far as a dynamic? From a problem standpoint, we've had some issues. We had our K-Rod thing. We had our Johan thing. We've had a Charlie Samuels thing. The Mets are no strangers to clubhouse drama. I think one good thing this front office will do, Terry Collins in particular, is give us some real stability.

Next year, do you think competing is realistic? What's your outlook going into spring training?

That's a tough question, because most teams, going into the season, are never real honest about what they think. For me, at least for the last half of my career, I've always tried to be really honest with whoever's asking me anything. And to be honest, I think we have presently potentially four All-Stars. So there's no reason why we shouldn't compete. Now, competing can look like all kinds of things. You compete when you lose 2–1, when you lose 80 or 90 games. You still compete hard. But if you mean win a championship, I think that we have a shot, because that's the beauty of the game. The San Diego Padres had a shot and they almost did it. And they hit what, .240 as a team? They just pitched well. We pitch well.

It's all about the culture of the clubhouse. Are the guys pulling for each other? There's so much that has to do with that. Really. It's not just an idiom. The clubhouse matters. If you've got a good work environment, where you can be honest, be yourself, not feel judged, where there's not all these little cliques that are back-biting each other, calling each other out, but are really being honest with each other, supporting each other, then you can do anything, regardless of who's on the team. At that level, you're not on the team because you stink. You're there because you can do it. So it's just a matter of getting the right mix of guys at that point.

I do want to press that a little. How does that manifest? What is the difference between a tight group and not?

I don't know if there's one difference. There's a few differences. For instance, knowing when and how to confront a teammate on an issue. Knowing how to do it in a gentle way that doesn't alienate him, that doesn't cause him to go grab another guy and turn his back on somebody else. In a real healthy way, be honest with him, put your arms around him, embrace him, say, "Look, I know you screwed it up. We need to do it better. This isn't a way we do things." Having guys in the clubhouse that know how to do that well, who can tell the truth, who don't run out of the room when you have a bad game and stay in the room when you're 4-for-4 and answer every question there is. Guys who are willing to stand up with integrity and say, "Hey, I blew it today. And this is why I blew it. And I'll try to be better next time, but today I sucked." Guys who are honest about the way they perform and the way they play. That's two or three instances right there that can really help the dynamic in a clubhouse.

If you've got the majority of guys in the clubhouse who behave in that manner, you're going to have a good team, because the other guys become the minority. And the majority always outweighs the minority, obviously. It's when the other guys are the minority that you have a lot of problems, when you have guys that aren't honest, who are contractually in a place where they're comfortable. And it doesn't matter from at-bat to at-bat or pitch to pitch what happens. And they play like that. Guys who are afraid to tell the truth, who are afraid for whatever reason to stand up and say, "Hey, guys, we need to be better and this is how we can be better." All those things play into it. And you've got to have good leadership. You have to have a good manager to steer the boat. That will really help.

When you came back to Nashville for a year, it seemed like you really became confident in the knuckleball. Obviously there was a practical reason to sign with the Brewers, being close to home. But was there extra motivation?

I think that was just the natural metamorphosis of what went on. In actuality, coming into the '06 offseason, preparing for the '07 season, the Milwaukee Brewers were my only offer. So if I wanted to keep playing Major League Baseball—or at least try playing Major League Baseball—that was my only avenue to do it. So here I was, having spent a year and a half trying to figure out the knuckleball with the Texas Rangers. There weren't a lot of teams out there that were going to take a shot on a 34-year-old knuckleballer who had very mediocre to below-mediocre statistics as a knuckleballer over the past year and a half. The Brewers were willing to do that. Ironically, the general manager of the Milwaukee Brewers was Doug Melvin, the same Doug Melvin who drafted me with the Texas Rangers, who proceeded to see fit that the condition of my elbow warranted a $800,000 reduction in bonus. There's a real neat story line there. But at the same time, it was the only opportunity I had. So when I got here, I really tried to embrace it fully, in that I wasn't ever in between being a conventional pitcher but a knuckleballer. I threw myself completely into throwing the knuckleball eighty to a hundred percent of the time. That was a big stepping stone—really committing to the pitch and really selling myself over to it.

Well last year you threw it 85% of the time, and you talked about not having your feet in two buckets. But a lot of people question the conventional wisdom that the knuckleball pitcher shouldn't mix in more pitches. Do you think you can have both the confidence that

you are a knuckleball pitcher and an expanded repertoire?

Let me answer that question in two parts—first, directly. For me personally, I can't do that, because the reason I went to that knuckleball anyway is because I didn't possess what I needed, as a conventional pitcher, anymore to get big league hitters out. If I wanted to stay in the big leagues and have success, I had to go full-time knuckleball, because what I had to offer wasn't going to cut it. That's one answer. What makes me successful as a knuckleball pitcher is that the hitter thinks the knuckleball is coming every pitch. He can't sit on a fastball in a 2–0 count or a 2–1 count or a 3–2 count or a 1–0 count. When he's got a count [in his favor], he can't just sit there and say, "Here comes a fastball. I'm going to crush it." There's that little seed of doubt in his mind that, "This guy is going to throw me a knuckleball; that's what he does." So I've had to really commit to that. Like you said, I threw it 85% of the time last year, which is a good ratio for me, 85–15 with the other stuff.

The second reason, and a more indirect answer to your question, is that when you're a knuckleball pitcher, it's a real tough thing to go back and forth and still keep the feel out of your hand of what it's like to throw a good knuckleball. So if I'm throwing fastball, fastball, fastball, and then I go to a knuckleball, it's a real tough thing to do, to repeat the mechanics that you need to throw a good knuckeball.

I had to learn this whole process. I learned with Charlie Hough, I learned with Phil Niekro, I learned with Tim Wakefield. You've got to be able to repeat your delivery and repeat your mechanics in a way that you can produce a ball that doesn't spin out of your hand, eight out of ten times. And if I'm constantly going from sinker to slider to knuckleball to sinker, I can't do it. And I know my own limitations, and that helps me to know that I need to throw a knuckleball 85% of the time.

You mentioned all those guys that you tutored under. Is that a fun part of throwing the knuckleball, that it's almost like a fraternity of the game's history? Are you going to reach out and try to pass it on?

I don't read the papers much, but I got a real interesting article sent to me by Rob Neyer [when he was at] ESPN. He kind of chronicled knuckleballers and the years that they were knuckleballers. And it seemed on paper like every knuckleballer had passed the torch to one guy—to one guy! And there's this thing set up where Tim Wakefield's kind of passing the torch onto me. If the situation arises that I can do that for another person, you bet your butt I'm going to do it. Simply because, one, that's the right thing to do, and, two, that's what's been modeled for me. These men who have poured themselves into me, whether it's been Phil Niekro, Charlie Hough, or Tim, have been so generous with their time and wisdom and secrets. It really does make for a real tight fraternity. There's very few people who walk this Earth that do what they do. They know what it's like to stand out there on the mound and feel like you don't have a good knuckleball that day. They know what that feels like. And there's only a handful of guys, literally, in existence on this planet that feel like that. So it's a real neat thing. It really does kind of bond you to another man.

Getting back to something else in your previous answer, you said you couldn't throw a fastball in a two-strike count. But one thing you did—and I think Keith Hernandez compared it to Phil Niekro—is you throw a hard knuckleball and then a softer one. Is that a conscious effort, or is that you just dialing up the same pitch?

It's become a conscious effort. It started as just something that happened. And then the better I've gotten with it.... That's one of the things that I've really discovered has been a component to the success I've had this last year, and something I can really build upon, is that I know how to do it now. I know how to throw one 81 miles per hour, and I know how to throw one 57 miles per hour. And that big gap, and all the speeds in between, are bullets in my gun, so to speak. So, if I've thrown five knuckleballs to Ryan Howard at 78 to 82 miles per hour, then all of a sudden, I throw him a 57 mile-per-hour knuckleball—if I know how to do that well, that's another bullet in my gun that I can get him out with. I really have worked hard to try to do that better. Before, when I was just kind of learning the pitch and learning the mechanics, I really couldn't do that well. I didn't have a feel for it. I didn't mechanically know how to do it. So, yes, now it is a conscious effort, but it's grown into one like it's something that had to be cultivated. It wasn't just [snaps] "Oh it happened." I had to really work on it.

Is there a next step? Are you experimenting with putting more spin on and off the ball?

I think what's next for me is just to really embrace the consistency that I need with it. I've always felt like last year is what I was capable of doing. Rightfully so, I'm sure there's a lot of people out there thinking that it was kind of a fluke year. And I get it. That's part of it. I've kind of been playing to that symphony my whole career, of people doubting what I can do. And that's all right. Truthfully, I'd probably ask the same question. So I think the next step for me is to just continue to be me with it. One of the things that allowed me to have a lot of success this past year is that I really stopped trying to be Charlie Hough, Phil Niekro, Tim Wakefield. I stopped trying to be them, and I really embraced who I was with the pitch and my own personality with the pitch, and that's that I can throw it harder than most guys. So why not throw it hard? I can change speeds with it. Well, so why not change speeds? I still have a good enough sinker to throw 85, 86 miles per hour. Why not use that as a weapon occasionally? So I really embraced who I was and what I had to offer with the pitch this past year, and that was a reason that you saw I had a lot of success. And part of the process of this whole thing is knowing that's what I did to have success. So now it's just a matter of continuing to trust the process and to become consistent. Because what everybody wants on any level of professional athletics is to be consistently good. And so I don't think there's anything that I'm going to have to learn that will make it better, because this year I threw a lot of really great knuckleballs. I just need to be able to throw that great knuckleball more.

What about game-to-game consistency, what's your preparation like? Because there's not a lot of "what pitch am I going to throw?"

Yeah. And that's what's beautiful about it. When I go on a mound, I don't have to work on fastballs down and away. I just throw knuckleballs... for an hour. And the great thing about it is I can throw off a mound more than conventional pitchers, because I'm operating at about 70% capacity, where they're operating at 100, max effort usually. That allows me to work on my craft off the mound more than most guys. And part of my preparation to be able to be consistent is taking advantage of what the knuckleball allows me to do. And that's to throw a lot, to really get a feel for what a great knuckleball feels like out of your hand.

And when you throw a good knuckleball, it's unlike any other pitch that you ever throw in that you know immediately that nobody's going to hit it. Like, you throw and you're like, "There's no chance that this is going to get hit." And it's different than any other pitch you throw. So, that's a neat sensation. It's a sensation that I really enjoy trying to duplicate over and over and over again.

I'll start, then I'll take a day of rest off, maybe watch some film, and then the very next day after that, I'm in the bullpen throwing again. Repetition, repetition, repetition is the name of the game for me. Continually getting off the mound, repeating my delivery, repeating my mechanics, in a way that I know when I get out there I wont have to be going through some mental check list: Is my hand in the right place? Is my stride-length long enough? Am I staying over the rubber long enough? Is my wrist position in the right place? I don't have to do that anymore. That's how I started, but it's really come to a place where it's pretty organic. Now I just react and can be instinctual with it. And that's really fun.

Could you pitch on much shorter rest than a typical five days?

Yeah, absolutely. In fact, last year I threw on two-and-a-half days rest once. The year before that, I threw countless times on no-days rest. I was out of the pen in Minnesota and threw three, four days in a row, no problem. And then in Seattle, I would start and then the very next day be in the bullpen. So it allows you to do some things that ordinary guys can't do and hopefully that's a real asset to a team. Last year, in fact, I started a game at the end of the season. That was my last start of the year, against Milwaukee. I was in the pen and threw an inning out of the pen two days later.

Are you going to talk to Terry? Jerry took you out a little earlier than you might have wanted last year.

I think Terry and I are going to start by having really open lines of communication, so he'll know what to expect out of me and I'll know what to expect out of him as a manager. With Jerry, it was such a learn-about-each-other-on-the-fly, that it was nobody's fault, just kind of the way it was. He didn't really know me or trust what I could do, because he didn't have a lot of exposure to me. Terry's been in the organization. He's seen me pitch quite a few times. He followed me last year, and he knows what I'm capable of doing. So I think there's going to be a real easy transition there. Throwing 130 pitches in a game is not a big deal to me, if I'm going good and keeping the hitters at bay. If I'm getting blown up, that's another thing—you've got to get me out of there, like anybody else. I think that it's going to be a nice transition. He knows I want the ball, I want to throw, and I want to finish what I start.

Do you know if you're having a good game, the same way you know

if you've thrown a good knuckleball—feel it or you can't?

I used to think that. I used to think that it was like that, because that was my experience. Another component to having success with this pitch is now I know that, if I don't have it for an inning or two, I can still find it. I remember a game in particular against the Houston Astros, where the first three innings were the worst I ever felt throwing a knuckleball. I was able to escape some jams and get out of some innings, because I threw enough of my other stuff to survive. But then, after the third inning came and went, I was able to find it again. So, to answer your question, I don't necessarily believe anymore that I have to go into an outing with my A+ knuckeball in order to win. I've gone out there, probably five out of the eleven times I won last year, with a "five out of ten" knuckleball, and it's kind of matured over the course of the game to an "eight out of ten." Which is great, that I can go in and still be confident I can get the job done, not having my best feel.

So mound presence is just as important, even though you're not throwing max effort? People might think you're more relaxed, but you're competing.

It's more important now than it ever has been for me. Phil Niekro shared with me a thing that I've really kept close to my heart, as far as pitching goes. And that is: I throw a bad knuckleball, or I throw a great knuckleball, or I throw one that goes behind the hitter's head, or throw one that he swings and misses and hits him, or whatever I do, always act like I meant to do it. Because the hitter doesn't know the difference, when you throw a knuckleball. That's what I've always tried to do. From one pitch to the next, it's always been because that's what I wanted to do to you. I've kind of taken that and tried to grow it and really feel like that's an important thing. You never want to give the hitter any inclination that you're not confident in what you're doing, or that you don't have it that day, or that you have no idea where it's going. Thusly, mound presence is a huge deal as a knuckleballer.

Armando Galarraga had perhaps the most famous moment of the year, when he lost his perfect game on the last out. But you let the first baserunner reach on an 0–2 count in Buffalo and then threw a perfect game afterward. What emotion is that?

To be honest with you, in the moment, I didn't know what was going on. I got the last out and then I started reflecting on it and I was like,

"I think I only gave up one hit." You're caught up in the game so much. Plus, the first guy's just gotten on, so all that goes out the window. It's not like you've gone seven hitless innings; you know what's going on during that time. The one-hitter against the Phillies? I knew I had a no-hitter in the fifth, when Cole Hamels came up. But the Buffalo game, it was so far out of my purview that I couldn't have cared less. And then at the end of the game, there's all this celebration, and I really started thinking about it, like "Yea, man, not even another baserunner after that guy." So, it was much more on reflection that I was able to enjoy that moment, rather than in the moment with it. With the Phillies game, I knew I had a great knuckleball, and I knew I was throwing well and a lot of strikes and what not. I knew that game was pretty neat.

Who caught the Buffalo game?

Thole.

Poor Thole, he's a convert to catcher. How's he doing?

He's great. And what makes him great is that he doesn't have an ego, which is a big deal. Not having an ego in this game is hard enough. But to be a catcher and to really be completely and utterly for whoever's standing out there on the mound, despite what you may or may not want, is a true gift. Thole offers that. He knows what I need to do, he knows what I'm trying to do, and he works his ever-living butt off to try to make sure that I can do it the best I can do it. He knows it's going to be a tough night behind the plate and he accepts it as a challenge, whereas a lot of guys dread it. He knows it's going to be tough, but he also knows it's going to be fun. We've had some fun outings together, he and I, already over the course of one year together.

You talked about the hard and slow knuckleballs being conscious now—do you start laying down fingers?

No, no, no. There's no game-calling element at all. It's all left up to me, as far as the speeds go. Now, of course, if I'm throwing another pitch, he needs to know that. So a lot of times, we have a way of communicating with each other, where he doesn't have to give me signs. I can do something with my body that will let him know what pitch I want next, and that really helps with a tempo. One of the things, I've always tried to do is work quickly. I am really a big believer in working quickly on the mound and keeping the pressure on the hitter, keeping my infielders on the bench, not out in the field, as much as possible. Thole's great with that. Blanco was great with that. Barajas struggled with it some; he didn't like catching it at all.

When did you throw your first knuckleball?

Oh man. Maybe nine or ten. Probably at MBA [Montgomery Bell Academy], when I was a freshman. 13 or 14.

It was a straight knuckleball? Not a hybrid?

No, just a knuckleball. I remember digging my fingers in the same way I do now and throwing it and having the same kind of reaction. A good knuckleball, whether I throw it or my daughter throws it, is a good knuckleball. That's the beauty of the pitch. That's why people really relate to it. It's almost a blue-collar pitch. You're in the seats and you watch me or Wake or whoever throw, and you're like, "There's a chance that I could do that."

Maybe not at your velocity.

Maybe not, but you could probably throw a baseball 60 miles per hour. A lot of guys in those stands can really relate to that. It gives them, in a very literary, metaphorical way, a link to being a professional baseball player. Because they look at you and think, "Man, that guy... I maybe could do it."

Do you think that's why the Mets fans are so drawn to you? It could be that you're good, too.

[Laughs] Yeah, could have been the other way. You know there's another side of the coin here. I've been on the good side these past few years, and I'm thankful for that. But I've also seen the other side too.

I don't know why. I think they really sense that I appreciate their plight. They just want to win. And they want ambassadors for the Mets that are really going to represent who they are. And I think who they are is a real blue-collar-type folk. [They want] people in the community, going to fire stations, caring about signing autographs. Real people, not superstars that act like superstars. I don't know; you'd have to interview some of them. But I know if I was a fan, that's who I would relate to. I would relate to the guy who had overcome a time to try to get there and when he got there, he really appreciated it, and you could see it in how he played.

I asked the fans what they wanted to ask you—and there was a lot of "what are you reading?"—but also a lot of "Why are you so awesome?"

[Laughs] That's sweet. I'm happy to answer whatever you want.

Well, what are you reading these days?

I'm reading a book called *The Tender Bar*. Actually, it's a memoir. It's a good book; really enjoy it.

My dad just read it.

Did he recommend it to you?

He loved it.

Yea, that's great. I just got finished reading the *2010 Greatest American Short Stories*. It's fantastic. It comes out every year and is edited by someone different each year. There's a great bunch of stories in there, I really enjoyed that. I read a history book about the Middle Ages, which is great. I just got a book from a friend called *The Long Walk*, that I haven't started yet. There's a book I recently read called *The Power of One*. Outstanding book. I recommend it to anybody. So there's a few.

Quite a few.

I've got some more lined up to read. I've just got to finish *The Tender Bar*.

PART 2: CHANGING OF THE GUARD

CHAPTER FOUR

CLEANING UP AFTER MINAYA

TED BERG

Omar Minaya's party in Flushing is over. What started as an enjoyable get-together in 2005 and swelled into a joyous throwdown in 2006 ultimately became crippled by lavish spending and irresponsible behavior. Though it remained at least somewhat enjoyable through 2007 and 2008, a series of myopic and desperate attempts to keep the party raging turned calamitous by the 2009 season.

When Minaya ran out of booze, he sent out for the most expensive liquor in the store without much regard for its quality. Then when he ran out of cups, he urged partygoers to somehow make do by reusing sticky old ones, drinking beer out of coffee mugs, and emptying out the fishbowl for mixing cocktails.

At some point, someone let Jeff Francoeur and some of his friends in, prompting an onslaught of wild and reckless behavior that destroyed half the furniture and shook the house's very foundation. By the end of the 2010 campaign, the keg was tapped dry, the drapes were shredded, and someone had peed in the coat closet (I'm looking at you, Rod Barajas).

With their place in disrepair, the Mets' owners—though they liked Minaya and were themselves present at the party—were forced to evict their GM and turn to Sandy Alderson to fix the place up. John Ricco was permitted to stick around, but really only because he stayed reasonably sober at the party and might be able to help locate the missing goldfish.

Or something like that. In truth, I haven't been to a house party in years. I spend my Friday nights crafting silly metaphors for Mets annuals now. Point is, Omar Minaya, for at least large parts of his tenure, spent his team's resources inefficiently and irresponsibly, apparently crippling the team's ability to add any big-ticket items this offseason and making Alderson's first winter as Mets GM a difficult one to judge.

Notwithstanding a flurry of activity immediately following Alderson's hiring—one that eventually introduced J.P. Ricciardi and Paul DePodesta to prominent front-office roles and Terry Collins as manager—the Mets have mostly been quiet. But under the magnifying glass conditioned by the lack of major acquisitions, Alderson's first series of minor roster moves appears strong.

Catcher Ronny Paulino has mashed lefties to the tune of a .382 wOBA across his career and provides a suitable backup or platoon partner to Josh Thole behind the plate. If Thole—a veteran of just 286 major league plate appearances—falters, the 30-year-old Paulino should be healthy and durable enough to be an adequate replacement on a regular basis.

Pitchers Chris Capuano and Chris Young, both signed to incentive-laden contracts coming off multiple injury-plagued seasons, enter spring training as the favorites for the two open spots in the team's starting rotation. The veterans force rookie Dillon Gee to earn his way into the mix despite his strong five-start audition in 2010.

New bullpen arm D.J. Carrasco proved both sturdy and reasonably effective over his first two full seasons in major league relief. A handful of reclamation projects and bargain-basement acquisitions—including the Taylors, Buchholz and Tankersley, and former Astros lefty specialist Tim Byrdak—will compete with the in-house options for roles in the relief corps.

Former Padre and lifelong Hairston Scott Hairston joins the Mets on a major league deal coming off his first bad season in four years. An obvious bounce-back candidate, Hairston suffered a career-low batting average on balls in play in 2010 despite maintaining his line drive rate, factors implying that he may have been the victim of misfortune. Hairston, with experience at all three outfield positions, was roughly a two-win player per season from 2007–2009.

Familiar NL East utility man and chronic thorn in the Mets' side Willie Harris, scooped up on a minor league deal, perhaps benefits the team most by not being able to play against them anymore. Taiwanese middle infielder Chin-lung Hu, acquired from the Dodgers in a deal for minor league lefty Mike Antonini, is unlikely to provide much offense in Alex Cora's old role but should offer the strong defense that Cora did not.

It always comes back to Cora, doesn't it? Truth is, Cora "earned" more money in 2010 to be a below replacement-level player than any of Alderson's new acquisitions is guaranteed in 2011. And nearly all the new faces offer the team something Cora never could: upside. Capuano and Young were once All-Stars. Hairston and Harris have both been multiple-win players within the past three years. Tankersley has at times sported an outrageous mustache.

Last winter, despite limited resources, Minaya guaranteed the then-34-year-old Cora $2 million and a baffling vesting option, even though the infielder had not been notably above replacement-level since 2004. The deal, though minor, exemplified so many of the failures of Minaya's administration. Not only were the Mets paying millions of dollars to a player almost guaranteed not to provide an adequate return on the investment, they had secured—and dedicated a roster spot to—a utility infielder with no chance of being anything more than that.

In this space last year, in a piece suggesting philosophical changes for the Mets organization, I reviled the Cora deal as indicative of that front office's inability to inform its decisions with statistical analysis. And I argued that the contract represented just one more float in Minaya's parade of multimillion dollar deals rewarding only nebulous qualities, specifically Cora's reputed grit.

I didn't cite Cora's deal as emblematic of one of the other listed organizational issues, a system-wide lack of depth, but probably could have. If the Mets had any major league-ready middle infielders inside the organization entering 2010, they might have allocated the $2 million given to Cora elsewhere. Recall that the 2009 club, once Jose Reyes went down with injury, had to trade for Wilson Valdez and Anderson Hernandez.

Alderson, with a stated commitment to bolstering depth, spent the winter bringing in players that will at the very least ensure that Mets prospects earn major league roles instead of inheriting them by default. As mentioned, Capuano and Young, if healthy, push Gee and top prospect Jenrry Mejia down the depth chart. The presence of Hairston and Harris likely means Lucas Duda gets time in Triple-A to prove his breakout 2010 was no fluke. Hu and Rule 5 draftee Brad Emaus give the Mets middle infield options so the young Ruben Tejada can play regularly in Buffalo.

Of course, Minaya—frequently criticized for his inability to develop good and cost-controlled complementary players—should be credited for keeping intact a farm system that now appears primed to produce viable major league contributors. Whether or not his power was checked within the organization (as has been rumored), Minaya, with the axe hanging over his head, did not trade any prospects to make short-term improvements in 2010. The team's farm system, normally top-heavy under the last administration, now boasts a reasonable crop of promising players in the upper levels. And rookies Thole, Ike Davis, and Jon Niese all performed like capable major league regulars last season.

Is that to excuse or apologize for Minaya's tenure in Flushing? Hardly. All general managers have hits and misses, but too often Minaya whiffed wildly. His failures hamstrung Alderson's offseason, and two of his most spectacular mistakes will test Alderson's ability to break with the Mets' tradition on the fourth charge levied here last year: their inability to understand sunk cost.

Since Oliver Perez and Luis Castillo are owed $12 million and $6 million respectively in 2011, they will be given every chance to fail come spring training. But once they do—and at this point, it looks likely that both will—Alderson will have to convince ownership that the team is best served eating their contracts and setting them free.

For now, we can hope that he will. Alderson, in his first year as Mets GM, still maintains something that Minaya had long since lost by the time he departed: the benefit of the doubt. We can still view Alderson's decisions through a filter of Mets-fan optimism that grayed with the failures of the last administration.

So while one could point out that Minaya's $1.25 million contract to Kelvim Escobar last offseason didn't look all that different from the ones handed to Young and Capuano this winter, I could counter that under Minaya, the Mets already had a history of neglecting medical due diligence, and that both Young and Capuano finished 2010 healthy and in their teams' rotations. And you can tell me that Minaya got all the production we can hope for out of Hairston and Harris from his own scrap-heap pickups like Jose Valentin and Endy Chavez, but I will counter that Minaya frequently became attached to those guys and committed to them too much money or playing time, and that Alderson—well, we don't know yet.

We are certain, though, that Minaya too often trotted out a thin roster on a massive payroll, and that he gave millions of dollars and an amazing 1,633 plate appearances to players with below-.300 on-base percentages in 2010, many of them to Francoeur's smile and Barajas's leadership and Cora's grit. We know he proved unwilling to cut bad players with big contracts and that he often seemed too eager to make meaningful decisions based on minuscule sample sizes. We remember that for all these reasons, the Mets fell apart in 2009 and 2010 and then finally sent Minaya packing.

There is evidence from Alderson's past to suggest he will rely on the full breadth of information at his disposal to inform his decisions and that he will invest the Mets' resources in players likely to provide adequate return. There are reasons to believe he is committed to fostering depth within the organization. And there is hope that, when faced with tough choices, Alderson will make decisions that best benefit the team instead of those aimed to help him save face.

But we don't know yet. Though he has been in and around Major League Baseball for 30 years, Alderson has not worked as a GM since 1998. His situation with the Mets is different, for a variety of reasons, than the ones in which he previously succeeded. The best thing we can say for certain about him is that we have not seen him fail yet.

Because of Minaya's myopia, we have so far seen Alderson work mostly as a maintenance man, called upon to straighten up the mess after that raucous party. And we are eager to see Alderson kick off his own shindig, one that we hope will be more satisfying and won't leave us with this awful hangover, and one to which we can now only assume fewer crappy old players will be invited.

CHAPTER FIVE

THE ESSENTIALS OF HAPPINESS

JEFF SULLIVAN

Greetings. I'm a Mariners fan. I know that makes me seem out of place, like I skipped a little too far on an alphabetized list of team annuals, but I promise I'm here for a reason.

I've been writing about the Mariners since the fall of 2003. When I got started, the M's were fresh off a four-year stretch during which they won 393 games. Spirits were high. The organization then hired Bill Bavasi to lead the front office, and, well, I don't think I need to go into too much detail here. The team made ill-advised moves, it fell on hard times, and it became a national punch line. In Bavasi's first year, the M's lost 99 games. In Bavasi's last year, the M's lost 101 games. There was no progress being made, at any level.

Bavasi made a number of poor decisions, but among the highlights were a $48 million, four-year contract given to Carlos Silva, an exchange of five prospects for fragile starter Erik Bedard, and two midseason trades in 2006 that sent a pair of top prospects named Shin-Soo Choo and Asdrubal Cabrera to the Indians for both halves of a designated-hitter platoon. His tenure is panned as one in which the organization failed to improve in either the short term or the long term.

In late 2008 the Mariners brought in a brand new front office, headed by Jack Zduriencik. And this is when everything began to turn around. The team started making moves which we, as a statistically oriented fan base, supported. It became evident that, after years of ineptitude, there were thinkers in charge. And not just thinkers, but people who thought the way we thought. People who thought the way successful front offices are supposed to think. Even though the M's just had a nightmare year in 2010, we still feel a lot better about the team than we used to simply because of the people running the show.

For the sake of underscoring the stark contrast between the two front offices, Zduriencik's first move was signing slugging, stathead-favorite Russell Branyan to a small contract. Shortly thereafter, he swung a three-way trade that sacrificed little and brought in a solid starting pitcher in Jason Vargas and a strong all-around center fielder in Franklin Gutierrez. Gutierrez had been targeted in large part because of his impressive defensive statistics. A year later, the team stole Cliff Lee from the Phillies. Where the Bavasi front office failed, the Zduriencik front office demonstrated an ability to make rational, helpful moves for the present while simultaneously building toward a bright future.

It's because of the Mariners' recent history that Eric asked if I'd be willing to write a chapter for this annual. As Mets fans, you're aware of the fact that, until recently, your front office was something of a joke. It was a unit lacking not in drama, but in acceptable roster-management intellect. And, as Mets fans, you're aware of the fact that the team has recently hired guys like Sandy Alderson, Paul DePodesta, and J.P. Ricciardi to take over the show. These new hires have gotten a lot of people excited, and Eric wondered if I could write a little something on—in his words—"what it was like to be a fan of a team that went from a bumbling front office to a stats-savvy one." I couldn't turn him down.

Reflecting on my own experience with the Mariners, I struggled for a long time to come up with the best way to describe the pronounced shift in outlook. I mean, a lot's changed. In 2008, the Mariners went 61–101. In 2010, the Mariners went 61–101. But while the records are identical, I—and others like me—feel a lot more positive about the team now than before.

I tried to come up with something profound. I argued with myself about the individual and specific ways in which I feel different as a fan than I used to. I even started making a list. But the list wasn't doing it. In the end I settled on something so simple that it feels like a cop out: As a Mariners fan now, I'm just a lot happier than I was as a Mariners fan under the previous administration.

I'll try to explain with a famous quotation. It's been attributed to a number of people, like Alexander Chalmers, Allan K. Chalmers, and Joseph Addison, but I picked it up watching *Greek*. Said the dean during a graduation speech: "The three grand essentials of happiness are: something to do, something to love, and something to hope for." The quotation presumably refers to happiness in one's own general life, but I think it also applies to happiness as a sports fan, and by breaking it down, hopefully I'm able to convey just how much better the whole baseball experience is for me now than it was in the middle of the decade.

The quotation is in three parts and I'll tackle them in order. The first part, something to do, has changed the least between the two front offices. "Something to do" refers to having something that occupies your time, and our time is occupied by being fans. I'm not more of a Mariners fan than I was. I watch them play and follow along now, just as I watched them play and followed along before. Baseball was already an occupation for me, just as it was for you even as you rooted for a team run by Omar Minaya. The only difference I can detect is that maybe now I follow along a little closer, or a little more intently.

It's when we move along in the quotation that the true differences are revealed. Second on the list is something to love. Now, I don't need to explain that, as fans, we always love our teams, no matter how bad or incompetent, or bad *and* incompetent, they may be. That's an unbreakable bond. But the bond can be weakened and strengthened to some degree, and I love—actually love—the Mariners more now than I did under the previous front office.

There are a lot of components to love, but I think two of them stand out. The first is compatibility. Opposites don't actually attract. In our teams, as with our partners, we often want them to think the way we think, and act the way we act. Well-informed fan bases simply don't mesh well with Bavasi- or Minaya-style front offices. But, for me, the Zduriencik front office is right up my alley. Even though we don't actually interact, we get along, and we have a lot in common. We both value defense, for example. We both value numbers and a strong farm system.

The second critical component is trust. With Bavasi—as, I'm sure, with Minaya—there was never any trust. I never trusted Bill Bavasi to make a smart move to help the team, and while he had his wins, I never saw them coming. With Zduriencik and his assistants, I believe in them and defer to their judgment because they earned my trust right away. In short, I assume that they know more than I do, which is something I could never say about the Bavasi administration. I trust the Mariners' current front office to lead the team in the right direction.

So the love is definitely stronger. Which brings us to the final part of the quotation: having something to hope for. And while, as a fan, I've always wanted the same things, the hope now feels more legitimate and far more realistic.

I think it comes down to the difference between hoping and dreaming. In the Bavasi years, I used to dream. I used to dream that the team would make some good moves. I used to dream that the team would play well, get into the postseason, and maybe win a championship. But dreams are shattered the instant you awaken.

Hope persists. With what I consider to be the right minds in charge of the team, these days I find myself hoping for success. Hoping for that championship. Where hopes and dreams share a common desire, hoping is done with a certain degree of confidence. No longer do I feel like hoping for success is akin to hoping for luck. I trust that these executives can put the right players together, and I hope that they're able to hit the right notes.

I suppose this explanation is only adequate if you believe that the quotation makes sense. I'm not going to sit here and pretend that Alexander Chalmers—or whoever—stumbled upon the irrefutable key to eternal happiness. He may be off-base. He may have left something out. Personally, though, I believe the line is pretty much spot-on, and I can't think of a better way to convey just how much better my day-to-day experience as a Mariners fan is now than it was before. One alternative would've been simply copying and pasting several things I wrote back while Bavasi was still in charge, but then this annual would've been given an NC-17 rating.

Ever since the new front office replaced the old one I've been a happier fan in just about every imaginable way. It hasn't, of course, all been peaches. The Mariners did just lose 101 games, embarrassing themselves at several stops along the way. There have been many occasions when I've been mad, and there have been many occasions when I've been disappointed. The Mariners' front office isn't flawless, and something you ought to know is that even an excellent, intelligent front office will have its deficiencies. It will make its mistakes. There will be issues you didn't foresee, and it won't all be smooth sailing.

But speaking as a fan who has been through something very similar to what you're going through now, let me tell you—it's much better this way. What you're feeling now doesn't get old. You'll become so confident in your organization that you might even start taking good moves for granted. Baseball is a pastime, and we choose pastimes for enjoyment. You're going to enjoy this.

CHAPTER SIX

REVENGE OF THE NERDS

SAM PAGE

Whenever a Mets fan used to evoke *Moneyball*, it was to disparage sabermetrics. One fan would cite an advanced statistic and another would say, "*Moneyball* ideas like that just lead to a team of fat base-cloggers! On-base percentage is stupid!" Then the first fan would dutifully retort, "You don't know anything! *Moneyball* was a book about market inefficiencies. Unless Sandy Alderson comes out of retirement to run the Mets, on-base percentage is beside the point!"

It's interesting how this deflection became the stock answer to sabermetric skeptics who would bring up *Moneyball*. There is a valid, practical concern behind this response: Defending *Moneyball* as an enumeration of sabermetric principles feeds the characterization of a cult following a set of ideas. Like in all academic fields, a subculture exists among those people on the cutting edge and some ideas are generally agreed upon. But intellectual curiosity and vigorous debate, not dogma, drive the sabermetric movement.

Yet, no one says, "*Moneyball* was just a good story about one front office and its use of sabermetrics." They say, "*Moneyball* was a book about market inefficiencies." The implication being, of course, the market inefficiencies exploited by Billy Beane in 2003 wouldn't be inefficiencies for long. Other teams would accept the value of on-base percentage, at which point the A's would have moved on to some new and exciting discovery. The answer betrayed a common hope that sabermetrics was on the side of progress and would be on the right side of history.

Since the publication of Michael Lewis's book, only one team with any discernible understanding of sabermetrics has won the World Series: the Boston Red Sox, who won it twice. In the past three seasons, two teams publicly contemptuous toward sabermetrics, and *Moneyball* in particular (the Giants and Phillies), and another franchise too far removed from normal financial concerns to even understand market inefficiencies (the Yankees) have won it all. The three teams perhaps most closely identified with sabermetrics—the Athletics, Blue Jays, and

Mariners—have produced a series of mediocre, or worse, teams. (The Rays also come to mind as a sabermetric success, but they are easy for critics to excuse as having been built from the draft.)

And while these results have done nothing to slow the fervor with which baseball's statistical community pursues its ideas, it has nearly destroyed their ability to communicate those ideas. Every proponent of sabermetrics knows in his or her heart of hearts that there are two types of teams in baseball: those teams that accept the stats and those that don't. But they don't admit it, because to do so would lend credence to every critic who has cited the Athletics' failures and the Giants' successes.

Instead, sabermetricians respond with a lot of false compromises and misplaced smugness. The most famous lie is "statistics and scouting are both important." This statement carries two distinct meanings and, consciously or not, people hide behind its ambiguity. To a critic of sabermetrics, it is an admission that what sabermetricians conclude and what they, the critic, believe are of equal weight. In actuality, all the sabermetrician has said is that scouts play an important role in successful baseball organizations—something no one disputes. Good amateur scouting provides the cost-controlled talent that is the very currency of baseball.

Critics of sabermetrics, however, are not scouts and they rarely (or never) debate sabermetricians on the merits of amateur baseball players. Your average baseball fan debates the micro-movements of the general manager, not the overall direction of the franchise. Giving Ruben Amaro Jr. full marks for the Phillies' World Series win is like blaming a President-elect for a financial crisis set in motion by acts of Congress ten years ago.

The critics hide behind the veil of scouting because it is the black box of front offices. Really, they are just anti-sabermetric and often anti-intellectual, drawing on all of the scouting communities' credibility and none of its expertise. But proponents of sabermetrics refrain from calling these people on the carpet for fear of playing into the *Moneyball* stereotype of wanting scouts out of baseball.

Most sabermetricians, in their heart of hearts, know that scouts have no business evaluating major league talent. Sure, a team should bring in an expert to analyze the mechanics of a broken player, but asking a scout to evaluate two free agents is a terrible waste of man hours and can only lead to a wrong answer. Ryan Howard is better than Albert

Pujols? OK, thanks for your input, please go watch some high school games.

Watch the reality show *The Club* on MLB Network if you want to peek behind the curtain. In one episode, White Sox GM Kenny Williams goes around a conference table of his scouts, asking if he should go after Edwin Jackson or an unnamed "lefty hitter." They alternate, seemingly on cue, between the cliché "good pitching beats good hitting" and its converse. The ambiguity ends with Williams making a truly horrible trade for Jackson, on a whim, with no objections from his scouts.

Most players who reach free agency carry statistical major league track records, from which a general manager can project and identify trends. Asking a scout his opinion based on the few times he has watched a player is to deny the very point of sabermetrics: estimating a player's true talent level with empiricism. Even the new technologies sabermetricians cite as evidence for the supposed symbiosis of scouting—things like PITCHf/x and HITf/x—exist to make major league scouting obsolete.

Yet sabermetrics' proponents can't say these things. They know the "sabermetric GMs" are good, but their only proof is the data they've collected. And whatever crisis of conscience this flagrant begging-the-question creates in them quickly subsides when they hear their critics' alternative explanations: winning attitudes, grit, the field manager, and a bunch of other things Sandy Alderson characterized as "shit" in *Moneyball*.

The defenders of sabermetrics are losing the debate for baseball's hearts and minds. And, ironically, the problem centers around that mantra, meant to give critics a truer understanding of the movement: "*Moneyball* was a book about market inefficiencies." They're wrong. Eschewing fielding for hulking on-base machines wasn't just the market inefficiency of the day; it was a carefully formulated and implemented organizational philosophy that Sandy Alderson created and passed down to Billy Beane. And in Alderson's absence, Beane changed course and sabermetrics followed, believing his team of slick-fielding, low-OBP speedsters was the new market inefficiency.

Fans of sabermetrics are rightly eager to advance their field, but in their eagerness may have accepted some rudimentary steps as gospel or, at least, as something worth building a team around. They need to get back to basics, back to the ideas in *Moneyball*, back to page 58:

The first, short answer, according to a pamphlet commissioned by

Alderson, was to spend it on hitters. The pamphlet was written by a former aerospace engineer turned baseball writer, Eric Walker. Fielding, Walker wrote, was "at most five percent of the game." The rest was pitching and offense, and while "good pitchers are usually valued properly, good batters often are not."

The statistic du jour these days is Wins Above Replacement (WAR), which has obvious appeal as a supposed holistic measure of a player, expressed in baseball's most important unit: the win. WAR allows player comparison regardless of position—shortstop, relief pitcher, bat boy, whatever. WAR requires a hitter's batting and fielding performance expressed in equal terms. This requirement has granted newfound prominence to zone-rating statistics, like UZR, which measure a player's single-season fielding contribution expressed as a number of runs above or below average.

However, even UZR's creator, Mitchel Lichtman, often explains that single-season UZR is not representative of a player's true talent. Random variation and the changing baseline for "average" cause single-season UZRs to fluctuate wildly. From 2007–2009, Bobby Abreu was a remarkably consistent hitter, finishing with nearly identical lines. His UZR, however, went from average to terrible to below-average in those three seasons.

Let's use Orlando Hudson as another example. O-Dawg's a guy with a wide range of single-season UZRs (a +15.9 in 2004 , a -10 in 2008). He also has a reputation of being one of the game's best defenders, a consensus often challenged by some, citing said stats.

In both 2009 and 2010, Hudson had a chance to convert 380 balls into outs. In 2010, he made about 13 fewer plays than he had made in 2009. According to UZR, those 13 plays corresponded to about 13 fielding runs of value. In hitting terms, that's the difference between a .340 and .320 wOBA, or an .800 and .730 OPS. That's 70 points of OPS—the difference between Jose Guillen and Justin Upton—in 13 ground balls rolling just past O-Dawg's glove and into the outfield. Intuitively, 13 missed ground balls are not as important as a .730 OPS hitter adding eight homers or 30 walks to his game. No way.

Is UZR wrong? No, it's just a relative stat for comparing fielders. And in the span of one season, what is relatively good can change. And unlike with hitting, the difference between a good and poor second baseman isn't that much and, over the course of a season it's barely noticeable. Fielding may not be less than 5% of baseball, as Eric Walker's report claimed, but it certainly ain't much.

And building entire teams on the basis of this stuff, à la J.P. Ricciardi's Blue Jays, Billy Beane's recent A's, and Jack Zduriencik's Mariners, was begging for disaster. After all, fielding doesn't happen in a vacuum. Did these teams expect three center fielders to stake out three equitable portions of the field and catch every fly ball? Out-of-zone plays are a huge part of these zone ratings, and having better fielding teammates would seemingly hurt a player's out-of-zone chances, not help them. Just adding up a ledger sheet of UZRs doesn't make sense, but it's exactly the type of analysis WAR necessitates.

Before the 2010 season, FanGraphs.com, sabermetrics' most prominent voice, ranked the Mariners as the sixth-best organization in baseball. The decision drew instant criticism from fans, who cited the M's barren farm system and their highly questionable major league offense. For years, sabermetrically inclined Mariners fans had panned then-GM Bill Bavasi as someone who just didn't get it. Then, Jack Zduriencik replaced him and built a Mariners team that looked great in the UZR and WAR columns, FanGraphs' two biggest statistical offerings. Those fans went all in on the Mariners—a team that would prove a good GM, aligned with certain philosophies, could make a world of a difference. It was a bold and overdue statement from the sabermetric community, but a costly losing bet. Maybe they were just playing favorites, intoxicated by a short gasp of fresh air from a stagnant franchise. And maybe I'm making the exact same mistake with Sandy Alderson, the new GM of my favorite team. I guess we'll see soon enough, because I'm all in.

Unlike the "new Moneyball" that has won nothing, Sandy Alderson has the rings. In the parlance of sabermetrics' critics, he's a proven winner. At his introductory press conference, confronted with a predictable line of *Moneyball* questions, Alderson defied anyone to disprove his old Earl Weaver strategies. The out is the most precious capital, hitters should foremost demonstrate power and patience, speed is fool's gold, and if I made it work in Oakland's Coliseum I can damn well do it here.

The long-term vitality of the Mets will depend on the team's willingness to reinvest in its farm system, and that will depend on the performance of Paul DePodesta's scouts and the Wilpons' willingness to pay over-slot money for draft picks. In the short term, however, Alderson will have ample opportunity to reassert the superiority of his strategic position.

Although the "sabermetric front offices" have lost some footing in recent years, they remain on the side of logic and innovation. FanGraphs' bet was wrong, but their intentions were right. Having a GM who does more than pay lip service to sabermetrics remains an incredible advantage in the free agent and trade markets. With the number of major league front offices that will be decidedly anti-saber for years to come—the Giants and Phillies immediately come to mind—Alderson will be in a strong position to quickly build up the Mets' assets.

And for the statistical community at large, Alderson's Mets may finally be the shining example that emboldens them to tell the truth about *Moneyball* and sabermetrics in general: It's not a useful tool, and it's not something to consider. It's the truth. Reject it at your own risk.

CHAPTER SEVEN

HAVE HOPE, METS FANS

GRANT BRISBEE

The idea is that this is supposed to be an open letter from one Giants fan to all Mets fans to remind everyone that baseball is unpredictable, that if the 2010 Giants can win the World Series, it isn't out of the question that another team could surprise in 2011. Like, oh, the Mets. It makes sense, but I do have to start with a disclaimer. One of the most underrated components to the Giants' regular-season and postseason success was the team's health. Only two of their pitchers went on the DL in 2010: Dan Runzler, who hurt himself swinging, and Todd Wellemeyer, who hurt himself running the bases. The lineup was healthy for the most part, and when there were injuries—to Mark DeRosa, Aaron Rowand, and Edgar Renteria—they allowed the Giants to shuffle in better hitters. The injuries, in retrospect, were quite well-timed.

By contrast, the Mets have already lost a member of their starting rotation to a wheat-thresher accident since you started reading this. Don't ask which pitcher it was. It will just upset you. A couple of outfielders will probably go down in a tandem-bike mishap, and an infielder will suffer a rare and painful triple-hamstring pull. Asking Mets fans to hope for good health would be ridiculous. It would be overly optimistic nonsense. Why, it would be like expecting Brian Sabean to build a legitimate offense after he'd spent the previous five years collecting various pieces of flotsam and veteran, hoping for something competent to appear by magic.

Wait. That actually happened. Rooting for Sabean to build a decent offense without Barry Bonds was like rooting for light to slow down. It wasn't just unrealistic, it went against the laws of nature. And then it happened. The universe aligned, and somehow the Giants found themselves with an average offense. An average offense! When the offense took shape, the pitching got even better, and they mowed through three very good teams on the way to their first championship in San Francisco. The GM holding the trophy over his head in November, champagne cascading over him, was the same one whose Opening Day starting lineup just two years prior included Rich Aurilia at first, Jose Castillo at third, and Brian Bocock at shortstop. The mix of bumbling, perseverance, and eventual triumph was like watching *Ernest Goes to Shawshank*.

It wasn't just the multiple losing seasons that disillusioned Giants fans before last year. It was more than that. Prior to the Giants being awful, they were close. So dang close. They had the best player on the planet, and they contended year after year, only to completely collapse at the absolute worst times. In the last three seasons in which they contended during the pre-Lincecum days, the Giants

- were eight outs away from a title with a five-run lead;
- ended a playoff series when J.T. Snow—who ran like Bartolo Colon wrapped in flypaper—was thrown out at home plate;
- watched a hated player (Steve Finley) on a hated rival (the Dodgers) hit a walk-off grand slam against the Giants to clinch the division, eating a live human baby as he rounded the bases. Presumably. I didn't see it. My head was in my hands. But I have an idea how it all went down.

To butcher an old maxim, Giants fans wondered if it was better to contend and lose than never to contend at all. It was a deep and philosophical question. Then the team started to stink and the answer was clear. It was painful to watch a team collapse after investing 162 games in them, but it was far, far worse to watch a team play horribly for 162 games. All you would do during the horrible season was fantasize about them contending, but you knew that when they did start to contend, they would collapse, just like every other time they got your hopes up. The bad seasons just added a layer of pain.

Mets fans know the feeling. Every post-Buckner season would end with some measure of heartbreak, and right before the Mets were bad, they were close. So dang close. When they collapsed at the end of two consecutive seasons, allowing the Phillies to scamper past them, the pain must have been palpable and thick. There was no way to explain it to people who didn't care about sports. Hundreds and hundreds of hours invested in a team, only to watch it all melt when something called Logan Kensing shuts your team down. And your reward for suffering through that? Horrific, losing seasons of misery that made you yearn for the days the Mets would fritter away a September lead. Watching a bad team, especially one that also has a history of heartbreak when they're good, is like trying to climb a mountain with a plastic spork and flip-flops. Even if you somehow reach the summit after years and years of struggle, you have a feeling that all that's at the top is a patch of poison oak and an ornery ibex whose kickin' hooves are right at crotch-level.

Right now, it must feel like the Mets are cursed, like they're doomed to be another injurious mess, like they're never going to contend with this current group of cornerstone players.

Maybe. Maybe not. If you want to moon both pessimism and logic, though, you certainly can. It's baseball. Baseball is freaky. If the Mets were to rise up from the ashes and win it all in 2011, it would be but a blip on the all-time baseball freaky-o-meter. If you want optimism, it's there for you to find. There's no such thing as a curse, or a team identity that follows a franchise around from season to season. What the Mets did a few Septembers ago doesn't mean a thing to the Mets going forward. The fluky injuries the Mets slogged through in the past two seasons don't mean much to the 2011 club. There is no such thing as a cursed franchise.

Well, there's the Bills. But that's it. Baseball has built an elaborate mythology around curses and pain, and fans of the Cubs and Indians can wear their scars with a measure of pride. I so wanted to be a part of that Emo club. We'd all sit around in my fantasies, listening to Terry Cashman play Cure covers, drinking heavily and bemoaning our fates. Yep. It would be the Giants, the Cubs, the Indians, the White So… whoops, they're out. So it would be the Giants, the Cubs, the Indians, the Red So… dang, they're out, too. It would be the Gi… oh… sorry, fellas. Looks like we got the call. We'll write. Maybe.

I used to be sure that the Giants were cursed, even as I rationally knew that curses couldn't exist. Throughout the '60s, the Giants were producing Hall of Famers like wet Mogwai, but they never won it all. In 1993, they had the best second-place record in the history of the game. And missed the playoffs. In 2002, they suffered what might have been the worst-timed bullpen collapse in the history of the game. There's no reason to bore you with the complete list, so I'll just describe it in a way that Mets fans might be able to understand. The most complete Giants team I've ever watched—the best combination of starting pitching, relief, and hitting since the days of Mays—was bounced from the playoffs in 2000 when they were one-hit by Bobby Jones. One of the better offensive teams in baseball was one-hit by a pitcher who hadn't had an ERA under 5.00 for two years and never would again

When was the last time you thought of Bobby Jones? I thought about him every day this past October. It was disturbing. I'm over it now.

Here's another underrated component of the Giants' success last year: They had good players. Everyone likes to talk about the luck, the flukes, the serendipity of it all, but the Giants started the season with Matt Cain, Tim Lincecum, and Buster Posey waiting to unleash well-mannered fury on the rest of the league. It was a heck of a start to a roster, and when the fluky things started to happen—like when Florida teams started putting productive outfielders up for free on Craigslist—the Giants had a foundation of talent on which to build. The Mets also have an enviable core. David Wright, Jose Reyes, and Carlos Beltran have all performed at an elite, elite level. If they were to do so again, it wouldn't make the cover of the *Weekly World News*. And if that, or something even close, were to happen, there would be a chance that the complementary pieces would fall into place around them, Tetris-style. The Giants turned over five-eighths of their lineup from April to November, but the foundation is what allowed them to have a chance in the first place. The Mets aren't in a position that's too different.

So your thoughts might start to turn dark, and you could begin to think, "Oh, the Mets. They'll let a bunch of injuries ruin their season. And even if they do contend, they'll find a way to choke at the end." You might be right. But you might be wrong. If you can't produce bursts of spontaneous optimism in the spring, you and baseball might need to see other people for a while.

Part 3: Profiling The NL East & The 2011 Mets

CHAPTER EIGHT

Colossal NL East Adventure

Tommy Bennett

WELCOME TO NATIONAL LEAGUE EAST!! Would you like
instructions? (y/n)

>y

Somewhere nearby is an eternal flag, which has granted others
glory and riches, though it is rumored that some who have
sought it have never returned. Swagger is a powerful force
in NATIONAL LEAGUE EAST. I will be your eyes and ears.
Direct me with commands of 1 or 2 words.

(IF STUCK, TYPE "HELP" FOR SOME HINTS.)

You awake with a start in a cold room. Your head swells with
pain as you drift back out of consciousness....

Hours later, you find yourself face down on a spare cot.
There is no pillow, but your headache remains. As your
eyes adjust to the darkness, you struggle to remember the
nightmare that has only recently gripped you. You hazily
recall a middle-aged man removing his shirt and threatening
to fight a team of young baseball players, executives
backbiting in otherwise mundane press conferences, and the
incessantly incandescent face of a "SPORTS WEEKLY" cover
boy. The dream slips away into incomprehensible memory and
leaves only pain behind.

>take aspirin

Aspirin will not cure the type of headache you have.

>stand up

You lumber to your feet.

>light match

You reach into your pocket and feel a matchbook. You open
it and discover a single match. The packaging reads, "ALEX
CORA'S UTILITY OUTLET" and bears a handwritten price tag

of "$2,000,000.00." You light the match, illuminating a
colorful living room that could once have been suitable for
an entire family but is now in a state of obvious disrepair.
You notice a small ladder extending through the floor in
the corner. The match, which never did burn brightly, is
extinguished. You throw it down the hole.

>ladder

You feel your way along the wall to the corner, where you
nearly fall through the hole in the floor. As you clamber
down the ladder, you enter what appears to be a smoke-filled
back room. In the middle of the aged wood floor, you notice
shavings that you desperately hope are beard hairs. You hear
sobbing.

>investigate sobbing

You turn--nearly tripping over an oversized, foam Theodore
Roosevelt sitting at the foot of a large cherry credenza.
Far from the heroic TR of San Juan Hill, this meek facsimile
has never won anything in his life. He is still crying.

>investigate credenza

There is a framed picture of an enormous bald eagle
photobombing a picture of a hairy orange giant in a
Canadiens jersey. You rifle through the documents on the
credenza. There is a pair of medical reports titled
"STRASBURG" and "ZIMMERMANN." You find yourself disappointed
by the positive diagnoses the reports disclose, but
something tells you not to worry about the former, at least
not for several months. Peeking out of a copy of the "2011
ALMANAC OF AMERICAN POLITICS" is a folder with a pleasingly
designed title that simply reads, "HOPE."

There is also a smashed pink piggy bank that looks like it
could once have held approximately $126 million--you know,
just eyeballing it. There is no sign of the money, but you
are reminded of the hair clippings on the floor. This grosses
you out a little.

>open folder

On the left side, under a binder clip, you see dozens of
tear-stained pictures of a scraggly looking pitcher wearing
jerseys that bear the names of barely familiar teams
("AZTECS," "SENATORS"). On top is an 8" x 10" glossy photo
of the same man that someone has defaced fourteen times with
the letter "K" (two of them have been drawn backward).

On the right side, you see a magazine cutout of a fresh-faced adolescent with heavy eye black. The tag line reads "THE CHOSEN ONE." Your headache returns, this time accompanied by severe nausea.

>north

To the north sits Jason Marquis. You are completely indifferent to his presence. You wonder how long he has been there. Miraculously, Livan Hernandez has managed to hide behind Marquis. Where do they get these guys? John Lannan waves harmlessly nearby.

>east

A baseball rolls over your foot. You look to see where it came from and find Ian Desmond splayed on the ground with his glove extended. In this land where metaphors become reality, his glove is made of lead and he wears a butcher frock. Danny Espinosa strikes out in the distance.

>xyzzy

Nothing happens.

>up

You climb back up the ladder. You notice that the lights have come on. Sitting on the blue and orange love seat are Paul DePodesta and J.P. Ricciardi.

>Moneyball

With what? Your bare hands?

>Jeremy Brown

You don't have that.

>Chad Bradford

Your knuckles begin to hurt.

>Nick Swisher

Ew--and, okay, we get it. DePodesta and Ricciardi join your party.

>xyzzy

You are in a large, multi-use stadium. As you look around,

you notice about 2,000 people sitting in the warm April
rain. "Good turnout," you say to no one in particular.
In the distance, you hear the crack of maple on leather.
Seconds later, a ball soars over your head. To the north,
the Marlins Manatees, MLB's only all-male dance/energy
squad, practice their routine.

>go infield

As you jog toward the infield, you see an athletic Dominican
man running along the outfield wall. Well, maybe not running.
More like dogging it, really. You feel an urge to remove
him from the lineup, but you sense that you cannot do that.
Besides, the memory of your nightmare prevents you from
trying. As he runs past you--revealing the name "RAMIREZ" on
his uniform--the numbers .313/.385/.520 flash on DePodesta's
laptop screen. You hope someone else benches him.

>home plate

At the batting cage, you realize that Mike Stanton has
gotten himself into excellent shape and seems to have
spent a lot of time at the tanning salon. No, you think to
yourself, this can't be the reliever who was halfway decent
back in 2004. Then you realize that this Stanton was the guy
hitting the home runs a minute ago. DePodesta mentions that
Stanton hit 44 home runs between Double-A and the majors
last year.

A terrible thought occurs to you as a hazy memory of the
2007 draft enters your head. The names Eddie Kunz and
Nathan Vineyard invite themselves unwelcomed into your
consciousness. The pain in your forehead reasserts itself.
The magnificent homonym in the batting cage lifts another fly
ball into the cavernous outfield. You find yourself wishing
you cared more about strikeouts.

>fire sale

Nothing happens. It's funny--you could have sworn that
worked the last two times.

Ricciardi whispers in your ear that Ramirez is signed for
four more years, Josh Johnson for three, Ricky Nolasco for
three, and that Logan Morrison and Stanton are under team
control for at least five more. He adds that the team will
inaugurate its new name (the Miami Marlins) and ballpark in
2012. You curse fish for being so lean and healthy, and yet
completely unsatisfying.

>HELP

I know of places, actions, and things. Most of my vocabulary
describes places and is used to move you there. Usually
people trying to move around just need a few more words.

>turner cnn coca cola

Welcome to sunny Atlanta! You look around in what appears to
be a half-sized replica of Atlanta-Fulton County Stadium.
The grass is much better manicured than you remember the
original being. Behind you is the home team's bullpen, just
off the right-field foul territory.

>go bullpen

You wander over to the bullpen, where you see a miniature
Tommy Hanson in the middle of a throwing session. Beyond
him, a tiny Tim Hudson leans casually against the wall.
Roger McDowell--who appears to be the pitching coach--spits
sunflower seeds from a chair nearby. McDowell, you think to
yourself, used to be cool. Now look at him. Fans in the
seats mindlessly do the Tomahawk Chop.

As you stare into the stands--rage building--your head is
nearly taken off by a Craig Kimbrel fastball. This is not a
good place to stand.

>regress Jurrjens

It's super effective! Jurrjens induces fewer ground balls
and his modest peripherals catch up to him. Derek Lowe
comforts him nearby. Overhead, a group of Minors and Beachys
swarm. To the north is a nursery, where Frank Wren wraps
saplings marked "TEHERAN," "VIZCAINO," and "DELGADO" in
blankets to keep them warm for the cold spring.

>Roundup

You don't have any. Besides, you know the Braves would just
grow more. Their scouting and player development have always
been terrific. You remember the 1990s. You are sad.

>go dugout

In the dugout, everyone is waving goodbye to Bobby Cox. It
makes you feel strange to see him like this. You wish he
were arguing with an umpire. You respectfully wait to go
down the steps.

>go dugout

You find the stairs blocked by All-Star Omar Infante, on his
way south to Florida. Dan Uggla pushes past you into the
dugout with a bag full of $62 million in small, unmarked
bills. Home runs! Behind you, Martin Prado hustles his heart
out toward left field. You scratch your head. Back in the
dugout, Chipper Jones ices his knee, using both his left and
right hands. Versatility!

>LAAAAAAAA-RRY!

Chipper continues to wear his grimace. Your insults only
make him stronger. He appears to be healing.

>right field

You try to walk toward right field, but a hype barrier stops
you dead in your tracks. Beyond the fog, you see either
a Hall of Famer or an injury-prone and overrated corner
outfielder--you can't quite tell, but you know it can't be
anything in between. As you push on the hype wall, it slowly
gives way (somewhere, it is enveloping Bryce Harper). You
pull out the youngster's Strat-O-Matic card; an unsettling
number of the dice rolls are accompanied by the word "WALK."
Freddie Freeman jogs in from first base and asks Jason
Heyward if he can borrow some hype. Heyward obliges. What a
class act.

>north north north north north north

Leaving the miniature Fulton County Stadium, you realize the
fragility and the beauty of the Atlanta ball club. You also
realize you forgot about Brian McCann. Almost everyone does,
even though he's a catcher who had a better OPS than every
regular on the 2010 Mets except David Wright. Just as soon
as you get past the city limits, though, the realization
vanishes from your memory.

Traveling north on I-85 and I-95, you put on your audio
cassette of "NEBRASKA." The tunes are especially appropriate
as you moodily speed through Baltimore. Ricciardi pipes
up from the back seat: "Man, Bruce used to be so edgy."
DePodesta punches him on the shoulder. You threaten to pull
the car over, or worse yet, trade them to the Orioles.

As you pull into Lot K at Citizens Bank Park, the smell of
alcohol assaults your nose. The barely melodic strains of
"Fly, Eagles, Fly" remind you that Phillies fans can spell
at least one word. To the north stands the ballpark.

>north

As you approach the entrance, you see a newly erected
statue. It appears to be inspired by Mount Rushmore, only
the heads on the statue are those of Roy Halladay, Cliff
Lee, Cole Hamels, and Roy Oswalt. It is made entirely out of
Tastykakes. You notice it has been christened in vomit. You
feel an urge to contribute as well.

>enter ballpark

You pass through the turnstiles and proceed to the batting
cage. There, members of the Phillies offensive core take
turns facing live pitching while the rest joke around and
laugh. The players finish their practice, so you stroll out
to the pitcher's mound. As you stare down the batter's box,
you realize that the left side is worn--the lines blurred in
the dirt. The right side, on the other hand, is pristine.

>go dugout

At the top of the dugout stairs, you see Charlie Manuel
bobbing his way up and down the bench chatting with players.
His West Virginia drawl is viscous as he tells Wilson Valdez
that he'll be starting yet again today. Jimmy Rollins
clutches a Red Bull and an ice pack while Shane Victorino
holds up nearly identical Ed Hardy tee shirts for group
approval.

>run away

You pump your legs until you find yourself in the home
bullpen, under the watchful gaze of hundreds of surly
Phillies fans. While looking up at them, you bump into Jose
Contreras, who is engaged in a heated discussion with Danys
Baez about Raul Castro's economic policies--or so your high
school Spanish would have you believe. Nearby, Brad Lidge
quietly snaps off a few tight sliders. In the corner, Scott
Mathieson waits his turn to pitch.

>broadcast booth

At the Harry Kalas Broadcast Booth, you spot Gary Matthews
trading war stories with the Phillie Phanatic. You hear the
opening strains of the theme from "ROCKY" emanating from the
loudspeakers. You feel very woozy.

>get hat

You clutch after Sarge's fedora, only to be sideswiped by

Ryan Howard, who tackles you to the ground. Just before
losing consciousness, you realize that, however overpaid
Howard may be five years from now, he still packs a wallop in
the old-fashioned here and now. The last thing you remember
is his toothy grin as he trades high fives with Green Man
from "IT'S ALWAYS SUNNY IN PHILADELPHIA." You despise that
show.

Hours pass.

You are surrounded by darkness.

You awake with a start in a cold room. Your head swells with
pain as you drift back out of consciousness again....

Sandy Alderson is sitting next to you on the orange and blue
love seat. He drops two Alka-Seltzers into a tall glass of
water, which he then hands to you.

"Good morning."

CHAPTER NINE

Previewing The NL East Rivals

Satchel Price

O ver the past couple of years, the Philadelphia Phillies have put a lot of effort into making one thing clear to the rest of the division: The road to the National League East crown goes through Philly. With three playoff appearances, two National League pennants, and a World Series championship in the past three seasons, it's hard to frame the Phillies as anything but the class of the division. And they reaffirmed that title over the winter by landing Cliff Lee when essentially nobody had them pegged as a suitor. Now the Phillies boast a potentially historic starting rotation that features Lee, 2010 NL Cy Young winner Roy Halladay, Cole Hamels, Roy Oswalt, and Joe Blanton. The club's No. 4 and No. 5 starters, Oswalt and Blanton, could easily slot into the top two rotation spots for many non-contending teams.

But the rest of the division isn't simply bowing down to Philadelphia's brilliance. The Phillies may be on their way to a league-best fourth consecutive playoff appearance, but they're going to get some steady competition from their counterparts, particularly in Atlanta. The Braves weren't able to land an elite player this offseason like the Phillies—or even the Nationals—but they still addressed some of their principal issues from last year. Washington and Florida are long shots to be major contenders, barring some unforeseen events—like Mike Stanton being an MVP candidate, for one—but they're both solidifying long-term foundations that could foster extended periods of success later in the decade. This division isn't loaded from top to bottom going into next season like its American League counterpart, but the Phillies probably aren't going to saunter their way into the playoffs like some anticipate.

Coming into the offseason, some around the game were wondering if this would be the beginning of the end of a dominant era for the Phillies. Franchise stalwarts Ryan Howard, Chase Utley, and Jimmy Rollins began to show their age last season, and the club didn't appear to have much payroll flexibility given their numerous contractual obligations. But their outlook became infinitely brighter on a single day: General manager Ruben Amaro accomplished the truly improbable when it was announced in December that Lee, one of the best pitchers in baseball and the top player on the free agent market, had agreed to a five-year, $120 million contract with Philadelphia. Most of the industry was left stunned. For months the bidding for Lee was assumed to be a two-horse race, that the New York Yankees and Texas Rangers were jockeying to be the left-hander's top choice. But we've since learned that Amaro was simply waiting in the weeds, properly positioning his team to make the perfect pitch to Lee, even though the Yankees were reportedly offering over $30 million more in guaranteed money. In the end, Lee proved to be an exception to the rule that money trumps all else. It's one of the rare instances in baseball history where we've seen an elite player near the height of his earning power turn down significant money to sign elsewhere.

And after that signing, Philadelphia's roster once again slots firmly into the "stacked" category. Even after adding another year of age and removing Jayson Werth (more on him later) from the equation, the Phillies' lineup is still intimidating. Utley and Rollins may be in the early stages of decline, but they're still among the top players in the game at their respective positions. Howard may no longer be an elite player, even though he's paid like one, but he's still going to provide 30-plus homers and a solid on-base percentage. Toss in quality regulars like Shane Victorino, Carlos Ruiz, and Placido Polanco, and it's entirely reasonable to expect the Phillies' offense to be strong once again next season.

But we all know that run prevention wins games, and that's where the Phillies are likely to thrive. We've already touched on the starting rotation—it's loaded, and it's almost certain to be one of the best in the game. And while the club isn't built on defense, it shouldn't be a major liability. The team has its best defenders up the middle (Utley, Rollins, Victorino) and its worst defenders on the corners (Howard, Raul Ibanez). Overall, Philadelphia is obviously the favorite to win the division going into the season. The starting rotation is potent enough to beat any team, and they shouldn't lose many games due to a lack of offensive firepower. It's not clear if they'll have much flexibility during the season to make changes unless they can free themselves of Joe Blanton's contract, but even as presently constructed this team seems a lock for 90-plus wins.

And frankly, as clear as it is that the Phillies are the top team in the division, it might be clearer that the Atlanta Braves are their biggest threat. It's easy to forget that the Braves won 91 games last season, given their somewhat quick exit from the playoffs, but you could also make an argument that they've improved themselves since then.

One of the biggest issues that ailed the Braves last season was a lack of pop in their lineup: Brian McCann led the club with a .184 isolated power, which was good enough for 60th among all qualified major league hitters. Beyond anticipating improved power production from outfield prodigy Jason Heyward, Atlanta addressed the issue by trading for one of the top power bats available in former Marlins second baseman Dan Uggla. They subsequently signed the 31-year-old Uggla to a five-year, $62 million contract that covers his final season of arbitration eligibility and four free-agency years. Having McCann, Uggla, Heyward, and rookie first baseman Freddie Freeman around for the long run means that the Braves should have a far more powerful offense than they've had in recent memory.

Like Philadelphia, the Braves are a club built on strong starting pitching. Few teams possess the kind of pitching depth that Atlanta currently has. With a projected rotation of Tim Hudson, Derek Lowe, Jair Jurrjens, Tommy Hanson, and Mike Minor—not to mention Brandon Beachy, Kenshin Kawakami, and free-agent signing Rodrigo Lopez as potential alternatives—Atlanta has eight pitchers that would be considered quality MLB starters by most teams. Hanson, Jurrjens, and Minor are among the top young pitchers in the game, while Hudson and Lowe provide lots of innings and lots of grounders. The Braves' bullpen could be strong as well. Scott Linebrink and George Sherrill aren't exactly legitimate replacements for Billy Wagner and Takashi Saito, but with Craig Kimbrel, Jonny Venters, and Peter Moylan at the back of the bullpen, it's one facet of the team that could end up being a strength.

The Marlins and Nationals shouldn't provide as much competition for Philadelphia as the Braves, but these aren't 100-loss teams, and they both have the potential to play spoiler late in the season, thanks in part to aggressive offseasons. Florida clearly has the superior roster at the moment, but given the dearth of quality prospects in their farm system you have to wonder when the Nationals are going to surpass them. The Marlins lay claim to some of the best young players in baseball, such as Hanley Ramirez, Josh Johnson, Mike Stanton, and Logan Morrison, but an active offseason included some puzzling decisions and it's hard to see the Marlins keeping up with Philly and Atlanta. Washington similarly employs some top young players, particularly the eternally underrated Ryan Zimmerman, but they're going to be feeling the effects of Stephen Strasburg's 2010 elbow surgery all season long.

When it was reported that the Marlins had traded Cameron Maybin to the San Diego Padres for a couple relievers, it looked like a deal that could end up working in Florida's favor. Then we learned that the Marlins pegged Chris Coghlan as Maybin's replacement in center field. It's not that there's anything wrong with Coghlan as a player overall; he can actually be quite valuable if used properly. But we're talking about a player who spent his entire minor league career as an infielder before putting up well-below-average defensive marks as a left fielder over the past two seasons in Florida. He's never given a hint that he's capable of playing an adequate center field. It's precisely the kind of peculiar move that's unlikely to work out.

Nevertheless, the Marlins still have an outside shot at contending. They have two elite players in Ramirez and Johnson, and two more guys with elite potential in Stanton and Morrison. They have a promising rotation led by Johnson, Ricky Nolasco, and Anibal Sanchez, with the possibility of a resurgent Javier Vazquez taking the rotation's performance to another level. When you have that many players with big upside, there's always a chance that things come together and you win a ton of games.

The Nationals, on the other hand, probably aren't going to do much damage this season. With Strasburg on the mend, the club's lack of front-line pitching is painfully obvious: A rotation of Livan Hernandez, Jason Marquis, John Lannan, Jordan Zimmerman, and Tom Gorzelanny doesn't exactly scream "playoffs." The lineup is similarly underwhelming despite the signing of Werth, although Ryan Zimmerman has firmly established himself among the very best all-around players in baseball. Generally speaking, 2011 is just a transition year for Washington. They added Werth and Gorzelanny with their gaze set beyond 2011, and that seems to be the overall direction of the team. Strasburg should return at full health in 2012, and the team has numerous top prospects—especially young outfielder Bryce Harper—that they expect to begin contributing over the next couple of years. They may not be a good team right now, but they're pouring the concrete into a foundation that could result in some strong teams in D.C. a little down the road.

The bottom line is that this is Philadelphia's division to lose. Barring injuries or other unpredictable events, the Phillies are the best team in the division on paper—they can rack up runs and have arguably the best starting rotation in the game. As for predicting how the 2011 NL East will shake out, smart money is with the Phillies to win the division, though the Braves are closer than most think. Behind those two, the Mets and Marlins should fight for third place with the Nationals likely to finish last for the fourth straight season and the sixth time in the seven years they've been in Washington.

CHAPTER TEN

MEET THE NEW BOSS

ALEX NELSON

When Jerry Manuel was fired at the end of 2010, many Mets fans rejoiced. When Terry Collins was hired in his place, many of those same Mets fans went right back to groaning. Despite not yet making a single decision as manager of the Mets, Collins was already guilty of two crimes: not being a member of the 1986 Mets, and never previously managing a winner. Unfortunately for Collins, another finalist for the job, Wally Backman, was a familiar face from the glory days, and many fans threw their support behind him for that very reason. The fact that Backman might not have been first runner-up, or even second runner-up—many reports had scout Bob Melvin and third-base coach Chip Hale finishing second and third for the job—is inconsequential to those fans. The fans wanted Backman, and no one else was going to do.

Collins probably does deserve a share of the blame for what happened during his previous managerial gigs in Houston and Anaheim. From 1994 to 1996, the Astros finished second each year under Collins, but there was always the expectation that the team should have been more successful. It was a very talented team, featuring players like Jeff Bagwell and Craig Biggio, but also Derek Bell, Luis Gonzalez, Shane Reynolds, Darryl Kile, and Mike Hampton. It probably should have performed better, and Collins was fired after a late-season collapse in 1996. But he was unemployed for just a month, as Bill Bavasi immediately hired him to run the Angels. The Angels didn't really fare any better under Collins, finishing second twice, and Collins found himself resigning during a disappointing 1999 season. The Angels were riddled with injuries, and newly signed slugger Mo Vaughn repeatedly rubbed a couple veterans the wrong way, leading to plenty of squabbling. Eventually, the players petitioned for Collins's dismissal. Feeling that he had lost the caustic clubhouse, Collins opted to give the players what they wanted despite the protests of Bavasi and team president Tony Tavares. Tim Salmon would later remark that the blame shouldn't have fallen squarely on Collins, but that doesn't mean Collins was blameless in allowing the team to fragment the way it did.

After leaving the Angels, Collins served as a scout for the Cubs and as the bullpen coach in Tampa, and he eventually landed as the field coordinator in Los Angeles, where he sufficiently impressed then-GM and current Mets player-development head Paul DePodesta that he was offered the managerial post. But a front-office shakeup ousted DePodesta before that could happen, and Collins moved on to Japan, where he managed with mixed success for three seasons. After a stint as the coach of China's World Baseball Classic team, Collins joined the Mets as their field coordinator for the 2010 season.

It is difficult to say how, exactly, Collins will manage. After all, it's been over a decade since he last managed a major league team. In the past, he's been known for having a fiery persona and as a guy whose brand of baseball is intense, gritty, and disciplined. And while most thoughts of fiery managers conjure images of Larry Bowa-types, men who put hard-nosed play above the talented play that actually wins ball games—in other words, men who tend to manage solely by gut instinct—Collins has always drawn raves for his preparation and intellect. Compared to Manuel's often haphazard approach to lineup construction and bull-pen usage, Collins should be a welcome change. When dealing with the bullpen, he will likely use his closer traditionally, but he has expressed no reservations about using his best setup men at high-leverage points, regardless of the inning in which they occur. In Houston and Anaheim, he displayed a preference for guys who got on base, and he transitioned nicely from an organization with lots of speed (Houston) to a team that didn't have much at all (Anaheim). He didn't try to force one philosophy onto a team ill-suited for it. That said, he did like small ball and was liberal in his use of the bunt while in Houston. Considering that the bunt is rarely a play that improves a team's chances of scoring runs, it will be something to keep an eye on this season. But what will be most interesting is how Collins interacts with his players. In the past, he often let his fiery side irritate the players he was supposed to be managing. He did soften up a little in Anaheim, and he claims to have learned further from his experiences there.

What might be the most beneficial aspect of the Mets' new manager is his relationship with the organization's young players, who appear to have an increased role under this new regime. As the Mets' field co-ordinator, Collins worked with each of these players. He knows their strengths and weaknesses, and many have learned to trust him. An outsider to the organization, or a hire from another department, wouldn't have that, and it could prove to be a critical resource when managing the clubhouse.

The Mets have also brought aboard a mostly new coaching staff. While third base coach Hale and pitching coach Dan Warthen are returning, Dave Jauss, Howard Johnson, Razor Shines, and Randy Niemann will not be. Instead, Mets fans will see a familiar face in Mookie Wilson manning the first base coach's box, and Triple-A Buffalo manager Ken Oberkfell will serve as Collins's bench coach. Jon Debus will be the bullpen coach, and Dave Hudgens will take over as hitting instructor. Warthen should be a known quantity for most Mets fans. He has a very hands-off style that appeals to some pitchers but leaves the more stubborn ones guessing his thoughts. Unlike Johnson, Hudgens has a very systematic, almost scientific, approach to hitting, one that reminds some of how former Mets coach Rick Peterson approached the art of pitching. It's a drastic difference from what Mets hitters are familiar with, and, much like how Peterson couldn't work well with certain pitchers, some hitters may be left with their heads spinning if Hudgens indulges in too many details.

Collins will be working on a two-year contract, so he and his staff will have a long leash this season. Nobody's expecting him to work miracles with a team hamstrung by a lack of financial flexibility, so 2012 should be the true test of Collins's style. But if he can demonstrably manage the egos that come with a big league clubhouse, there's no reason he couldn't impress and earn an extension before his two years are up.

CHAPTER ELEVEN

PLAYER PROFILES AND PROJECTIONS

L ast season, we included player profiles for every player in Mets camp, save two catchers. That meant that there was about as much content for nonentities Jack Egbert, Shawn Riggans, Arturo Lopez, and Alex Cintron as there was for Carlos Beltran, Angel Pagan, Johan Santana, and Jason Bay.

While there's something to be said for including information about every soul with a remote chance of latching on with the Mets, in retrospect it didn't appear to be the most effective use of our time. It's nice knowing that Jack Egbert posted some above-average ground ball rates in the minors, but he never had a prayer of making the team, so that information never became relevant.

This year we've narrowed our focus to provide more substance for the players who are more likely to see time with the team, and we hope the 2011 profiles are a little more interesting and a little more helpful. And if we've missed somebody who will appear on the 25-man roster on April 1, here's an apology in advance. Know that our hearts were in the right place.

For most players, the profile is split into three parts: statistics, commentary from one of the Amazin' Avenue writers, and a custom graphic. Our statistics this year include a simplified approach over last year when we included two tables of numbers—one for traditional stats and one for more advanced metrics. Showing that much data was unwieldy and confusing. And probably overkill.

We've reduced the number of tables to just one. Inside each, you'll find the player's biographical information at the top, followed by his key 2010 data. Players who split 2010 between the majors and the minors— or who spent time at multiple minor league levels—show numbers from whichever level we think is most significant, generally where the player had the most playing time. The final line of the stat table is the player's 2011 ZiPS projection. For a description of ZiPS, as well as all of the other statistics we provide, see the Statistics Glossary at the end of the book.

Player commentaries include information about the player's background, an analysis of his recent production and overall skill set, and a description of what the player is likely to provide as a member of the

Mets in 2011. You'll get a great idea of where each player has been and what to expect of him.

The final component of our profiles is a player-specific graphic created by the fantastic Justin Bopp of Beyond the Box Score. Each is unique and highlights something of particular interest about the player. Graphical illustrations are an efficient way of getting information across, and Justin did a wonderful job making certain they were visually appealing. Note that a handful of players who were signed to minor league deals do not have a corresponding graphic. Sorry, Blaine Boyer!

Also note that the Mets' top prospects are not included in this section. You can find them in Chapter 14, "Prospect Profiles And Predictions."

Before we dip into the profiles, we thought it might be useful to take a quick look at some numbers summarizing last year's team.

2010 TEAM & PLAYER PITCHING: ORDERING BASED ON FIP

2010			METS PITCHING						Min. 40 IP	
NAME	K/9	BB/9	K/BB	BABIP	LOB%	GB%	IFFB%	HR/FB	FIP	xFIP
Francisco Rodriguez	10.52	3.30	3.19	.294	84.6%	42.1%	14.0%	5.3%	2.63	3.30
Pedro Feliciano	8.04	4.31	1.87	.348	77.5%	56.0%	10.3%	2.6%	3.22	3.86
Johan Santana	6.51	2.49	2.62	.272	79.1%	34.5%	8.6%	6.0%	3.54	4.32
R.A. Dickey	5.37	2.17	2.48	.276	77.3%	55.1%	10.5%	8.5%	3.65	3.88
Hisanori Takahashi	8.41	3.17	2.65	.298	76.7%	38.4%	8.3%	8.3%	3.65	4.01
Mike Pelfrey	4.99	3.00	1.66	.300	73.7%	47.8%	6.7%	5.7%	3.82	4.46
Jon Niese	7.67	3.21	2.39	.324	70.6%	47.7%	9.4%	11.8%	4.10	3.94
Raul Valdes	8.59	4.14	2.07	.310	71.1%	33.7%	13.3%	8.4%	4.31	4.69
2010 Mets	7.20	3.37	2.03	.281	74.0%	43.9%	9.5%	10.7%	4.34	4.31
Elmer Dessens	3.06	3.06	1.00	.239	84.6%	42.2%	10.4%	6.0%	4.72	5.56
Fernando Nieve	8.14	4.71	1.73	.239	70.2%	37.0%	11.1%	18.5%	6.08	4.47
Oliver Perez	7.19	8.16	0.88	.317	72.1%	35.4%	10.4%	13.4%	6.99	6.43

2010 TEAM & PLAYER BATTING: ORDERING BASED ON wOBA

2010 NAME	AVG	OBP	SLG	OPS	OPS+	BABIP	BB%	K%	wOBA
David Wright	.283	.354	.503	.856	131	.335	10.3%	27.4%	.364
Ike Davis	.264	.351	.440	.791	115	.321	12.0%	26.4%	.345
Angel Pagan	.290	.340	.425	.765	108	.331	7.0%	16.8%	.341
Jason Bay	.259	.347	.402	.749	105	.329	11.0%	26.1%	.336
Carlos Beltran	.255	.341	.427	.768	109	.275	11.8%	17.7%	.332
Jose Reyes	.282	.321	.428	.749	103	.301	5.1%	11.2%	.329
Josh Thole	.277	.357	.366	.723	99	.305	10.6%	12.4%	.327
Chris Carter	.263	.317	.389	.706	92	.274	6.7%	10.2%	.309
2010 Mets	**.249**	**.314**	**.383**	**.697**	**90**	**.287**	**8.2%**	**20.0%**	**.308**
Rod Barajas	.225	.263	.414	.677	82	.219	3.0%	15.7%	.289
Jeff Francoeur	.237	.293	.369	.662	80	.259	6.5%	19.0%	.287
Luis Castillo	.235	.337	.267	.604	68	.269	13.0%	10.1%	.285
Ruben Tejada	.213	.305	.282	.588	62	.250	8.6%	17.6%	.266
Jesus Feliciano	.231	.276	.287	.563	55	.258	5.0%	11.1%	.256
Henry Blanco	.215	.271	.300	.571	56	.248	7.6%	20.0%	.252
Alex Cora	.207	.265	.278	.543	49	.226	5.3%	9.5%	.246

MANNY ACOSTA

Bat/Throw: S/R		RELIEF PITCHER						Born: 05/01/81					
	G	IP	H	BB	K	BB/9	K/9	HR	ERA	FIP	BABIP	LOB%	LD%	GB%	WAR
2010	41	39.2	30	18	42	4.1	9.5	4	2.95	3.63	.280	83%	18%	42%	0.6
2011	54	60.0	57	31	53	4.6	7.9	8	4.50	4.61	.281	71%	---	---	0.1
Career	144	153.2	136	77	127	4.5	7.4	17	3.40	4.47	.279	80%	18%	49%	1.4

Signed by the New York Yankees as an amateur free agent in 1998, it took Manny Acosta a while to make his way to the big leagues. He was released by the Yankees in July 2003, but the Atlanta Braves signed him only a few days later. In 2007, the hard-throwing righty finally reached the majors, and over the course of three seasons and 103 appearances he posted a 3.55 ERA despite high walk rates. Just before the 2010 season started, the Mets claimed Acosta off waivers from the Braves.

Acosta's 2010 was spent between Buffalo and the Mets, but he tallied

41 appearances out of the Mets' bullpen. Those 41 games constituted what was probably the best season Acosta has had thus far in his career. As has always been the case with Acosta, he walked over four batters per nine innings, but that rate was still a marked improvement over anything he'd done to date. He also struck batters out at a career-high clip, significantly lowering his FIP and xFIP and making his ERA look a lot more sustainable that it did during his years with the Braves. In terms of splits, there wasn't a huge difference between Acosta's performance against lefties and righties. He struck out and walked right-handed hitters more often than left-handed hitters.

Based on last year's performance, the Mets could do worse in filling their bullpen than giving a spot to Manny Acosta. Despite walking lots of batters, he does throw hard. Unfortunately, the strikeout and walk rates from last year are probably unsustainable, as both were career bests. Some regression seems inevitable, but Acosta could put together a respectable season out of the bullpen. Even if the Mets find they can fill their bullpen with other pitchers in spring training, it wouldn't be surprising to see Acosta eventually get called up if someone else in the bullpen falters or gets hurt. —*Chris McShane*

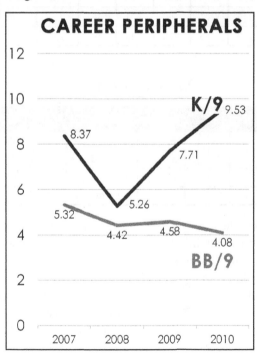

JASON BAY

Bat/Throw: R/R				LEFT FIELDER								Born: 09/20/78		
	G	PA	R	HR	RBI	BB%	K%	AVG	OBP	SLG	BABIP	wOBA	SB	SB%	WAR
2010	95	401	48	6	47	11%	26%	.259	.347	.402	.329	.336	10	100%	1.1
2011	122	515	71	20	76	12%	24%	.252	.349	.455	.306	.353	9	90%	2.0
Career	1017	4298	627	191	657	12%	27%	.278	.374	.508	.327	.380	76	84%	18.9

Back in 2002, Mets GM Steve Phillips acquired Jason Bay from the Omar Minaya-led Expos for the laughable price of utility man Lou Collier. Of course, Phillips then traded Bay away a few months later to the Padres for the almost-as-laughable price of Steve Reed.

So when Omar Minaya signed Bay to a four-year, $66 million deal before last season, it appeared like two giant mistakes were rectified. After years of building an accomplished offensive resume with the Pirates, Bay moved on to Boston where he put up some more MVP-type statistics. While there were flaws in his game, he seemed like a safe bet to produce with the bat, at least as far as 2010 was concerned.

Instead, Bay continued to haunt the Mets, "hitting" to the tune of a .259/.347/.402 line and missing almost the entire second half of the season after suffering a whiplash-induced concussion after colliding with the wall in Dodger Stadium in late July. Now that contract is looking like one of the larger albatrosses on a team with enough of them to make up an aviary. The near-total disappearance of Bay's power is most troubling, obviously, as it represents the bulk of his value to the team. Let's face it: He's not in the lineup every day for his defense, which is well below average at a position that only requires marginal defensive ability to begin with. The first place many critics turned to was Citi Field. Surely the cavernous dimensions of the new park were to blame for Bay's struggles, just as they were when David Wright's power vanished in 2009. Unfortunately, the numbers don't quite back that up: Bay didn't hit great at Citi Field (.277/.371/.459), but they were the second-best home numbers on the team, and they positively dwarf his numbers on the road (.243/.326/.356). Now, it's possible that Bay made some adjustments at home that threw off his production on the road. But that seems like a little bit of a stretch, and there could be any number of simpler explanations for Bay's difficulties, not the least of which is small sample size.

So what's the verdict? Is Jason Bay just the latest in a string of big-ticket acquisitions the Mets have brought in only to fail miserably upon arrival? Or is he a Carlos Beltran type, a guy who bounces back from one poor, injury-plagued season to put up the MVP-type numbers everyone expected? It's impossible to know which for sure, but Bay has just too much history to suggest he's as bad as he looked in 2010. Look for new hitting coach Dave Hudgens to make Bay a priority this spring. It's reasonable to expect a bounce-back season, though at his age—Bay is entering his age-32 season, so he's on what's typically the downward slope to his career—probably not to the heights he achieved in Pittsburgh or Boston. —*Alex Nelson*

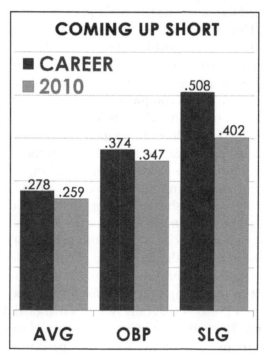

PEDRO BEATO

Bat/Throw: R/R					RELIEF PITCHER								Born: 10/27/86	
	G	IP	H	BB	K	BB/9	K/9	HR	ERA	FIP	BABIP	LOB%	LD%	GB%
2009 (A+)	20	105.1	125	40	70	3.4	6.0	12	4.53	4.75	.328	73%	14%	45.5%
2010 (AA)	43	59.2	49	19	50	2.9	7.5	4	2.11	3.50	.271	87%	16%	44.3%
2011	45	56.2	59	26	36	4.2	5.7	6	4.76	4.78	.286	67%	---	---

The Mets attempted to right a past mistake this offseason when they plucked Beato from the Orioles organization in the Rule 5 Draft. The

Mets held the rights to the Brooklyn-born Beato back in 2005 after selecting him in the 17th round of the amateur draft as a "draft-and-follow," where they had no intention of signing him immediately but saw enough talent to warrant keeping an eye on his progress. It was a smart move: By the following spring Beato's arm strength had improved dramatically, his fastball frequently touching the mid-to-upper-90s. The problem? It had improved so much that Beato had worked himself into first-round consideration for the 2006 draft. In other words, there was no chance he'd sign. He returned to college and was drafted by the Orioles in the first round. The next spring, he placed 99th on *Baseball America*'s prospect list and played in the Futures Game that summer.

Unfortunately for Beato and the Orioles, his development stalled in the minors. Actually, it was worse than that. He took a step backward. His fastball stopped hitting those high-90s, forcing him to rely on a 90-mph sinker. And his breaking stuff never really progressed. As a result, he never displayed the strikeout numbers in the minors you'd want out of a dominant pitcher, and without pinpoint control, it was clear by the end of 2009 that Beato was not going to make it as a starter.

The transition from starter to reliever went well. The fastball velocity went up a little, the strikeout rate climbed, and the walk rate dropped. It's unlikely that he'll ever evolve into any other role than middle relief, but he could be a righty specialist with an affinity for getting ground outs.

As a Rule 5 pick, Beato needs to make the 25-man roster or be offered back to the Orioles for half his purchase price. If he were to make the Mets' roster, the idea would be for him to assume the role the team envisioned for Sean Green last year, which was more or less the same role Chad Bradford once filled in the past: a guy who can come in and pitch to a couple tough righties and grab a key ground out. He's far from an automatic to land the job, however, and he'll probably be competing directly with non-roster invitee Blaine Boyer for the same position. The fact that the Mets will lose him entirely if he doesn't land the gig does work in his favor, but he'll still need a solid spring. —*Alex Nelson*

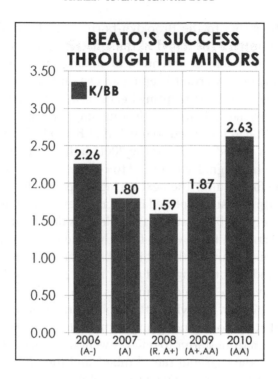

BEATO'S SUCCESS THROUGH THE MINORS

K/BB

Year	2006 (A-)	2007 (A)	2008 (R, A+)	2009 (A+,AA)	2010 (AA)
K/BB	2.26	1.80	1.59	1.87	2.63

CARLOS BELTRAN

Bat/Throw: S/R				CENTER FIELDER								Born: 04/24/77		
	G	PA	R	HR	RBI	BB%	K%	AVG	OBP	SLG	BABIP	wOBA	SB	SB%	WAR
2010	64	255	21	7	27	12%	18%	.255	.341	.427	.275	.332	3	75%	1.8
2011	99	429	52	13	54	11%	15%	.270	.354	.447	.297	.344	10	83%	3.3
Career	1626	7132	1106	280	1062	11%	18%	.282	.359	.494	.301	.371	289	88%	56.5

After his historic playoff run with the Astros in 2004 when he belted eight home runs, knocked in 14 runs, drew nine walks, and reached base more than half the time, Carlos Beltran inked a massive free-agent contract with the Mets. For seven years and $119 million, the Mets had secured the budding superstar. To this day Beltran is still booed in Houston and, on many occasions, inexplicably booed in his home park. Six seasons into his Mets tenure, Beltran has had one subpar campaign (2005), three outstanding ones (2006–2008), and two that were injury-shortened (2009–2010). He is now 33 years old and entering his contract walk year amid plenty of health-related concerns, positional uncertainty, and the stark reality of a career in decline. Less than two years ago, he was generally considered the best center fielder in the game and was in the midst of what figured to be a career year. However, baseball fortunes can turn on a dime.

Beltran was hitting .336/.425/.527 in late June of 2009, when a right knee contusion put him on the shelf for nearly three months. He was hardly the same player after returning, as he hit just .284/.377/.403 over the season's final three weeks. Last offseason he caused a stir when he underwent arthroscopic surgery on his bothersome knee, allegedly without first getting the Mets' blessing. He would miss the first half of 2010 recovering from the surgery, though the Mets were in good hands, as Angel Pagan performed splendidly in his absence. Beltran made his 2010 debut after the All-Star break and it took longer than expected for him to hit his stride. Through the end of August, he was batting .218/.329/.331, and casual observers could have been forgiven for suggesting that Beltran's days as a productive hitter were running short. September brought with it better days for Beltran, though, as he hit .321/.365/.603 in 21 games before knee soreness forced him out of the final meaningless week of the season.

Things seem to be back on track for Beltran in 2011, though his knee will probably never be perfectly healed and he'll certainly never have the body of his 28-year-old self again. Since this may very well be his final year with the Mets, fans should make it a point to really watch the man play, on television or in person, wonky knee or not. While Beltran has professed a desire to remain with the Mets after this season, many circumstances beyond his control—Mets payroll flexibility, team needs, and the voracious march of Scott Boras, free agent opinion-maker—could lead him elsewhere in 2012 (or sooner). If that's the case, whether you think he's overpaid or if you've never forgiven him for that time he struck out looking in the playoffs, Beltran should nevertheless be remembered as one of the best all-around players the Mets have ever had. —*Eric Simon*

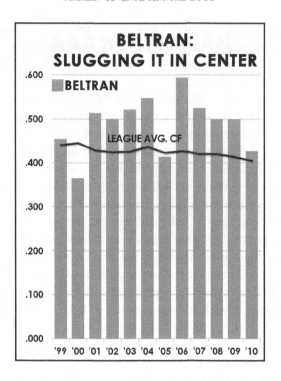

BLAINE BOYER

Bat/Throw: R/R					RELIEF PITCHER								Born: 07/11/81	
	G	IP	H	BB	K	BB/9	K/9	HR	ERA	FIP	BABIP	LOB%	LD%	GB%	WAR
2010	54	57.0	59	29	29	4.6	4.6	3	4.26	4.32	.296	67%	13%	66%	-0.3
2011	59	62.7	64	26	44	3.7	6.3	5	4.31	4.08	.290	69%	---	---	0.2
Career	228	227.1	234	93	161	3.7	6.4	15	4.63	3.89	.305	63%	16%	56%	-2.0

The 29-year-old Boyer, who signed a minor league deal with the Mets in January, was originally drafted by the Braves in 2000, just one of the seemingly countless Georgia players whose high schools have become a feeder system to their local big league team. Boyer spent parts of six seasons in the minors before the Braves called him up midway through the 2005 season. Shoulder tendinitis nagged him late that season and during the following spring, and after making just two appearances in 2006, he opted for surgery that would keep him out of action for the rest of the year. He was shuffled back to the minors for most of 2007 but returned to the Braves in 2008, a season defined by great process—8.4 K/9, 3.1

BB/9—which nevertheless resulted in a disappointing 5.88 ERA.

Boyer had a rough time with the Diamondbacks in 2010, walking the same number of batters as he struck out—29—in 57 innings of work. His walk rate was quite a bit better in 2009, a year he split between Atlanta, St. Louis, and Arizona, but his strikeout rate was still a shamefully low 4.77 per nine innings.

Why would the Mets even bother with a pitcher like Boyer, a seemingly mediocre pitcher with spotty peripheral stats and a season-ending shoulder surgery on his record? Well, there's one thing Boyer does extraordinarily well, and that's generate ground balls. His 3.08 ground ball ratio was the fourth-best mark in baseball last season, and the corollary is that he also does a fine job preventing home runs. As with most right-handed ground ball pitchers, Boyer is very effective against right-handed batters and much less so against lefties. In short, he's a ROOGY—a Righty One Out GuY—and while he's certainly an underdog to make the team out of spring training, if he can keep the walks to a minimum, the Mets could have a decent double play-producing pitcher for the middle of their bullpen. —*Eric Simon*

TAYLOR BUCHHOLZ

Bat/Throw: R/R					RELIEF PITCHER						Born: 10/13/81			
	G	IP	H	BB	K	BB/9	K/9	HR	ERA	FIP	BABIP	LOB%	LD%	GB%	WAR
2010	9	12.0	10	6	9	4.5	6.8	2	3.75	5.25	.250	83%	12%	36%	0.1
2011	44	49.1	47	17	39	3.1	7.1	4	3.65	5.25	.283	70%	---	---	1.1
Career	135	285.0	267	78	203	2.5	6.4	36	4.39	4.28	.268	65%	18%	42%	0.7

Every time Buchholz's career seems to be taking off, it gets grounded. Buchholz was drafted by the Phillies in the sixth round of the 2000 draft, and he quickly established himself as a top prospect. In the minors, he had a good fastball, a great curve, and excellent control. He wasn't a dominant pitcher by any means—his strikeout rates never stood out enough for that—but he did look like a future mid-rotation starter. However, he was dealt to the Astros as the main component in the Billy Wagner deal, and he struggled in Triple-A for his new organization. He still made the club in 2006, pitched poorly, then was summarily demoted. He was nearly traded to the White Sox, but he failed a physical and was instead dealt to the Rockies for Jason Jennings.

He failed as a starter once more for the Rockies before they decided to make him a reliever. And then he blossomed, posting a 2.17 ERA in 2008 while putting his trademark control on display. In shorter outings, his velocity crept back into the mid-90s and his curve proved to be an outstanding weapon against both right- and left-handed hitters. Buccholz is odd in that he has always shown a reverse platoon split, but that normalized some when working out of the bullpen. And just when the Rockies were patting themselves on the back, Buchholz blew out his elbow, requiring Tommy John surgery which forced him to miss all of 2009 and most of 2010. The Rockies cut him during the season, and the Blue Jays, who picked him off waivers, followed suit shortly after the season. The Red Sox claimed him but didn't tender him a contract.

The Mets signed him in January to a one-year deal. How effective he is depends on how well he has recovered from surgery. If he's healthy, he could be an extremely useful setup man who can pitch to both righties and lefties. If not, it only cost the team $600,000.
—*Alex Nelson*

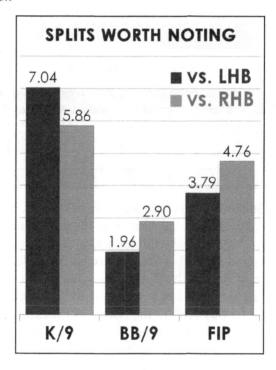

TIM BYRDAK

Bat/Throw: L/L					RELIEF PITCHER							Born: 10/31/73		
	G	IP	H	BB	K	BB/9	K/9	HR	ERA	FIP	BABIP	LOB%	LD%	GB%	WAR
2010	64	38.2	40	20	29	4.7	6.8	4	3.49	4.48	.308	83%	19%	29%	0.5
2011	63	47.1	44	25	41	4.8	7.8	6	4.37	4.70	.274	71%	---	---	0.1
Career	343	266.2	251	164	242	5.5	8.2	39	4.35	5.15	.280	76%	18%	41%	0.6

It's difficult to get excited about Tim Byrdak. After all, the Mets will be the 37-year-old's seventh organization since first coming up with the Royals in 1998, and that doesn't include his various stints in the independent leagues. A cursory glance at his statistics will make some wonder why the Mets are even giving him a chance. The strikeout rate is fine, but we're talking about a guy who's walked 5.5 batters per nine innings over nine big league seasons—by comparison, Oliver Perez's career rate is 5.1—while sporting a 4.35 ERA. He's also a fly ball pitcher who can be prone to giving up homers.

But Tim Byrdak is left-handed, so everything goes out the window. If you're left-handed and you can still throw 80, there's a good chance of a job waiting for you somewhere. Byrdak's never been any use at all against righties, but he's death to southpaws, holding them to a .213/.271/.373 line in 2010. A look at his arsenal tells you all you need to know: He pairs a 90-mph fastball with a slurvy breaking pitch that doesn't have enough late bite to fool right-handed hitters. When he is called upon to face righties, he'll rely more upon a forkball which he uses as a changeup. It doesn't appear to be doing the trick, though, as righties hit .333 off him last year.

With Pedro Feliciano out of the picture, the Mets find themselves in need of a lefty specialist for the first time in years. Sandy Alderson is hoping that either Byrdak or Taylor Tankersley, or possibly both, will step up in spring training and be able to fill that void. In Byrdak's case, he has the ability to get those tough lefties out, but he will need to watch his control to have a strong chance of making the team. Nobody wants a lefty specialist who walks the one batter he's supposed to get out.
—*Alex Nelson*

CHRIS CAPUANO

Bat/Throw: L/L					STARTING PITCHER							Born: 08/19/78			
	G	IP	H	BB	K	BB/9	K/9	HR	ERA	FIP	BABIP	LOB%	LD%	GB%	WAR
2010	24	66.0	65	21	54	2.9	7.4	9	3.95	4.22	.290	78%	17%	43%	0.8
2011	28	110.2	112	35	89	2.8	7.2	12	4.15	3.95	.292	69%	---	---	1.8
Career	148	777.2	794	261	639	3.0	7.4	110	4.35	4.47	.297	73%	20%	40%	8.4

Chris Capuano was drafted by the Arizona Diamondbacks in 1999 and traded to the Milwaukee Brewers shortly after the 2003 season as part of the package for Richie Sexson. It was in Milwaukee that he really blossomed into a pitcher that few could have predicted. In 2005, he won 18 games, and he might have even been better in 2006 despite winning fewer. Then injuries happened, as they inevitably do with pitchers. In 2007, it was a torn labrum. In 2008, Tommy John surgery.

Capuano finally returned to action last June after two full seasons off, and after initially trying him in the rotation for one catastrophic start, they inserted him into the bullpen. He pitched much like he had pitched before his injury. Although he only pitched 66 innings, the results suggest that Capuano may still be the pitcher that he was before the two surgeries. His strikeouts and walks per nine were on par with his pre-injury numbers. On top of that, his average fastball velocity in 2010 was 87.4 mph, higher than it had been in any of the 2005–2007 seasons.

Despite his success, with the Brewers trading for Zack Greinke and Shaun Marcum, they didn't see any room for Capuano, at least not in the starting rotation. Capuano did not want to move to the bullpen, and the two sides decided to part ways. Shortly thereafter, Capuano signed an incentive-laden deal with the Mets, a seemingly perfect fit since the Mets' starting rotation was in need of arms and Capuano was in need of an opportunity to start.

The red flag with Capuano is that he's missed so much time as a result of Tommy John surgery. Throw in his age, and there's no guarantee that he can pitch a full season as a member of a major league rotation. Because of this, Terry Collins has indicated that Capuano might begin the season in the bullpen. But there were plenty of positives to take out of his return to the Brewers last year, and if he's able to stay healthy, he may fulfill his desire to be a starter. —*Chris McShane*

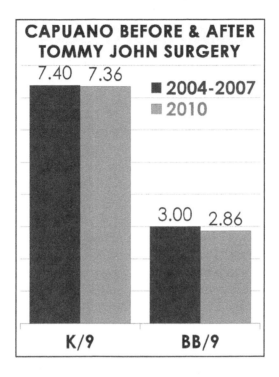

D.J. CARRASCO

Bat/Throw: R/R					RELIEF PITCHER					Born: 04/12/77				
	G	IP	H	BB	K	BB/9	K/9	HR	ERA	FIP	BABIP	LOB%	LD%	GB%	WAR
2010	63	78.1	68	34	65	3.9	7.5	5	3.68	3.74	.285	68%	21%	48%	0.5
2011	51	75.2	72	29	59	3.4	7.0	6	3.81	3.86	.282	70%	---	---	0.5
Career	244	440.2	453	183	285	3.7	5.8	36	4.31	4.27	.300	71%	20%	51%	4.6

At first blush, Carrasco's profile doesn't leap off the page. He'll be 34 years old in April, and he features a low-90s fastball, a high-80s cutter, and a mid-70s curveball. He'll also mix in the occasional slider. He's never been a dominant strikeout pitcher, though he did improve a bit in that department last year, notching a career-best whiff rate of 7.5 per nine innings. He doesn't have great control and actually walked hitters more frequently in 2010 than he had in any season since 2005.

Two things stand out positively for Carrasco. The first is his tendency to keep the ball on the ground and, by extension, in the ballpark. Merely decent strikeout and walk rates coupled with an above-average home run rate can add up to a solid reliever. Ground ball pitchers limit home runs in particular, and extra-base hits in general, since grounders are less likely to find gaps than their airborne brethren. More ground balls usually mean more double plays, too, so that's another bonus. The second point for Carrasco, albeit an ethereal one, is that he was very effective against lefties in 2010, which is exceedingly rare for right-handed pitchers. Unfortunately, he hasn't historically been strong against lefties, and was awful against them in 2009 (.317/.392/.463). He did throw far more curveballs last season than ever before, but it's not clear how that would serve him well against lefties. The bottom line is that Carrasco has been an above-average pitcher over the past three seasons.

Carrasco made $950,000 in his first season of arbitration eligibility last year, splitting time between the Pirates and the Diamondbacks. He was a non-tender victim in Arizona this offseason, and the Mets scooped him up. It might seem unnecessary to give Carrasco two years, but $2.5 million for two seasons isn't much more than $1.25 for one. Plus, it's a hedge against Carrasco having a decent year and then seeking a bit more money in 2012. If he's terrible in 2011, then the Mets can either dump him or trade him, and all they've wasted is a million bucks. If he's even remotely useful, then the Mets have an inexpensive bullpen arm locked up for another season. —*Eric Simon*

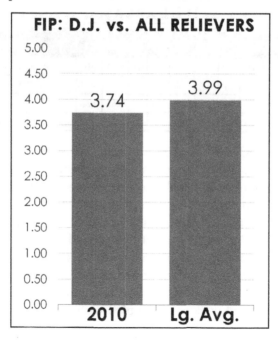

LUIS CASTILLO

Bat/Throw: S/R					SECOND BASEMAN						Born: 09/12/75			
	G	PA	R	HR	RBI	BB%	K%	AVG	OBP	SLG	BABIP	wOBA	SB	SB%	WAR
2010	86	299	28	0	17	13%	10%	.235	.337	.267	.259	.285	8	73%	-0.1
2011	103	410	49	1	27	11%	9%	.259	.345	.308	.277	.294	12	75%	-0.3
Career	1720	7471	1001	28	443	11%	13%	.290	.368	.351	.329	.328	370	72%	24.5

Luis Castillo spent the first ten years of his career with the Marlins, and in doing so he won three Gold Gloves, went to three All-Star games, and celebrated two World Series championships in Florida. In 2006 he signed a free-agent contract with the Twins, who dealt him to the Mets a year and a half later for minor leaguers Drew Butera and Dustin Martin. Castillo hit well enough down the stretch—and the Mets were increasingly desperate to find a decent second baseman—that he managed to coerce a four-year, $24 million contract out of then-GM Omar Minaya. In the three years that have transpired since, when Castillo hasn't been either hurt or healing, he has been dropping game-ending fly balls or forcing the Mets to consider a host of inadequate contingency plans at second base. When not busy with all of that, he has occasionally been able to reach base just often enough to be marginally useful.

Last year was more of the same for Castillo, who missed the better part of two months with a foot contusion and, upon returning, lost his starting job due to ineffectiveness. As unremarkable as Castillo has been since re-signing with the Mets, his injuries and ineptitude forced him to cede second base to the underwhelming triumvirate of Alex Cora, Luis Hernandez, and Ruben Tejada. In fact, at age 34, Castillo most assuredly had the worst season of his modestly successful career, setting low-water marks in plate appearances (299), batting average (.235), on-base percentage (.337), and slugging percentage (.267). He continued to be unflappably disciplined at the plate, drawing walks as frequently as ever, but that was scarcely enough to offset an offensive profile that was otherwise inert.

Castillo's four-year contract has been a sunk cost practically since the day it was signed. While a couple of years ago he might reasonably have been counted on to mitigate his considerable offensive shortcomings by coaxing enough walks to remain moderately useful, his baseball expiration date is rapidly approaching. While the Mets are contractually obligated to pay Castillo for one more year, the $6 million they still owe him isn't so much that Sandy Alderson won't consider jettisoning him if he thinks the roster spot is more valuable than the player consuming it. Each of the last three springs began with an assumption that Castillo would be the Opening Day starter at second base. This year, with competition coming from Justin Turner, Brad Emaus, Luis Hernandez, Daniel Murphy, and Chin-lung Hu, the odds are no longer in Castillo's favor. If his health problems are behind him, Castillo's impeccable strike zone judgment could still make him a useful part-time player under the right circumstances. If he continues to be nagged by injuries, the Mets may well be better off without him altogether. —*Eric Simon*

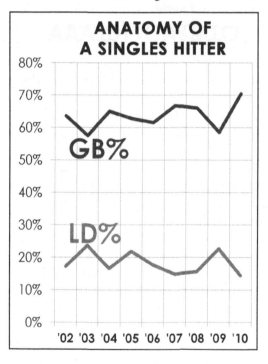

IKE DAVIS

Bat/Throw: L/L					FIRST BASEMAN							Born: 03/22/87		
	G	PA	R	HR	RBI	BB%	K%	AVG	OBP	SLG	BABIP	wOBA	SB	SB%	WAR
2010	147	601	73	19	71	12%	26%	.264	.351	.440	.321	.345	3	60%	2.5
2011	152	635	76	22	79	11%	24%	.257	.342	.447	.318	.342	2	50%	2.0
Career	147	601	73	19	71	12%	26%	.264	.351	.440	.321	.345	3	60%	2.5

When the Mets drafted Davis in the 2008 amateur draft, he was the fifth of six college first basemen taken in the first round. Shockingly, he's also been the most successful, at least so far. While it's unlikely that he'll maintain that distinction—Yonder Alonso and Justin Smoak are very talented, and both should improve in 2011—he has made the Mets look very smart for picking him 18th overall. At the time, Davis was considered a strong all-around player for a first baseman, if slightly unrefined. He was a good athlete for a corner infielder, and he could also throw 90. He made good contact at the plate. He had some power. However, there were flaws in his swing that made some scouts skeptical over whether he'd hit for power or contact like he did in college. When Davis struggled in his professional debut in 2008 and early in 2009, many felt vindicated.

But Davis, to his credit, adapted. He started squaring up the ball better and using his lower body to generate the power he'd been lacking. He had a big second half in 2009, and he followed that up with a monster spring training in 2010. Davis began the year at Buffalo, but he was quickly called up and made an immediate impact. On the whole, though, Davis's rookie season was up and down. There were times when he appeared to be pressing by expanding his strike zone—he struck out 138 times, and patience would disappear entirely for stretches at a time—but you have to be impressed with 53 extra-base hits. And he did rebound to have a stellar September. Davis also provided something many weren't expecting: tremendous defense at first base. Agile, soft-handed, and strong-armed, Davis might be the best defender the Mets have featured at first since John Olerud departed for Seattle.

Davis now figures prominently in the Mets' plans going forward. But questions do remain. Is Davis a future star or is he more of a solid everyday regular? If he can improve his contact ability from last season, it seems possible that he could be a star player. Unfortunately, few players improve in that regard without advance signals, and it's unlikely that we'll see his other skills radically evolve overnight. At the same time, it shouldn't be surprising if pitchers start exploiting Davis's weaknesses at the plate a little more aggressively, causing him to take a small step back production-wise. Mets fans should be patient. Like most youngsters, he's learning on the job. —*Alex Nelson*

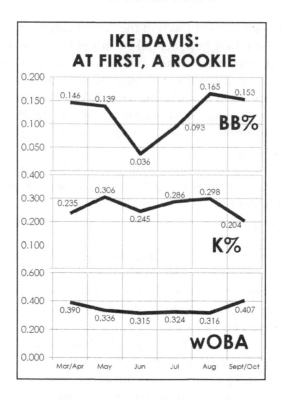

IKE DAVIS:
AT FIRST, A ROOKIE

R.A. DICKEY

Bat/Throw: R/R					STARTING PITCHER								Born: 10/29/74	
	G	IP	H	BB	K	BB/9	K/9	HR	ERA	FIP	BABIP	LOB%	LD%	GB%	WAR
2010	27	174.1	165	42	104	2.2	5.4	13	2.84	3.65	.276	77%	17%	55%	3.4
2011	28	170.0	173	46	100	2.4	5.3	17	3.86	4.12	.275	71%	---	---	3.4
Career	171	617.0	684	219	375	3.2	5.5	82	4.70	4.75	.300	72%	20%	47%	4.7

Port St. Lucie had an unusually intemperate March in 2010. The normally sunny Mets' spring training home experienced driving rains and gusting winds. The hard, fast knuckleball thrown by R.A. Dickey can cut through most weather, but it spun out of control in his Mets' audition. Dickey's chances to make the Mets were literally gone with the wind, but fate has never really seemed to be on his side. On a Mets off-day a month later, SNY aired the Buffalo Bisons game. Dickey was pitching and again it was windy. The first batter singled on an 0–2 pitch. The next twenty-seven went down in order. Dickey had just missed a perfect game, but immediately moved up several spots on the Mets' starting pitcher depth chart. A month later, when the Mets needed a starter, Dickey got the call up and made a better first impression. In his second start, the knuckleballer threw a six-inning shutout against the division rival Phillies. It would be the first of six times Dickey would surrender no runs in a start, including another one-hitter. And he showed no signs of slowing down either, excellent right up to his final appearance—a scoreless inning of relief in the season's last weekend.

Mike Pelfrey may be the Opening Day starter in 2011, but Dickey may have a better chance of being the team ace. Terry Collins having already named Pelfrey the Opening Day starter seems like baseball's equivalent of the young NHL phenom being named captain—it's a challenge to the athlete to fulfill potential as much as it is a reward for a job well done. Yet it may again be Dickey, not Pelfrey, that has the untapped potential.

Many fans, seeing Dickey's career-best performance at age 35, are predicting regression, but it's not a sure bet, if history is any guide. Every year since Dickey became a full-time knuckleball pitcher, his performance has improved. Skeptics might also point to his .275 batting average on balls in play, a low mark, but there's nothing out of character about it, as knuckleballers routinely outperform their pitching brethren in this area.

The upside in 2011 for Dickey is playing time, as his low-effort pitch and ulnar collateral ligament-free pitching arm could allow him to shoulder a lion's share of innings for the Mets, well over 200. If he combines that durability with quality—an ERA somewhere in the 3.00s— and if some other players have stronger than expected seasons, the Mets could have legitimate postseason aspirations.

Ironically, the arm deformity that was supposed to end his career, may enable him to become the Mets' most valuable player. And in the fact that knuckleball pitchers typically have uncommon aging curves— Charlie Hough and Phil Niekro pitched well into their forties—and last year may have been just the beginning for Dickey. Though it seems counter-intuitive, for Dickey and the Mets, the best may be yet to come.
—*Sam Page*

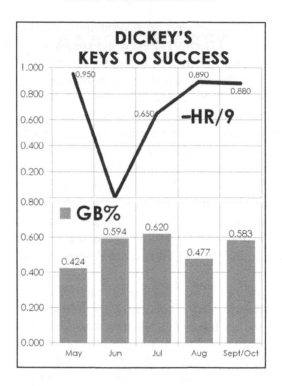

BRAD EMAUS

Bat/Throw: R/R				SECOND BASEMAN								Born: 03/28/86		
	G	PA	R	HR	RBI	BB%	K%	AVG	OBP	SLG	BABIP	wOBA	SB	SB%
2008 (A+)	124	543	87	12	71	11%	12%	.302	.380	.463	.320	.387	12	75%
2009 (AA)	137	581	67	10	67	10%	14%	.253	.336	.376	.271	.329	10	77%
2010 (AAA)	87	364	58	10	49	14%	16%	.298	.395	.495	.327	.394	8	80%

It's been quite a while since the Mets grabbed a player in the Rule 5 Draft who stuck around for the whole season—catcher Kelly Stinnett in 1994, to be precise—but this year the Mets have two in camp, both of whom have legitimate opportunities to make the team. Of the two, Emaus and Pedro Beato, it's Emaus who has the better chance of sticking with the club. Emaus came from the Blue Jays organization, where he was drafted by current Mets special assistant J.P. Ricciardi. Things were looking good until Toronto soured on him after a disappointing 2009 season in Double-A. He bounced back in 2010, but found himself on the wrong side of a roster crunch this offseason, as Toronto could not clear a spot for him on their 40-man roster.

Looking at his minor league career, one thing becomes clear—he can take a walk. Last year at Double-A and Triple-A, he walked 18.2% and 13.7% of the time, respectively. He pairs that patience with a low strikeout rate, making him a very disciplined hitter. It's the rest of his game that's a question mark. His power—very solid in 2010—may have been inflated by the ballparks in which he played. In Triple-A, where his .197 isolated power (ISO) looks enticing, he was playing in the PCL, the fifth-most hitter-friendly league in the minors, where the average ISO was .156. In the Eastern League, where he put up a more modest .162 ISO, the average ISO was .134.

Further damaging is the fact that he was also old for his leagues. There's definitely some power there, but it might simply play as above-average for an infielder rather than as impressive. Defense is a question, too. TotalZone had him as a positive in New Hampshire at Double-A, but a negative at Dunedin in High-A. Marc Hulet, prospect maven at FanGraphs.com, said that the Jays may have felt that "his defense is below average for second base and his offense is below average for third base." Perhaps this is an indication the Mets' new regime has a slight preference for offense over defense.

When it comes to Emaus's sticking on the major league roster—a must if the Mets are to keep him—the question then becomes who he would best complement. Unfortunately, if the defense is a question mark, Daniel Murphy might not be the best mate. If the team wants to bring Ruben Tejada north with the major league team, and he can simultaneously serve as the backup shortstop, all three could be used to fill in at second and back up around the infield. But Terry Collins has stated a preference to keep Tejada in the minors for 2011. All that said, Emaus's best chance rests with his ability to convince management that he deserves the job all to himself. —*Eno Sarris*

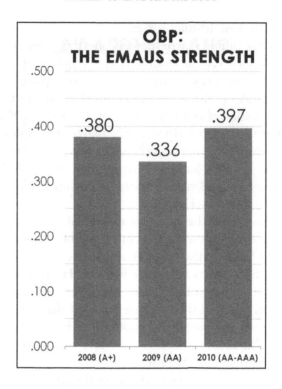

NICK EVANS

Bat/Throw: R/R				UTILITY MAN							Born: 01/30/86		
	G	PA	R	HR	RBI	BB%	K%	AVG	OBP	SLG	BABIP	wOBA	SB	SB%
2008 (AA)	75	326	52	14	53	8%	22%	.311	.365	.561	.353	.403	2	67%
2009 (AAA)	66	261	27	10	30	9%	23%	.211	.280	.414	.231	.306	0	N/A
2010 (AA)	88	391	62	17	55	10%	19%	.294	.366	.527	.317	.390	0	0%

You have to figure that Evans is looking forward to spring training more than ever. If he's lucky, he might even get released. Evans was drafted by the Mets in the fifth round of the 2004 draft, and he moved quickly through the system. After a great .311/.365/.561 season at Double-A Binghamton, Evans jumped directly to the big leagues. There, he occasionally looked overmatched, but he did demonstrate an ability to mash left-handed pitching, a skill he brought with him from the minors. If nothing else, Evans appeared to be a capable reserve or platoon option. Of course, Jerry Manuel and Omar Minaya instead relegated him to a season at Buffalo in 2009, where his batting average suffered despite his patience, power, and contact rate holding steady. The low batting average was mostly just bad luck.

In 2010, Evans was almost completely ignored in camp, and this time he wasn't even assigned to Buffalo. They sent him back to Binghamton instead. There, he bashed Eastern League pitching and was promoted to Buffalo in July, where his performance was even stronger. Eventually, even Manuel and Minaya couldn't ignore him, and his banishment came to an end. He was called up to the majors in late August, and he batted .306 the rest of the way, in sparse duty. Evans has his uses. He's nothing special against right-handed pitching, but he crushes lefties and is versatile enough to play the corner outfield positions or either corner infield positions. He doesn't have a ton of patience at the plate, but he's not a strikeout machine either.

Once again, Evans will find himself fighting for a spot on the team this spring. The situation is complicated by the presence of Scott Hairston, who has many of the same attributes that Evans has but is also capable of playing center field. Even worse: Hairston is working on a guaranteed contract. Evans is also out of options, so the Mets will not be able to stash him away in the minors as they did in 2009 and 2010. It seems very likely that Evans will either be traded or be released, in which case he'll be able to pick his landing spot. He could certainly help augment some team's bench. —*Alex Nelson*

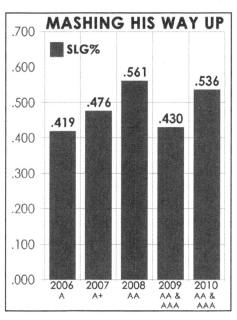

SCOTT HAIRSTON

Bat/Throw: R/R					OUTFIELDER						Born: 05/25/80			
	G	PA	R	HR	RBI	BB%	K%	AVG	OBP	SLG	BABIP	wOBA	SB	SB%	WAR
2010	104	336	34	10	36	9%	23%	.210	.295	.346	.236	.290	6	86%	-0.4
2011	110	371	44	12	44	8%	20%	.254	.316	.423	.291	.324	6	86%	0.3
Career	564	1856	204	68	198	7%	23%	.245	.303	.435	.278	.320	25	76%	3.8

Hairston comes from a family steeped in hardball tradition. His .190 isolated power is above average, and the fact that he managed 45 homers in 1,009 plate appearances while playing for San Diego also speaks to the same fact that he's got some pop. He even managed 24 in 528 PETCO plate appearances; kudos to him for muscling it out of that tough park. Along with the power, you get mediocre plate discipline with Hairston. He walks a little less than average and strikes out a little more than average. But neither number is too far from the median, and his low batting averages are probably more the result of low BABIPs built on hitting the ball in the air more often than not.

All of these statistics are better when Hairston is facing lefties. In 634 plate appearances against southpaws, Hairston has hit .278/.331/.498, compared to .227/.288/.402 against righties (in 1,222 plate appearances). That's not quite statistically significant, but he's been better against lefties in every year of his career, so it looks like a legitimate trend. For a team that had the fourth-worst wOBA in the National League against left-handed pitchers last year (.309), this is an interesting skill to own. Defense is a plus for Hairston as well. In 125 games in center field, he's managed a positive UZR/150 (+7.7). On the other hand, he's probably not as good as that number suggests, given his UZR/150 in 275 games in the corner outfield (+6.6). In any case, he can play center in a pinch and is a boon on the corners, which can be important in a big ballpark.

Hairston's track record and defense put him ahead in the battle for the fourth outfielder spot. While many of Hairston's numbers have been deflated by playing in pitcher's parks most of his career, that much isn't likely to change in New York. What we can glean from his past is that he'll likely make the team because of his prowess hitting lefties and his ability to play every outfield position. —*Eno Sarris*

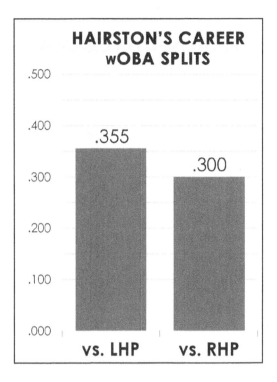

WILLIE HARRIS

Bat/Throw: L/R				OUTFIELDER								Born: 06/22/78		
	G	PA	R	HR	RBI	BB%	K%	AVG	OBP	SLG	BABIP	wOBA	SB	SB%	WAR
2010	132	262	25	10	32	13%	27%	.183	.291	.362	.199	.294	5	71%	-0.8
2011	131	340	41	8	33	12%	18%	.224	.326	.378	.257	.307	9	69%	0.0
Career	895	2484	324	37	187	11%	20%	.239	.327	.352	.281	.308	101	74%	3.8

Twice Willie Harris robbed the Mets of a sure walk-off hit in front of the home crowd—once with the Braves in 2007 and again with the Nationals in 2010. On two other occasions in 2008, he victimized the Amazins with similarly spectacular catches again that were close and late. A running joke between fans suggested the Mets should sign Willie Harris and stash him in the minors. If you can't beat him, sign him to an incentive-laden minor league deal, right?

Who knows if Sandy Alderson knew this history when he signed Harris, but the once-loathed outfielder will indeed compete for a job in Port St. Lucie this year. Unlike most light-hitting, slick-fielding fourth outfielders, Harris relies on walks and power for his offensive game. And like many hitters of the same mold, a propensity toward the strike-out brings down his batting average and leads to prolonged slumps. For instance, last year's preseason release of Elijah Dukes should have meant more playing time for Harris, but he failed to capitalize, hitting just .183/.291/.362 for the year. Luckily for Harris and the Mets, that slump seems to have been of the bad luck variety, not a Nate McLouth-kind of breakdown. The power and patience were still there, and Harris's .199 BABIP should regress toward his career .281 mark, raising his average well over the Mendoza Line. As a fielder, Harris has the range to play any of the three outfield positions with aplomb, though his weak arm keeps him from all-around excellence in center field. Harris even has experience at second base, third base, and shortstop, having broken into the league as a second baseman for the White Sox.

The sum of Willie Harris's tools isn't enough to construct a starting-caliber player at any position, but he can still be a good utility man capable of serving a variety of roles. Scott Hairston is ahead of him on the depth chart, but if the Mets carry five outfielders on the roster this season, Harris has as good a shot as anyone to fill that last outfielder spot. His handedness (lefty) and fielding ability should set him apart in spring training from players like Nick Evans and Lucas Duda. —*Sam Page*

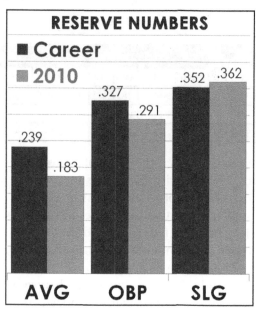

LUIS HERNANDEZ

Bat/Throw: S/R				MIDDLE INFIELDER						Born: 06/26/84			
	G	PA	R	HR	RBI	BB%	K%	AVG	OBP	SLG	BABIP	wOBA	SB	SB%
2008 (AAA)	57	216	18	0	11	4%	13%	.185	.216	.220	.213	.198	2	50%
2009 (AAA)	55	223	24	1	26	7%	9%	.303	.356	.369	.326	.325	1	25%
2010 (AAA)	47	208	25	0	12	5%	16%	.280	.319	.376	.329	.301	2	67%

The Mets signed Hernandez before last season knowing, or at least strongly suspecting, two things: He had a very good glove at shortstop and he had virtually no hitting ability. Hernandez came up through the Braves organization, and though scouts loved his defense, the club grew tired of waiting for the offense to appear and lost him to the Orioles on a waiver claim in 2006. The Orioles watched him for a year, and though he only hit .242 for Double-A Bowie, he earned a September call-up. By some small sample-size miracle, Hernandez hit .290 in 71 plate appearances. That was enough to fool Dave Trembley, who guaranteed Hernandez the starting job in 2008. That lasted a little more than a month, and the Orioles cut him loose after the season for the Royals to pick up. They, too, promised Hernandez a starting job only to give up when he failed to hit once again.

Hernandez showed some offensive improvement in Omaha to close out 2009, and Omar Minaya took a flier on him and assigned him to Binghamton at the start of the season. And something funny happened: Hernandez didn't fail miserably with the bat. In 225 at-bats, Hernandez hit .298/.343/.427, perfectly respectable numbers. True, he was a 25-year-old playing Double-A ball, but those numbers were leaps and bounds better than almost anything he'd done before. He moved up to Buffalo, and while he didn't hit as well, he continued to make regular contact at the plate. He returned to the majors at the end of the season and, if nothing else, enjoyed at least one memorable moment when he hit a home run moments after breaking his foot on a foul ball. His season ended as soon as he hobbled across home plate.

The Mets have a crowded middle infield situation headed into spring training. There's almost no chance he'll win a starting job, and you'd have to figure that Chin-lung Hu, Brad Emaus, Daniel Murphy, and Justin Turner are ahead of Hernandez on the depth chart. And with Hernandez being out of options, it seems most likely that he'll again be looking for another organization. —*Alex Nelson*

CHIN-LUNG HU

Bat/Throw: R/R					SHORTSTOP						Born: 02/02/84		
	G	PA	R	HR	RBI	BB%	K%	AVG	OBP	SLG	BABIP	wOBA	SB	SB%
2008 (AAA)	41	168	21	1	15	4%	12%	.295	.323	.385	.328	.313	2	100%
2009 (AAA)	130	544	66	6	53	5%	11%	.294	.332	.393	.318	.326	14	74%
2010 (AAA)	58	223	37	4	25	4%	8%	.317	.339	.438	.326	.345	8	89%

It's easy to jump to conclusions and form two very different opinions about Hu going off either his major league career or his recent minor league data. The major league line is, to put it bluntly, abominable. In fact, abominable might be too kind a word. In 191 plate appearances at the major league level, spread out over four seasons with the Dodgers, Hu has hit .191/.241/.283. Now, the sample size there is awfully small, and he's rarely had an extended opportunity in which to prove himself, but .191, in any package, isn't good. Hu's supporters, on the other hand, might point to his impressive minor league numbers last season. In 223 plate appearances for Albuquerque, Hu batted .317/.339/.438. That's a small sample, too, but Hu has always been a good minor league hitter, hitting .298 over his career. The problem? A huge chunk of that hitting has come at places like Albuquerque and Las Vegas, both of which are tremendous hitter's parks.

So what is he? This will come as a surprise, I'm sure, but his true skill level falls somewhere between a .191 hitter and a .317 hitter. He has very little power and marginal patience, but he does bring two things to the table. First, he's a smooth-fielding infielder, someone who should be able to handle shortstop more than capably and third or second base with aplomb. Second, at least in the minor leagues, he's been very good at making contact with the ball. He's never struck out more than 12.9% of the time in any Triple-A season, a fantastic rate. The number's been much, much higher (22.0%) in the majors, but I'd expect that to fall over time, especially if hitting coach Dave Hudgens can persuade Hu to stop over-swinging.

Hu may not be a long-term answer at any infield position, but his glove and ability to consistently hit for contact may make him a capable backup who can be trusted to start for stretches at a time. In 2011, expect him to compete with Luis Castillo, Brad Emaus, Daniel Murphy, and perhaps Luis Hernandez for the starting job, and while he might not win, he should be the favorite for the backup gig. —Alex Nelson

PAT MISCH

Bat/Throw: R/L				STARTING PITCHER								Born: 08/18/81		
	G	IP	H	BB	K	BB/9	K/9	HR	ERA	FIP	BABIP	LOB%	LD%	GB%	WAR
2010	12	37.2	43	4	23	1.0	5.5	4	3.82	3.64	.307	66%	15%	52%	-0.1
2011	34	134.2	154	35	72	2.3	4.8	16	4.75	4.45	2.95	65%	---	---	1.3
Career	72	193.2	216	53	111	2.5	5.2	27	4.60	4.74	.295	72%	20%	45%	0.3

The San Francisco Giants drafted Pat Misch in 2003. During his years in the Giants' minor league system, Misch was primarily a starter, and he distinguished himself as a pitcher with good control who also induced some ground balls. Strikeouts were never a strength, but the Giants were impressed enough to give him his first shot in 2006 and chances to make an impact over each of the next four seasons. When the Giants would call Misch up, he typically pitched in long relief with the occasional start mixed in. Making an impact is not easy in such a role, and, when his ground ball rate slipped at the next level, the Mets were able to claim him off waivers during the 2009 season.

Misch eventually found his way onto the 25-man roster and pitched out of the bullpen and the rotation with mixed results. He did not make the Opening Day roster in 2010 and spent most of the season playing in Buffalo. He was eventually recalled and made a handful of appearances, again both starting and in relief. In a small sample of just 37.2 innings with the Mets, Misch posted pretty good numbers. As before, he didn't strike out very many batters, but he was also extraordinarily stingy with walks.

Whether Misch ends up with the Mets or in Buffalo to begin the year, he'll provide some depth for the rotation. When a starting pitcher inevitably goes down with an injury, there's a good chance that Misch will be the first to get an opportunity to make some starts. He's definitely not a spectacular pitcher, but at the very least he's not going to walk many batters. Keeping walks down is important for all pitchers, but Misch doesn't strike very many batters out or generate a ton of ground balls, so it's incredibly important that he avoid issuing free passes in order to succeed. —*Chris McShane*

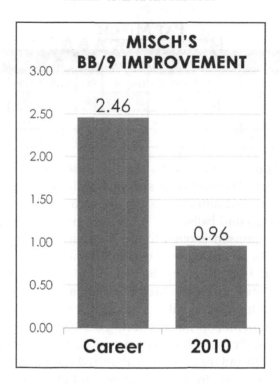

DANIEL MURPHY

	G	PA	R	HR	RBI	BB%	K%	AVG	OBP	SLG	BABIP	wOBA	SB	SB%	WAR
Bat/Throw: L/R				**SECOND BASEMAN**								**Born: 04/01/85**			
2010	DID NOT PLAY DUE TO INJURY.														
2011	97	366	42	8	55	7%	13%	.278	.329	.435	.301	.328	5	71%	1.2
Career	204	707	84	14	80	8%	15%	.275	.331	.437	.303	.330	4	50%	1.5

Entering the 2010 season, opinions were sharply divided on Murph. Some fans saw his .313 rookie average in 2008 and his marked second-half improvements in 2009 and predicted future stardom. Others saw his unimpressive overall 2009 batting line and his inability to stick at any position but first base as portending an end to his Mets career. They agreed on one thing, however: In 2010, these questions about Murphy's ability and future would be answered.

Whoops. A right knee sprain, suffered during spring training, forced him to cede his presumed starting gig at first base to Mike Jacobs. Jacobs himself lost the job before Murphy could return. Ike Davis received the call from Triple-A instead and quickly entrenched himself as the Mets' first baseman of the future. Without an opening in Flushing, Murphy returned to the Triple-A Buffalo Bisons, where he began trying other positions, notably second base, at the Mets' behest. The Mets reasoned that the ability to play second, his natural position (third base), and his assumed positions of left field and first base, would at least make Murphy a jack-of-all-trades, Mark DeRosa-type utility player. There was also the tacit hope that if he really took to his new assignment, Murphy could unseat Luis Castillo and become a long-term solution at second base, a position of chronic need. Unfortunately for Dan, however, an awkward double play turn at second ended his season when he tore the medial collateral ligament in his knee.

So Daniel Murphy enters 2011 with the same uncertain potential but now with an even harder road to the big leagues. This offseason, Murphy worked as a second baseman in the Dominican Winter League. If he hopes to crack the Mets' Opening Day lineup, he'll have to beat out newcomer Brad Emaus and incumbent Luis Castillo for the second base job. Castillo is one bad spring from the Mets releasing him and eating his remaining $6 million salary. Emaus, on the other hand, brings a fresh face to the organization and potential favor from the new front office. Murphy and Emaus are, interestingly, both bat-first, glove-second players, but that's where the similarities stop. While both players control the strike zone well, Murphy relies on lots of contact to buoy his batting average, while Emaus draws more walks. And unlike Emaus, who lacks some range, Murphy's fielding provides range but is error-prone. At the very least, Murphy's positional flexibility and familiarity with the Mets' staff should increase his chances of landing a spot on the Mets' bench.
—*Sam Page*

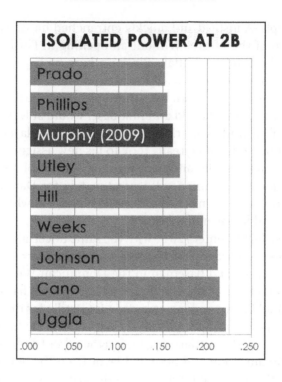

ISOLATED POWER AT 2B

Prado
Phillips
Murphy (2009)
Utley
Hill
Weeks
Johnson
Cano
Uggla

.000   .050   .100   .150   .200   .250

MIKE NICKEAS

Bat/Throw: R/R					CATCHER							Born: 02/13/83		
	G	PA	R	HR	RBI	BB%	K%	AVG	OBP	SLG	BABIP	wOBA	SB	SB%
2008 (AAA)	54	184	16	2	17	8%	26%	.215	.275	.307	.268	.257	0	0%
2009 (AA)	18	67	3	0	7	13%	16%	.182	.292	.200	.213	.248	0	N/A
2010 (AA)	82	318	27	5	33	15%	16%	.283	.403	.396	.323	.371	1	50%

In last year's annual, there were a grand total of two players in camp we didn't cover in profile form: Kai Gronauer and Nickeas, the eighth and ninth catchers in camp. We figured there was pretty much no chance for either player to make the team or do anything of note. After all, there were seven guys ahead of them on the depth chart and both were only invited to camp to catch all the extra arms present at the onset of spring training. Of course, Gronauer had a breakout season in 2010 and Mike Nickeas ended the season on the Mets' roster, as almost every other guy ahead of him on the depth chart faltered in one way or another. They did it just to spite us.

Nickeas came to the Mets organization in August of 2006, sent over by the Texas Rangers in exchange for Victor Diaz. He was hitting .297 at the time of the trade but was known primarily as a defensive player. And while he's shown some occasional promise in his bat, that's pretty much what he's been as a member of the Mets organization: a good defender with apt handling of the pitching staffs and zero offense. At bat, he's just a .239 hitter in his minor league career, and he has no power to speak of, but he mitigates the damage, at least a little, by being extremely patient at the plate. 2010 was his most successful campaign to date, and Nickeas, after hitting .283 with a .403 on-base average in Binghamton, was promoted twice to find himself on the major league team when rosters expanded in September.

Nickeas now finds himself with an excellent chance of making the Opening Day roster in 2011, thanks to Ronnie Paulino's lingering eight-game suspension. As of this printing, Nickeas is one of just three catchers on the 40-man roster and, even after Paulino returns, will continue to serve as the first line of defense in the event of a catching injury. If he does play, don't expect much more than a good glove, because he probably won't provide anything else. —*Alex Nelson*

JON NIESE

Bat/Throw: L/L					STARTING PITCHER									Born: 10/27/86
	G	IP	H	BB	K	BB/9	K/9	HR	ERA	FIP	BABIP	LOB%	LD%	GB%	WAR
2010	30	173.2	192	62	148	3.2	7.7	20	4.20	4.10	.324	71%	21%	48%	-0.3
2011	29	164.1	171	59	131	3.2	7.2	17	4.27	4.09	.298	68%	---	---	2.4
Career	38	213.1	239	79	177	3.3	7.5	23	4.39	4.06	.327	70%	21%	47%	-0.3

Drafted by the Mets in the seventh round of the 2005 amateur draft, Jon Niese advanced to Triple-A in his fourth season with the organization. Although he may not have been considered a top prospect during those years, Niese steadily improved each year. His first cup of coffee in the big leagues came in September 2008, when he was thrown into the fire for three starts as the Mets attempted to get into the playoffs. One of those three was excellent, the other two were downright awful. He made a couple of starts early in 2009 and was called back up to the Mets in July. His season came crashing to an end, however, when he suffered a gruesome hamstring injury during his third start after being recalled.

After earning a spot in the rotation for 2010, Niese pitched very well for the majority of the season, but faltered quite a bit in September. One explanation for the decline that month is that Niese wound up throwing over 70 more innings than he threw in 2009 and hit a wall. Despite pitching so poorly toward the end of the year, Niese's numbers for the season were still solid. Neither his strikeout nor his walk rate was spectacular, but each one was definitely good enough for major league success, especially when coupled with an above-average ground ball rate. Niese was also a bit unlucky in 2010, judging by the difference between his ERA and xFIP.

Since Niese only has one full year with the Mets under his belt, there's plenty of room here for either improvement or a step in the wrong direction. Although his major league experience is still limited, the numbers he generated last year make sense when compared to his progression through the minors. Much will depend on walks. If he's able to cut down on how many he issues, Niese could have a very good year. Of course, Niese could also benefit from things that have little to do with his actual abilities, such as improved luck on fly balls or an upgrade to the team's defense. —*Chris McShane*

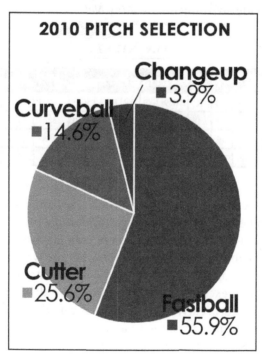

2010 PITCH SELECTION

Changeup ■3.9%

Curveball ■14.6%

Cutter ■25.6%

Fastball ■55.9%

ANGEL PAGAN

Bat/Throw: S/R					OUTFIELDER							Born: 07/02/81		
	G	PA	R	HR	RBI	BB%	K%	AVG	OBP	SLG	BABIP	wOBA	SB	SB%	WAR
2010	151	633	80	11	69	7%	17%	.290	.340	.425	.331	.341	37	80%	4.8
2011	114	459	60	8	52	7%	15%	.278	.326	.424	.312	.321	21	78%	1.8
Career	418	1462	195	26	153	7%	17%	.285	.335	.435	.325	.338	63	77%	9.5

Originally drafted by the Mets in 1999, Angel Pagan spent two years in the Chicago Cubs organization before returning to the Mets via trade in 2008. He didn't play very much in the majors until 2009, but since then he has taken advantage of his opportunities and turned into a valuable outfielder. Pagan showed promise in 2009 as he filled in for the injured Carlos Beltran, and in 2010, he was able to shed the "fourth outfielder" moniker that had been bestowed upon him in the past. Pagan quickly overtook Gary Matthews Jr. as the starting center fielder in April, and when Beltran returned from knee surgery in the middle of the season, Pagan became the everyday right fielder instead of Jeff Francoeur.

Pagan racked up 633 plate appearances last year, which was by far his career high, and he produced. At the plate, he hit .290/.340/.425. None of those numbers are elite in their own right, but his production at the plate was well-rounded. On the base paths, he excelled. He stole 37 bases and was caught only nine times, good for an 80.4% success rate. Pagan did well in all aspects of base running, and the same speed he combined with heads-up decisions on the base paths helped his defense, too. He was top notch in both center field and right field.

Pagan seems to have reached his potential and should provide the Mets with a great deal of value moving forward. Terry Collins pegged Pagan as the second hitter in the lineup heading into the season, a role for which he is well suited with his fairly good on-base skills and elite ability to run the bases. Defensively, the Mets could maximize their return on his talent by putting him in center field and convincing Carlos Beltran to move to right field. While 2010 was the first full season Pagan has played in the majors, the results were generally consistent with what he had shown in 2009. It's perfectly reasonable to expect more of the same, or numbers pretty close, out of Pagan in 2011. —Chris McShane

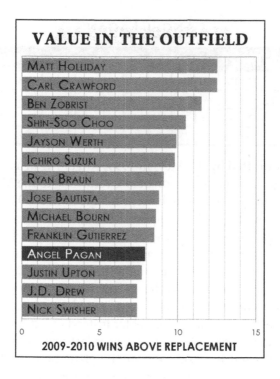

VALUE IN THE OUTFIELD

Matt Holliday
Carl Crawford
Ben Zobrist
Shin-Soo Choo
Jayson Werth
Ichiro Suzuki
Ryan Braun
Jose Bautista
Michael Bourn
Franklin Gutierrez
Angel Pagan
Justin Upton
J.D. Drew
Nick Swisher

2009-2010 WINS ABOVE REPLACEMENT

BOBBY PARNELL

Bat/Throw: R/R					RELIEF PITCHER						Born: 09/08/84				
	G	IP	H	BB	K	BB/9	K/9	HR	ERA	FIP	BABIP	LOB%	LD%	GB%	WAR
2010	41	35.0	41	8	33	2.1	8.5	1	2.83	2.25	.374	76%	26%	56%	0.4
2011	61	69.1	66	26	62	3.3	8.0	6	3.76	3.56	.293	71%	---	---	0.8
Career	115	128.1	145	56	110	3.9	7.7	9	4.63	3.69	.338	69%	19%	49%	-0.4

Bobby Parnell is a bona fide homegrown New York Met. He was picked by the Mets in the ninth round of the 2005 amateur draft and posted strong strikeout numbers throughout his minor league career, earning his first cup of coffee with six appearances in 2008. His rookie campaign of 2009 was a bit of a mixed bag. Toward the end of the season, with the rotation in shambles and the season long gone, the Mets decided to give Parnell a shot at starting. He did so five times and the results were not good, to put it mildly. Any issues Parnell may have had while he was coming out of the bullpen were exploited in the new role, as those five starts were enough to skew Parnell's season statistics significantly. As a relief pitcher he managed a 3.46 ERA, but as a starter it was an appallingly Ollie-esque 7.93. His overall stats from 2009 mask that he fared reasonably well when he was used as a reliever.

Perhaps unfairly, Parnell began the 2010 season in the minors, but it didn't take him long to rejoin the Mets bullpen. He returned and racked up 41 appearances, looking very good in the process. Parnell raised his strikeouts, lowered his walks, and finished with a 2.83 ERA that was actually higher than his FIP would suggest it should have been. In the process, he was throwing his fastball a little more frequently than he had in 2009 while nearly abandoning his rarely-used changeup.

Parnell will again be an important piece of the Mets' bullpen. Last year was a step in the right direction, but he hasn't established enough of a track record to be a sure thing just yet. There's no question that Parnell throws hard, and keeping his walk rate down will go a long way toward determining how good a reliever he will be. Heading into the season, Parnell will likely be entrusted in high-leverage situations. And should Francisco Rodriguez miss any time, Parnell is the logical choice to fill in as the closer. If Parnell improves upon his impressive 2010 campaign and the Mets are able to free themselves of Rodriguez's outrageous vesting option, Parnell could well establish himself as next in line for the closer gig. —*Chris McShane*

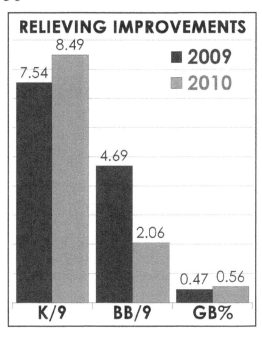

RONNY PAULINO

Bat/Throw: R/R				CATCHER							Born: 04/21/81		
	G	PA	R	HR	RBI	BB%	K%	AVG	OBP	SLG	BABIP	wOBA	SB	SB%	WAR
2010	91	344	31	4	37	7%	16%	.259	.311	.354	.295	.293	1	100%	0.6
2011	30	329	30	6	37	7%	16%	.257	.310	.370	.293	.299	1	50%	0.8
Career	475	1720	157	31	192	8%	18%	.273	.328	.383	.314	.312	4	67%	4.1

Paulino was drafted by the Pirates and debuted with the team at the end of the 2005 season. His rookie campaign was impressive, but it was heavily fueled by a high batting average on balls in play. Once his luck started to even out, Paulino's overall numbers took a nose dive. By 2008, the Pirates expressed concerns about his conditioning and work ethic and sent him to the minors. They more or less gave up on him, and he began a trek during the winter and spring of 2008–2009 that sent him first to Philadelphia, then to San Francisco, and finally to Florida. He stuck with the Marlins, playing there for the 2009 and 2010 seasons before the Mets signed him this winter.

Overall, Paulino's 2010 season was not that impressive. Despite his poor production, Paulino maintained an ability to mash left handed pitching, as his wOBA against lefties was still .383. Over his career, he's hit .338/.390/.491 with a .382 wOBA against them. Unfortunately, against right-handed pitchers, Paulino has been pretty awful. Paulino missed the final 42 games of the season as a result of a 50-game suspension by Major League Baseball after testing positive for a banned performance-enhancing drug. Paulino later claimed the substance was a dietary pill.

Paulino still has eight games to serve on his suspension, so the Mets will be without his services to start the season. After that, with Josh Thole as the starter and Paulino as the backup, the Mets have the ingredients for a strong platoon behind the plate. While Thole must continue to see left-handed pitching to further his development, Paulino figures to face some of the tougher left-handed starters the rest of baseball will have to offer. It's also worth noting that Paulino will turn 30 shortly after the season begins, making him a far younger backup than the Mets had last year in Henry Blanco. Paulino figures to be a good backup option behind the plate, provided he's properly inserted into the lineup by Terry Collins. —*Chris McShane*

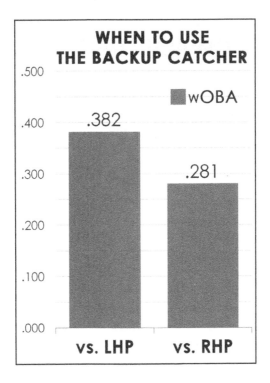

MIKE PELFREY

Bat/Throw: R/R					STARTING PITCHER							Born: 01/14/84			
	G	IP	H	BB	K	BB/9	K/9	HR	ERA	FIP	BABIP	LOB%	LD%	GB%	WAR
2010	34	204.0	213	68	113	3.0	5.0	12	3.66	3.82	.300	74%	20%	48%	2.5
2011	32	192.1	203	65	115	3.0	5.4	15	4.12	4.05	.289	68%	---	---	2.4
Career	116	683.0	745	249	388	3.3	5.1	49	4.31	4.18	.308	71%	20%	49%	4.4

When Mike Pelfrey was the ninth player selected in the amateur draft way back in 2005, there were two primary paths he could take toward becoming a legitimate major league pitcher. While there are dozens of different ways all pitchers can fail entirely—injuries, an inability to adjust, loss of command, whatever—if Pelfrey succeeded he was most likely going to be one of two types of pitchers. One path would take him to stardom, the other merely toward being a very capable starting pitcher. The first path was the Kevin Brown path, and it required Pelfrey to develop a true swing-and-miss pitch. Very few pitchers in major league history have been able to combine dominant sinkers with the ability to garner strikeouts, and there was hope that Pelf could become one. Without that vital out pitch, Pelf would end up on the Derek Lowe path for ground ball specialists.

The 2010 season might have represented the last chance for Pelfrey to move off the Derek Lowe path and onto the Kevin Brown path. Pelf's always had the ground ball rates, but his strikeout rate remained pitiful as he played around with a curve and slider. In fact, he had survived entirely by mixing variations of his fastball. In 2010, he added a splitter to his repertoire, and after a brief spike, his strikeout rate settled right back near his career levels. It's time to admit that Pelfrey is what he is, a dependable workhorse who gets a good number of ground balls with superior fastball command, and no more. His reliance on his infield defense will prevent him from being great and keep his ERAs fluctuating as it's done over the past three seasons. And there's absolutely nothing wrong with that, because even someone who isn't quite as good as Lowe—Pelf's career ground ball rate of 49.4% pales in comparison to Lowe's 62.9%—is still a strong mid-rotation starter.

Some things should be set in stone: Almost half of the balls put into play against Pelfrey will be on the ground, he'll give up very few home runs, and he'll continue to strike out virtually no one. Those numbers have been very stable ever since he broke into the league, but one thing to keep an eye on is his walk rate. Pelfrey has generally been good at not walking hitters, but given how many balls he puts into play—and how many of them wind up as base hits—he can't afford to give up free bases. As for his ERA, it will depend largely on how well the fielders behind him perform and how many bad bounces those ground balls take. Terry Collins has already named Pelfrey the Opening Day starter in Johan Santana's absence. While he may be unspectacular to watch, the pre-spring training announcement is a testament to the organization's belief in Pelfrey as the their most dependable starter.—*Alex Nelson*

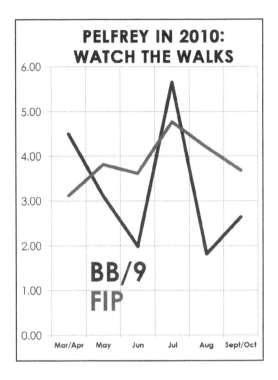

OLIVER PEREZ

Bat/Throw: L/L					STARTING PITCHER						Born: 08/15/81				
	G	IP	H	BB	K	BB/9	K/9	HR	ERA	FIP	BABIP	LOB%	LD%	GB%	WAR
2010	17	46.1	54	42	37	8.2	7.2	9	6.80	6.99	.317	72%	19%	35%	-1.5
2011	22	96.2	95	67	87	6.2	8.1	15	5.40	5.55	.284	70%	---	---	-0.7
Career	206	1111.2	1019	628	1126	5.1	9.1	167	4.63	4.87	.287	73%	20%	33%	3.6

Back in 2004, Oliver Perez had a great year. He was striking out batters at an incredible clip, his walk rate was high but manageable, and he
finished with a 2.98 ERA, still his career-best mark. Perez was a Pirate
at the time, having been traded from the Padres along with Jason Bay in
2003. He wasn't very good in the years after that, so the Mets were able
to pick him up in a trade in the middle of the 2006 season. He continued
to struggle after the trade, but he did make one great start: Game 7 of
the NLCS. Perez improved in 2007 but regressed a bit in 2008 before
infamously signing a three-year, $36 million contract with the Mets. In
2009, the already-wobbly wheels completely fell off, as he walked nearly

eight batters per nine innings and wound up with a 6.82 ERA.

In the second season of his contract, Perez somehow managed to do worse. His average fastball velocity clocked in at 88.0 mph, a full 2.0 mph lower than the year before. His walk rate increased. And after it was apparent that Perez wasn't going to improve, the Mets asked him to go work things out in Buffalo. He refused and instead chose to ride the pine in the bullpen. And ride it he did, making just six appearances after the All-Star break. He made the occasional appearance as the ultimate mop-up man, but for the most part Perez spent his 2010 season in oblivion.

Perez should be released. His name hasn't been included in the discussion for the Mets rotation—nor should it be—and he's not even a realistic fringe candidate to make the bullpen. Perhaps if he's offered a one-way ticket to Buffalo again, Perez will accept, but the Mets may not even give him that choice. At this point, the only unanswered question about Perez is when the Mets will release him. —*Chris McShane*

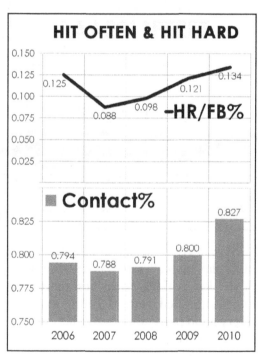

JOSE REYES

Bat/Throw: S/R					SHORTSTOP							Born: 06/11/83		
	G	PA	R	HR	RBI	BB%	K%	AVG	OBP	SLG	BABIP	wOBA	SB	SB%	WAR
2010	133	603	83	11	54	5%	11%	.282	.321	.428	.301	.329	30	75%	2.2
2011	122	567	80	11	54	7%	11%	.284	.337	.439	.303	.335	39	78%	2.7
Career	924	4254	634	74	379	7%	12%	.286	.335	.434	.308	.340	331	80%	23.3

Ever since he made his debut with the Mets in 2003, Jose Reyes has been one of the most exciting players on the team. The main draw early in Reyes's career was that he was fast—really fast. He struggled with injuries in 2003 and 2004, but from 2005–2008 he averaged over 158 games per season. Reyes began to realize his potential in 2005, but it was in 2006 that the shortstop emerged as a star. Suddenly, he was getting on base a lot more frequently and hitting for power. With improved plate discipline and more pop in his bat, Reyes wound up with an excellent .367 wOBA that season. 2007 wasn't quite as good as the year before, but in 2008, Reyes managed to put up numbers nearly identical to those from 2006. For three years straight, Reyes produced at an elite level for his position. Like many of his teammates, however, Reyes was bitten by the injury bug in 2009. He played well in 33 games but missed the rest of the season with a calf injury.

As Reyes was recovering from the injury and preparing for the 2010 season, it was discovered that he had a thyroid condition, sidelining him for the few weeks leading into the season. Reyes got back out on the field a handful of games into the season, but he would miss more time later in the year with oblique injuries. Despite those injuries, Reyes managed to play 133 games, but his production was down across the board. He attempted stolen bases less frequently than he had in the past, and his on-base percentage was its lowest since 2005. A big reason for that was Reyes swinging at an alarming 32.1% of pitches outside the strike zone. On the upside, he still hit 11 HR and slugged a decent .428.

Reyes heads into 2011 in the last year of his contract with the Mets. His season will depend upon whether or not he can stay healthy and regain the plate discipline he appeared to have learned in 2006. Assuming he is healthy, Reyes could drastically improve his offensive output simply by swinging at fewer pitches outside the strike zone. It's probably also safe to assume that Reyes will be trying to steal bases at a higher rate than he did last year. Reyes is now two years removed from a 6.0

WAR season, but entering his age-27 season, it's entirely possible that he regains that form. —*Chris McShane*

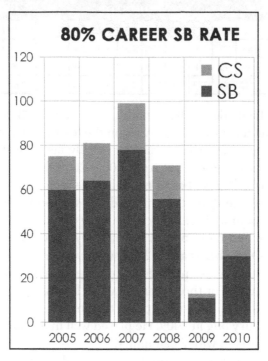

FRANCISCO RODRIGUEZ

Bat/Throw: R/R					CLOSER							Born: 01/07/82		
	G	IP	H	BB	K	BB/9	K/9	HR	ERA	FIP	BABIP	LOB%	LD%	GB%	WAR
2010	53	57.1	45	21	67	3.3	10.5	3	2.20	2.63	.294	85%	19%	42%	2.1
2011	61	60.1	48	29	71	4.3	10.5	5	3.13	3.25	.280	76%	---	---	2.3
Career	531	577.0	401	257	727	4.0	11.3	44	2.50	2.96	.268	81%	18%	42%	20.3

Francisco Rodriguez spent six seasons with the Angels and spent the great majority of that time as the team's closer. He sported incredibly high strikeout rates, good enough to make up for the fact that he also amassed far too many walks per nine innings over the course of those years. In 2008, K-Rod tallied 62 saves, setting an all-time single-season record. During that same season, however, his velocity dipped nearly 2.0 mph and his strikeout rate followed suit, dropping nearly 2.0 K/9. Despite those red flags, the Mets decided to bring Rodriguez in on a monster contract for three guaranteed years with an even more monstrous vesting option for a fourth year. In his first year with the Mets, Rodriguez wasn't necessarily awful, but he set a career low in strikeout rate and a career high in walk rate. On the upside, his fastball velocity did bounce back a bit from 2008.

As a result of his somewhat underwhelming performance, there were already questions surrounding Rodriguez as he entered the 2010 season. Rodriguez responded by posting his best strikeout rate since 2007 and a career-low walk rate. Despite the fact that his fastball velocity once again dropped, this time to a career low, Rodriguez was doing something right on the mound: For the first time since his fastball velocity began to decline, Rodriguez also threw his changeup slower. Perhaps the increased difference between the two pitches helped Rodriguez miss more bats, improving his effectiveness. Although there were still signs of decline, his performance made it seem plausible that he could remain an effective closer for at least one or two more years. Unfortunately, the slight positives from 2010 were overshadowed when Rodriguez's year came to a screeching halt on August 10 as he was arrested after a physical altercation with his girlfriend's father outside the Mets clubhouse. He made one appearance after that, but he discovered he'd injured his hand when he allegedly landed a punch during the altercation.

The Mets attempted to void the remainder of his contract, but an off-season settlement dashed any hopes of escaping the remaining year and the potential vesting option. Instead, the Mets merely avoided paying Rodriguez the roughly $3 million in 2010 salary he would have received while on the disabled list for the hand injury.

Regardless of what happens this year, it is unlikely that Rodriguez will provide enough value to justify his salary. Despite that fact, Rodriguez should still prove to be a capable relief ace for the Mets, provided he is fully recovered from his hand injury. While he will probably walk opposing batters more frequently than he did last year, if he can continue striking them out with the same frequency, he should remain generally effective. That vesting option for 2012 is more troublesome, and it will be interesting to see whether management lets it guide how he is used. If the team is willing to make the effort during games, they could limit the number of games Rodridguez finishes, taking the team off the hook for $17.5 million in 2012. —*Chris McShane*

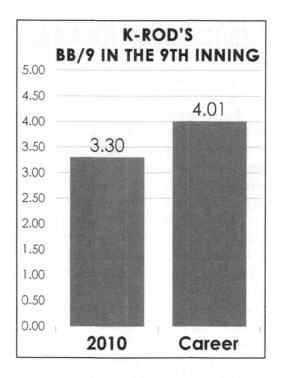

JOHAN SANTANA

Bat/Throw: L/L					STARTING PITCHER							Born: 03/13/79			
	G	IP	H	BB	K	BB/9	K/9	HR	ERA	FIP	BABIP	LOB%	LD%	GB%	WAR
2010	29	199.0	179	55	144	2.5	6.5	16	2.98	3.54	.272	79%	20%	35%	4.4
2011	27	180.1	168	49	145	2.5	7.3	17	3.39	3.65	.276	74%	---	---	4.0
Career	339	1908.2	1609	528	1877	2.5	8.9	203	3.10	3.40	.275	78%	20%	38%	46.5

Johan Santana was acquired prior to the 2008 season when he was clearly one of the elite pitchers in baseball, coming off four-plus stellar seasons with the Minnesota Twins. The Mets were willing to do what the Twins would not and signed Johan to a seven-year extension. Many thought Santana would put the Mets over the top in 2008 after a dismal end to the 2007 season. That proved false as 2008 also ended miserably, but Santana produced and pitched one of the more memorable regular-season games in recent history on the penultimate day of the season. Unfortunately, Santana's 2009 and 2010 seasons ended early because of injury, the latter requiring major surgery on his pitching shoulder.

In his three seasons with the Mets, Santana's ERA has remained low despite a significant drop in strikeouts per nine innings from 2007 to 2008 and again from 2009 to 2010. His pitch velocities have decreased by nearly 2.0 mph since his first year with the Mets, and he missed fewer bats in 2010 than in the past. Santana's ground ball rate is also concerning: He has always been a fly ball pitcher, but he induced few ground balls in 2009 and 2010, even by his standards. While Santana has almost always outperformed his FIP and xFIP, the margin between his ERA and those numbers has been increasing in recent years. One of the reasons Santana has continued his success despite these drop-offs is he has kept his walk rate low and remarkably consistent over the last three seasons.

In 2011, there's no timetable for Santana's return from shoulder surgery, and the guess from the Mets' front office has been somewhere around the All-Star break. Assuming Santana even comes back this season, there are no guarantees how he'll recover from his surgery. Was his alarmingly low strikeout rate in 2010 a sign of a continued decline, or was it because of his ailing shoulder? And what might his velocity look like when he returns to the mound? The answers to these questions will go a long way toward developing realistic expectations for Santana. Even in the best-case scenario, the Mets should not expect Santana to be their best pitcher immediately upon his return. —*Chris McShane*

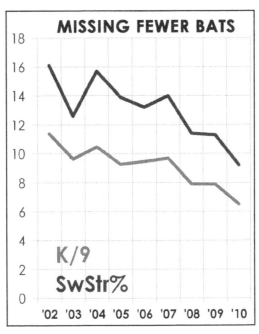

TAYLOR TANKERSLEY

Bat/Throw: L/L					RELIEF PITCHER						Born: 03/07/83			
	G	IP	H	BB	K	BB/9	K/9	HR	ERA	FIP	BABIP	LOB%	LD%	GB%	WAR
2010	27	12.0	12	7	7	5.3	5.3	4	7.50	8.25	.211	63%	17%	26%	-0.4
2011	63	47.1	45	25	41	4.8	7.8	7	4.75	4.98	.274	70%	---	---	0.0
Career	168	118.0	109	70	115	5.3	8.8	18	4.58	5.14	.289	76%	18%	36%	0.5

Tankersley is a good exhibit of why it can be dangerous to take a college reliever in the first round of the amateur draft. The Marlins took Tankersley 27th in the first round of the 2004 draft after an up-and-down career at Alabama that ended on a positive note after he was sent to the bullpen. To be fair to the Marlins, they intended to make Tankersley a starter, as his 88–93-mph fastball never screamed closer. But they gave up on that dream in 2006 after some shoulder issues and converted him full-time to relief. The problems are that he throws from a low arm slot, his breaking pitch is pretty slurvy, and he doesn't have a great changeup. It all adds up to a LOOGY (Lefty One-Out GuY). While guys like that can have value, they have relatively little impact, making the choice a poor allocation of a first-round draft pick.

Tankersley pitched pretty well in his rookie and sophomore campaigns of 2006 and 2007, but there were some holes in his game. While he dominated lefties, he struggled against batters on the opposite side of the plate, as expected. He also tended to give up a lot of fly balls, and his command, in general, stunk. The house of cards he'd built all came crashing down in 2008. His ERA ballooned to 8.15 over 25 appearances, almost solely the result of a sky-high home run rate. He was probably more than a little unfortunate, but when 75% of your balls in play are in the air—an astronomical rate—you're going to give up plenty of home runs. And when you're also walking more than five batters per nine innings, those home runs aren't going to be solo shots. The next spring, doctors discovered a stress fracture in his forearm, requiring him to undergo season-ending surgery. He returned to the club briefly in 2010 and was once again roughed up.

The Marlins designated him for assignment after the season, and Tankersley opted for free agency. The Mets picked him up on a minor league deal, hoping to find a lefty-relief replacement for Pedro Feliciano, who vacated for the Bronx. Tankersley is expected to compete with Tim Byrdak for the job and is probably the favorite, as of this printing, to land it. He has youth on his side—he's nine years younger than Byrdak—and, if nothing else, coaches have always praised his makeup and demeanor, both on the mound and in the clubhouse. Call it a tie-breaker. —*Alex Nelson*

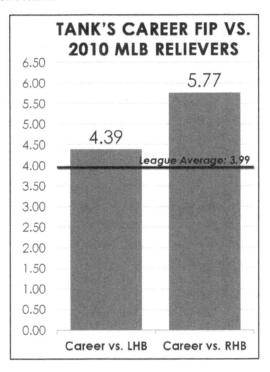

JOSH THOLE

Bat/Throw: L/R						CATCHER						Born: 10/28/86		
	G	PA	R	HR	RBI	BB%	K%	AVG	OBP	SLG	BABIP	wOBA	SB	SB%	WAR
2010	73	227	17	3	17	11%	12%	.277	.357	.366	.305	.327	1	100%	1.4
2011	140	516	48	5	49	9%	11%	.273	.342	.380	.304	.324	4	67%	2.7
Career	90	286	19	3	26	10%	12%	.286	.357	.373	.313	.328	2	100%	1.7

Thole really snuck up on the organization. The Mets drafted Thole out of a high school in rural Illinois with a 13th-round draft pick. And while Thole had been a catcher in high school, his receiving skills were considered below average, so the Mets immediately made him a regular at first base. The problem with Josh Thole the first baseman was that he didn't fit the prototype you'd expect to find at the position. He wasn't a big, lumbering guy with lots of power. Actually, Thole didn't have any power—he knocked just two home runs over his first 700 plate appearances in the minors. After his 2007 season at Savannah, it became overwhelmingly clear that first base wasn't going to be a long-term option, so they moved him to St. Lucie in 2008 and made him a full-time catcher. Smart move. His catching skills still weren't great, but he stood a chance to improve, and the position profile made him much more appealing as a hitter. He moved steadily through the system and became the Mets' regular catcher in early July 2010.

At the plate, Thole has two primary strengths. He almost never strikes out, and he draws tons of walks. He has a fantastic approach at the plate, never trying to do too much while taking whatever the pitcher is willing to give him. The home run power will never come, but he has matured into a hitter who will occasionally slash the ball into the gaps. Behind the plate, he has seen fast improvement under the tutelage of catching instructor Bob Natal, to the extent that coaches were raving about him last spring. It's still not quite a strength, but it's getting there. And his throwing might have been the biggest surprise. That was always the most problematic aspect of Thole's defensive game behind the plate, but he managed to remove an impressive 44% of would-be base stealers in 2010. The sample size isn't large enough to get overly excited yet, but it is an encouraging signal.

Sandy Alderson hedged his bets a little by signing Ronny Paulino this offseason. Thole has traditionally struggled against lefties, the same pitchers Paulino has traditionally mashed. And even if Thole gets off to a rough start, the team can feel somewhat comfortable depending on Paulino to fill in. But the plan is for Thole is begin the season as the team's principal catcher, and if successful there's no reason Thole couldn't become a modern, left-handed-hitting equivalent of Don Slaught—a catcher with adequate defense, little power, and lots of on-base ability. —*Alex Nelson*

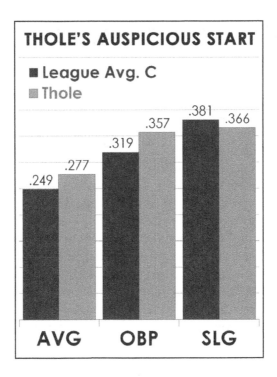

THOLE'S AUSPICIOUS START

■ League Avg. C
▨ Thole

AVG: .249 / .277
OBP: .319 / .357
SLG: .381 / .366

JUSTIN TURNER

Bat/Throw: R/R					MIDDLE INFIELDER						Born: 11/23/84		
	G	PA	R	HR	RBI	BB%	K%	AVG	OBP	SLG	BABIP	wOBA	SB	SB%
2008 (AA)	78	323	45	8	42	10%	19%	.289	.359	.432	.326	.360	2	67%
2009 (AAA)	108	441	54	2	43	8%	10%	.300	.362	.388	.320	.340	9	69%
2010 (AAA)	101	443	69	12	43	6%	18%	.316	.374	.487	.325	.389	7	70%

The Mets could have used somebody like Turner in 2010. Maybe somebody should have told Omar Minaya that they actually had him sitting in Buffalo for most of the season. Turner was a seventh-round pick by the Reds in 2006, but he's always been seen by scouts as a guy short on raw talent. However, he's also been an extremely consistent hitter no matter where he's played, and 2010 was no exception. Minaya picked Turner off waivers from the Orioles organization in May, and he hit .333/.390/.516 for Buffalo after coming over. While those numbers are better than anything Turner's ever done before, they aren't too far off his career line of .309/.373/.442 in the minors, either. On a team where Luis Castillo (.604 OPS), Ruben Tejada (.588), Alex Cora (.543), and Joaquin Arias (.483) saw significant action at second base, it's a little shocking that an established minor league producer like Turner wasn't given more than nine plate appearances in the majors.

Turner is one of those guys who often gets undervalued in the minors because he's not a specialist. There's nothing he does exceptionally well. While he's shown a consistent ability to hit for contact, he also hasn't had a season where he's posted a gaudy batting average. He doesn't have blazing speed or tons of power. He's nothing special as a defender, lacking the range to be an above-average second baseman or even a capable shortstop. But at the same time, he won't clog the bases, he does have a little bit of pop, he's pretty disciplined at the plate, and he has the versatility which enables him to fill in at any infield position. With his track record, he deserves the chance to earn a reserve infield spot, at the least.

Hopefully, the new regime will give Turner a chance to compete for what will be an open audition at second base this spring. There are a lot of bodies in camp eyeing the same job, so he'll need to make his performance stand out. But even if he fails to beat out Brad Emaus, Daniel Murphy, or Luis Castillo for the job, he could still help the team as a backup or as an insurance plan in Triple-A. —*Alex Nelson*

DAVID WRIGHT

Bat/Throw: R/R					THIRD BASEMAN						Born: 12/20/82			
	G	PA	R	HR	RBI	BB%	K%	AVG	OBP	SLG	BABIP	wOBA	SB	SB%	WAR
2010	157	670	87	29	103	10%	27%	.283	.354	.503	.335	.364	19	63%	3.9
2011	155	679	94	25	99	11%	21%	.282	.361	.481	.334	.362	23	72%	3.3
Career	1004	4335	639	169	664	11%	21%	.305	.383	.516	.343	.387	138	77%	31.1

When Mike Hampton fled for the thin air and ostensibly superior schools of Colorado following the 2000 season, the Mets were awarded two compensatory first-round picks in the subsequent amateur draft. They took Aaron Heilman with the first of those picks and with the second, the 38th-overall selection, they grabbed David Wright. Wright spent the next three-plus years humbling minor league pitchers before being summoned to the majors midway through the 2004 season. In the ensuing four years, Wright went about humbling big league pitchers while establishing himself as the preeminent all-around third baseman in the National League. He ran aground somewhat in 2009, falling shy of his own superstar standards and failing to find his power stroke inside the yawning expanses of Citi Field.

In 2010, Wright rediscovered most of the power he had lost the previous year, but in an apparent swap of one struggle for another, his on-base prowess tumbled considerably en route to a career-low .354 OBP. However, the season wasn't a total wash for Wright, who hit splendidly in the first half—.314/.392/.532—buoyed in no small part by an unsustainable .398 batting average on balls in play. That mark dropped to .261 in the second half and Wright's offensive output predictably followed suit. Whether by coincidence or by the strength of team solidarity, the other Mets hitters echoed Wright's decline, as the whole team offense wilted over the final ten weeks of the season. Of particular concern for Wright was the continued upward trend of his strikeout rate, which climbed to a career high in 2009, only to further its ascent in 2010, a season which saw Wright strike out more than once for every four turns at bat. The correlation between Wright's rising strikeouts and a tendency toward greater offensive futility is difficult to ignore.

The 2011 season is shaping up to be a pivotal one for forecasting the remaining trajectory of Wright's career. His 28th birthday, celebrated in December, is the one that usually coincides with the beginning of a hitter's prime years. Another merely good season from Wright in 2011—along the lines of his previous two—might cast Wright along the path to a very good career once his final story has been written. There's nothing wrong with being very good, but it wasn't long ago that Wright seemed destined for greatness, and falling short of that, even if only a notch or two, would be at least a minor disappointment to Mets fans. Nothing has been cast in stone yet, but it might be worth keeping an eye on the frequency of Wright's strikeouts this season. If they veer toward his pre-2009 rate—around 19% of his at-bats—then things are probably looking up. If his strikeout rates is substantially higher, don't be surprised if 2011 turns out to be another very good—not great—season for Wright.
—*Eric Simon*

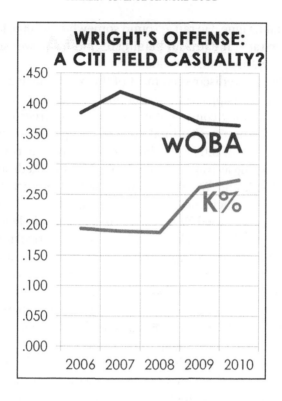

CHRIS YOUNG

Bat/Throw: R/R					STARTING PITCHER									Born: 05/25/79
	G	IP	H	BB	K	BB/9	K/9	HR	ERA	FIP	BABIP	LOB%	LD%	GB%	WAR
2010	4	20.0	10	11	15	5.0	6.8	1	0.90	3.88	.164	97%	16%	29%	0.9
2011	10	51.2	48	25	42	4.3	7.3	7	4.53	4.81	.264	71%	---	---	0.6
Career	135	751.2	614	295	653	3.5	7.8	90	3.80	4.22	.251	74%	19%	29%	10.7

From 2005–2007, Chris Young was quietly one of the better starters in baseball. Over those three seasons, he was 32–20 with a 3.60 ERA, striking out 8.1 batters per nine innings while walking just 2.5. Young wasn't a traditional ace, but his peripherals and ERA firmly suggested he was a top number-two starter in the game. After that, he couldn't stay healthy. First it was a freak injury, a line drive off Albert Pujols's bat that hit his face, shelving him for a couple months in 2008. He came back only to strain his forearm. In 2009, it was a partial tear in his shoulder labrum. He returned in April 2010 but was pulled from his first start with a shoulder strain that sidelined him until mid-September. He pitched well when he returned, but he made just three starts.

Young has never pitched as he looks like he should, a big reason why the Pirates, Expos, and Rangers gave up on him before he landed in San Diego. At 6 feet 10 inches, Young looks like he should be a flamethrower, but he barely throws 86 mph. But don't assume he's a junkballer. He lives off his fastball, throwing it nearly 80% of the time, while using a slider as his primary—and often sole—off-speed pitch. Young has a power pitcher's mentality with a finesse pitcher's arm. So how does he get so many strikeouts? An answer rests in the past: Sid Fernandez, stalwart of late-1980s and early-1990s Mets rotations, didn't throw terribly hard, but his fastball was described as "sneaky fast" due to a deceptive delivery and late rise. Young's fastball shares these properties. And like Fernandez, Young has benefited from a pitcher-friendly environment where his fly ball tendencies don't hurt him.

Young signed a one-year deal with a $1.5 million base value and incentives that could elevate it to $4.5 million. All his past injuries make it unclear what sort of performance the Mets will receive for their investment. It's a bit of a gamble, perhaps even more so when you consider that Young never fit a traditional mold. It's always difficult to predict a player's performance, and Young's injury history complicates this. But the risk and expectations are minimal since Sandy Alderson was just looking for a back-of-the-rotation starter, not a staff ace. —*Alex Nelson*

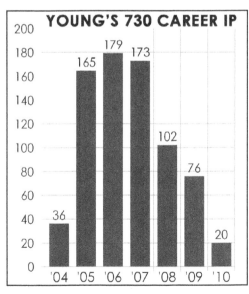

YOUNG'S 730 CAREER IP

PART 4: THE REMNANTS OF MINAYA

CHAPTER TWELVE

LEGACY OF A SCOUTING DIRECTOR

ALEX NELSON

While the changes at the top of the front office garner the most attention—and rightfully so—some new faces lower down in the food chain can have a profound organizational impact that might not be immediately noticed by the casual fan. One of those faces—probably the most important one—belongs to the director of amateur scouting, a man whose entire body of work is in service to a single event in early June: the amateur draft. A scouting director is generally seen as one of the three or four most important decision-makers in an organization. A good one can keep an organization supplied with inexpensive talent and useful trade chips for years to come. A poor one will keep his general manager scrambling for free agents to fill out the major league roster. The scouting director needs to be able to evaluate talent, find scouts he can trust to be his eyes and ears, coordinate those scouts, evaluate players' signability, negotiate with players, and make the appropriate budget allocations based on all of that information. It's a complicated process that requires months and months of preparation. The worst part? Due to the nature of baseball's development cycle, it takes years for a GM to confidently know whether or not this key lieutenant is performing his duties satisfactorily.

During the majority of the Omar Minaya era, the director of amateur scouting position was held by Rudy Terrasas. On November 20, after five years of more criticism than praise, Terrasas became one of the first casualties of the Sandy Alderson takeover. The vacancy created by his departure was filled two weeks later by Chad MacDonald, the Arizona Diamondbacks' Director of International Scouting. With so much of a franchise's future depending on the competency of its scouting director, there are some very important questions to consider in order to evaluate Terrasas's legacy. For starters, did he really deserve to get axed? What were his drafting tendencies? Can MacDonald be expected to stay the course, or will he introduce a dramatic shift in philosophy? Is such a shift even desirable?

I'll attempt to tackle each of these questions, but let's begin with a review of the five drafts Terrasas oversaw.

2006 Draft Class

Terrasas was given the job after previous scouting director Russ Bove, who had followed Minaya to New York from Montreal, was reassigned with just one draft under his belt. It's unclear why Bove was ousted; in retrospect, the 2005 draft doesn't look half bad, having produced major leaguers Mike Pelfrey, Jon Niese, Josh Thole, Bobby Parnell, and Drew Butera. It is extremely unusual for a scouting director to be dismissed after just one draft, but the move came alongside large-scale changes to the entire department, suggesting the organization felt the command structure from top to bottom was faulty. Whatever the reason, Minaya turned to Terrasas, an old ally from his days in Texas, to oversee the reformed department.

Terrasas was given a difficult task right off the bat: The team had no first-round pick after signing Billy Wagner, and 61 players came off the board before Terrasas finally made his first selection.

The First-Rounders: With no first-round pick, the team made college righty Kevin Mulvey its number one. Mulvey was a solid choice, featuring a low-90s sinking fastball, an above-average slider, and good college performance. Mulvey was considered a fair bet to become a mid-rotation starter and was a key chip in the Johan Santana trade two years later. Now 26 and in the Diamondbacks organization, Mulvey still hasn't made much of an impact at the major league level.

The Highlights: Third-rounder Joe Smith, a sidearming righty, has a 3.57 ERA through 181 major league innings. Daniel Murphy was taken in the 13th round, and while he should never have been trusted with a starting job at an offense-first position like first base, he still has a chance to stick as a utility player. Tobi Stoner, a college pitcher taken in round 16, has virtually no upside as a finesse righty, but there are probably worse insurance policies to keep in Triple-A. Dustin Martin, a 26th-round outfielder, did just enough to be packaged with Butera in a trade for Luis Castillo. Butera subsequently hit a wall in Triple-A and is unlikely to advance any further. Josh Stinson, a 37th-round righty, probably doesn't have enough stuff to make it in the bigs for any extensive period of time, but he's still hanging around and is on the Mets' 40-man roster. If we're feeling generous we might count those last two as mild successes.

The Lowlights: Oh, just about everyone else, though some of it was simply bad luck. Talented fifth-rounder Stephen Holmes signed but immediately handed back his signing bonus, quit baseball, and returned to school due to personal issues. Sixth-rounder Scott Schafer had a live arm, but his one DUI matched his total for games pitched in the organization. Ninth-rounder Jeremy Barfield didn't sign after an unfortunate altercation during which he pushed his father, former big leaguer Jesse Barfield, down a flight of stairs.

The other selections were clearly poor choices whose failings can't be charged to the account of Fortuna. Take fourth-rounder John Holdzkom, a righty from a Utah junior college who was tall and young and not much else. He had inconsistent velocity, lousy control, no good breaking pitch or changeup, and a reputation for being difficult to coach. Through 126 minor league innings, the 6-foot-7 Holdzkom has a 5.57 ERA. And you know what else? Terrasas drafted almost the exact same guy in ninth-rounder Nathan Hedrick. Not as talented as Holdzkom but three inches taller and a lot less surly, he walked 46 batters in 52 Gulf Coast League innings before promptly retiring. Seventh-rounder Dan Stegall? Lots of athleticism but terrible swing mechanics. Few could have been surprised when he was released in 2009 with a .219 career minor league batting average.

The Tendencies: Very few useful players emerged from this draft. In fact, only Holdzkom, Murphy, Stoner, Stinson, and 36th-round reliever Edgar Ramirez (struggling some in Double-A) remain with the organization. While you certainly don't expect to get much in the way of impact talent out of a draft after the first round, it was surprising how quickly most of it sputtered. In fact, every player signed between Smith in the third round and Murphy in the 13th was out of baseball by the end of 2009, or, as in the case of Holdzkom, might as well have. Even as volatile as baseball prospects are, that was a dreadful return.

As he often would, Terrasas focused the top of his draft on college pitchers, grabbing six of them among his first nine selections. Of the team's 35 signees (including Holmes), 24 came from four-year college programs, five from junior colleges, and six from high schools. However, despite the heavy leanings toward college-aged players, it was a draft light on refined skill. Through the top 10 rounds, only three picks—Mulvey, Smith, and Holmes—had any sort of polish.

2007 DRAFT CLASS

Terrasas was given far more to work with in 2007 despite still not having a true first-round pick after Minaya signed Moises Alou. However, the Mets received two sandwich-round picks—a second-rounder and a third-rounder for losing relievers Roberto Hernandez and Chad Bradford. There wasn't a great chance at landing a blue-chipper with either selection, but it presented Tarrasas with an opportunity to add some much-needed depth to the system and perhaps make a splash or two with signability picks that other teams had passed on.

The First-Rounders: The Mets' first pick came at number 42 overall, and they selected... Eddie Kunz? A college reliever? Big-bodied, Kunz had a starter's frame, a heavy sinker, and an above-average slider, but since he lacked a third pitch, he was more or less stuck in the bullpen. Kunz's career at Oregon State had been a little lackluster: The ERAs were shiny, but he didn't have the dominant strikeout numbers you'd expect a closer to have. Add in his mechanical flaws and Kunz profiled as a setup guy, at best. And that best-case scenario didn't exactly work out, as Kunz walked more than he struck out as a swing man in Double-A last season.

The Mets used their second sandwich-round pick on Nate Vineyard, a lefty from a Georgia prep school. Vineyard had a good build, average velocity, and a promising slider, but his career ended two games into the 2008 season when he left for home to rehab a shoulder injury and never reported back.

The Highlights: Fifth-round infielder Zach Lutz can certainly hit, having compiled an .870 OPS during his minor league career. A slew of injuries have been holding him back, however. The addition of power in 2010 to Lucas Duda's skill set has made the first baseman/outfielder and seventh-round pick a legitimate prospect after years sitting on the edge of noteworthiness. Robert Carson, taken in round 14, has a very heavy sinker, and if he can continue to corral his stuff he could be a mid-rotation starter. Tarrasas also took a trio of finesse pitchers in the middle rounds—southpaw Mike Antonini (round 18), righty Dylan Owen (20), and righty Dillon Gee (21). While Gee is probably the only one with a chance to crack the back end of a rotation, Antonini brought shortstop Chin-lung Hu over in a trade with the Dodgers, and Owen does provide some pitching depth. Roy Merritt, a 29th-round lefty, still has a chance at a middle-relief career.

The Lowlights: Kunz and Vineyard were big busts. Second-rounder

Scott Moviel, at 6 feet 10 inches tall, falls into the Holdzkom–Hedrick category of tall righties with underwhelming results. The Mets picked Moviel hoping he'd add some velocity and learn how to throw a better breaking pitch, but neither happened. He posted a 5.56 ERA at pitcher-friendly St. Lucie in 2010. Righty Brant Rustich still has a chance, but he was another college reliever, and an older one at that. He will already be 26 with barely any time in the Florida State League. Third-round relievers Eric Niesen and Stephen Clyne both hit the wall in Double-A, and Clyne is no longer with the organization. Fourth-round third baseman Richard Lucas has struggled mightily in two attempts at full-season ball. Eighth-round finesse-righty Dan McDonald was hurt from 2008 through 2010 before being released in November. Righty Cole Abbott was considered a top prep talent who fell to the 25th round due to signability, but injuries ended his pro career after just 16 innings pitched.

The Tendencies: Terrasas called it quits early in this draft, making just 39 picks (the draft is 50 rounds long). It's not that unusual to see one or two teams head home before the draft is over, though it is a little odd for one to bow out quite that early. However, Terrasas still had a full draft class, signing 32 players, a clear indication of a reliance on pre-draft deals. Even Abbott, considered the toughest sign in the Mets' class, agreed to a deal almost immediately after the draft. Once again, Terrasas was generally focused on pitching at the top of the draft, though this time he did take a couple of prep arms that blew up in his face. Only a dozen players from the class remain in the organization, and it's likely that just five have a reasonable chance at making even a small impact: Duda, Lutz, Gee, Carson, and Merritt. One or two others have remote chances at relief roles, but they're still a good distance away.

In the end, Terrasas aimed very low in this draft, with two relievers in his top four choices, and he still missed on every pitcher until hitting on Carson in the 14th. However, he does deserve some credit for also grabbing underwhelming talents with superior control, like Antonini, Owen, and Gee.

2008 Draft Class

2008 represented Terrasas's best chance to make an impact on the Mets' system. The team had three first-round picks, two of which were awarded to them after losing Tom Glavine to the Braves via free agency.

The First-Rounders: The Mets' first pick was the 18th overall, and Terrasas selected the best player to emerge from his tenure: Ike Davis.

Ike had a solid rookie campaign in 2010 and figures to be a good-bat, great-glove first baseman over the next six years. With some refinement in his plate discipline and the further development of his power he could be a very good player, though perhaps short of being a perennial All-Star.

Four picks later the Mets took Reese Havens, a shortstop from South Carolina. Havens had been on scouts' radars for a long time and he had a monster season as a junior. Since being drafted, he's shifted to second base, as expected, and has played well when healthy. That last part has been the catch. He's been hampered by hamstring and oblique injuries over the past three seasons.

In the sandwich round the Mets took UNC-Wilmington righty Brad Holt, a tall pitcher with tremendous arm strength and endurance. However, his command could be iffy at times, and his breaking stuff and changeup lagged behind his fastball. At the time, I viewed the Holt pick as a good gamble—his upside was pretty high, and the bullpen was always a possibility for him if the secondary pitches never arrived—but the command issues and a velocity dip caused Holt to completely implode and he was last seen struggling to throw strikes after being demoted to St. Lucie.

The Highlights: Terrasas did a great job selecting hitters in this draft. Both Davis and Havens have been as good as advertised, if not quite as healthy. Third-rounder Kirk Nieuwenhuis has been a steady performer and has speed and power. A high strikeout rate might keep him from succeeding as a regular, but he should be a good reserve at the very least. Fourth-rounder Sean Ratliff, a Stanford product, has somewhat unexpectedly been a Nieuwenhuis clone. Josh Satin, taken in the sixth, is an on-base machine with some pop and versatility in the field. Eighth-round third baseman Eric Campbell has exceeded expectations after showing some power in St. Lucie and Binghamton last season. Even second-round choice Javier Rodriguez, a very talented but also very raw outfielder from Puerto Rico, has recently gotten into the act. After a horrendous start to his pro career, he hit .319 and slugged .500 in Kingsport last season. Terrasas deserves a lot of credit for these picks.

On the pitching side there's been less to applaud Terrasas for. Mark Cohoon, their 12th-rounder, is another control artist who was unhittable at Savannah last year and earned a promotion all the way to Binghamton, where he was merely competent. Brandon Moore, taken in the 14th, has posted some outstanding strikeout-to-walk ratios, but he's now 25 and will begin 2011 in Binghamton. It's early, so there's still a chance that one or two other draftees emerge from this class.

The Lowlights: Holt is the big failure here but hardly the only one. Fifth-round catcher Dock Doyle was a pick I liked a lot, but he hasn't had much playing time and hasn't impressed when he's found it. Prep lefty Brian Valenzuela and college righty Jeff Kaplan, the club's 10th- and 11th-round picks, have barely pitched due to injuries and never realistically projected as anything more than middle relievers. Kyle Allen, a prep talent that fell until late in the draft due to signability concerns, was disappointing in 2010 but was previously promising and still has plenty of time to turn things around.

The Tendencies: One thing was never more apparent about Terrasas: The guy often made smart decisions about drafting college hitters. Ike Davis is looking like one of the best picks in a first-base-heavy draft, Havens and Rodriguez have lots of promise, and Terrasas found gems in Nieuwenhuis, Ratliff, Satin, and Campbell. It really makes you wish he had taken more college hitters in previous (and later) drafts.

A staggering 39 players signed, but the team needed to grab a lot of organizational filler when so many players from the 2006 draft were going belly-up. Only four signees came from the high school ranks and, as a result, the Mets started drawing criticism for being cheap drafters. A total of 23 players remain with the organization.

2009 DRAFT CLASS

Once again, Terrasas was given the challenge of finding talent without the luxury of a first-round pick. His first pick, No. 72 overall, came even later than it did in 2006.

The First-Rounders: With no first-round choice, Terrasas grabbed Steven Matz, a local southpaw from Long Island with projection, an above-average arm, and no refinement. You know, all those things scouts love. Unfortunately, no one has seen him pitch yet as a pro— Tommy John surgery swallowed up his 2010 season. Nevertheless, it was a perfectly reasonable selection at 72.

The Highlights: It's very early, so I'll just put the most promising guys here. Injuries have slowed third-round shortstop Robbie Shields, but he rebounded to put up a decent .290/.331/.457 line at Savannah. He won't make it as a defender at short, but his bat could still be above average at second. Athletic outfielder Darrell Ceciliani was picked in the fourth round out of a Washington junior college, and though he could use some more power and patience, he batted .351 in the New York-Penn League. Terrasas took soft-tossing southpaw Darin Gorski in the seventh, who pitched capably at Savannah in 2010. Zach Dotson, who the Mets went over slot to sign out of the 13th round, is talented, but has had some difficulty staying on the field (injuries and a 50-game drug suspension).

In the Hail Mary Division, third baseman Joe Bonfe (round 21) has hit .320 since going pro and has nice size, but third is a crowded position in the organization and Bonfe doesn't really provide the power you'd like to see from the position. John Church (23) doesn't have much in the way of stuff, but he did have a sparkling 2.64 ERA at Savannah in 2010.

The Lowlights: Lacking a first-round pick, Terrasas made matters even worse with two absolutely boneheaded decisions. First, he took Texas prep righty Damien Magnifico in the fifth round. The kid had two things going for him: He could touch 97 with his heater and he had one helluva name. Unfortunately, he couldn't consistently hit 97, he had no control, no breaking stuff, and no changeup. What's more, he was short, and he wanted a cool million dollars for signing. Guys like Magnifico regularly get selected in the later rounds by organizations who have no interest in giving them much money. Teams just have picks to spare and prayers that the player will either get a lot better or a lot more realistic. Magnifico simply had no business being drafted when he did, and it was a fundamental error by Terrasas.

He made another mistake with the very next pick when he selected David Buchanan, a junior college pitcher with some talent, with his sixth-round pick. It was a fine choice. The problem? He reportedly took so long in offering a contract to Buchanan that he had already written off the Mets and committed to transfer to the University of Georgia. It's a simple idea: Keep the lines of communication open. The inability to do this is an inexcusable error.

There were other mistakes, like taking a pair of underwhelming catchers in the eighth and ninth rounds, but they pale in comparison to the other two gaffes.

The Tendencies: Terrasas was a little more willing to find help from the prep pool. Seven of his 35 signees were high school athletes. Matz hasn't played yet and Dotson has barely played, but the other five have all been underwhelming one year in. Those five still have time, but I'm not optimistic. Once again, Terrasas did his best work with college hitters like Shields and Ceciliani. Twenty-eight players are still with the club.

2010 DRAFT CLASS

There really isn't a fair way to even begin to evaluate this draft yet, so I'll just provide a summary. A down 2009 season for the Mets meant Terrasas had a high first-round pick—seventh overall—at his disposal, and he used that selection to take Matt Harvey, a tall righty with a sharp sinker. Reminiscent of Mike Pelfrey, Harvey has neither Pelfrey's history of college performance nor his fastball command. He'll need to work on his secondary stuff, so he's something of a high-risk, high-reward signing.

The Mets didn't have a second-rounder, but they took college catcher Blake Forsythe in the third. Despite Terrasas's history of solid college position-player choices, Forsythe does not look like one of them, as his strikeout rate, sky high in college, was crippling in the minors. Fourth-round pick Cory Vaughn, son of former All-Star Greg, looks like the gem of the draft right now, though he'll need to watch the strikeouts, too. He hit .307/.397/.557 in 2010, though I'd advise tempered expectations until he repeats the effort in full-season ball. Matt den Dekker (round 5) was likewise pretty successful in his debut. He has tons of speed and plays a great center field, but he's old for his level and he'll need to—surprise!—watch the strikeouts as he advances.

The Mets went over slot to sign UCLA starting pitcher Erik Goeddel. Terrasas deserves credit for signing what many considered an impossible sign, and Goeddel has enough talent that it's easy to envision him as either a potential front-line starter or a quality reliever.

This draft was even more college-heavy than previous ones, especially at the top. Just one of the first 20 picks came from the high school ranks—Akeel Morris, a tenth-round pitcher from the Virgin Islands. Morris was also the only high schooler Terrasas managed to sign. Much like before, however, there still wasn't a whole lot of refinement throughout the Mets' draft despite all the players with extra experience. Harvey's college performance left much to be desired, Forsythe's contact rate has really held him back, and the same has been true of Vaughn and den Dekker. Frankly, Terrasas picked up a lot of college players in this draft who didn't improve as much during their college careers as most teams prefer. It indicates a tremendous confidence in the organization's player-development system, a confidence that may or may not be misplaced.

What All This Means

I'm of the opinion that Terrasas absolutely had to go when the front office transitioned from Minaya to Alderson. The 2009 mishaps were a pair of inexcusable errors that would really make me question the competence of my scouting department on a fundamental level. This wasn't a difference of opinion but a question of preparedness and attention to detail. The fact that the 2006 and 2007 drafts were such disasters wouldn't make me feel any worse about the decision.

Just to sum up, here's how I would characterize the Rudy Terrasas era:

1. He had relative success at drafting college hitters.

In 2006, Terrasas brought home Daniel Murphy. In 2007, Zach Lutz and Lucas Duda. 2008? Ike Davis, Reese Havens, Kirk Nieuwenhuis, Sean Ratliff, Josh Satin, and Eric Campbell. 2009 gave Mets fans Darrell Ceciliani and Robbie Shields, 2010 Cory Vaughn and possibly others. In general, teams hit on college hitters the most often, but it does seem like the Mets have seen more than their share of domestic hitting prospects in recent years. Whether this is because Terrasas and crew have been scouting them more effectively or because the player-development system in place is better at refining their talent, I don't know. It's probably a little bit of both. Whatever the case, given his success with college hitters, it's a shame that Terrasas felt compelled to use most of his high draft picks on pitching.

2. He was not big on taking guys with lots of refinement, even when they were coming out of college.

Despite his successes, most of the hitters Terrasas grabbed were guys with major flaws that have flown under the radar somewhat. In fact, most of them have been guys with suboptimal contact rates in college. Nieuwenhuis, Ratliff, Satin, Shields, Vaughn, den Dekker, Forsythe, and Lutz were all college hitters with contact concerns. It didn't scare away Terrasas in the slightest.

He was less successful with the formula on the pitching side, which worries me a little about Matt Harvey's future. Terrasas loves size and he clearly believes in projection, but big pitchers are notorious for having mechanical issues and a lot of pitchers just never add the velocity you're expecting. He wanted guys like John Holdzkom, Nathan Hedrick, Scott Moviel, Eric Niesen, and Stephen Clyne to emerge as better pitchers in the pros than they had previously been. Most of them just never learned or never developed physically. It's been aggravating.

3. He had much more success with finesse pitchers than power pitchers.

Mark Cohoon, Dillon Gee, Mike Antonini, Dylan Owen, Kevin Mulvey, Tobi Stoner, Josh Stinson. None of these young men really lit up the radar gun and were more notable for their pitchability and mound presence than their arms. But they're the ones who have reached or will reach Triple-A, and they're the guys the Mets have traditionally had the most success developing into useful big leaguers. Considering that most of the player-development people have been in place since before Omar Minaya took over, this is an important consideration.

These are not the kinds of picks that get anyone excited. Their ceilings are lower, and it isn't uncommon for finesse pitchers to stall at higher levels. But sometimes you have to draft to an organization's strengths, and control pitching has been one of the Mets' biggest.

4. He loved taking college pitching at the top of drafts.

College and junior college pitchers generally dominated Terrasas's top ten rounds. On the whole he wasn't very successful with the philosophy, though he didn't have much more success with the few high school pitchers he grabbed in the same spots, either. Part of the reason he had so little success drafting college pitchers in the top rounds was his refusal to use his early selections on control pitchers. The nicest thing about college pitching toward the top of the draft is the presence of pitchers with wide arsenals and command but lesser upside. Terrasas avoided these pitchers like the plague until well after the tenth round. I understand the reasoning—pitchers with upside can be impossible to locate late in the draft—but Terrasas failed to hit on any of these types of pitchers.

5. He wasn't afraid to draft college seniors or players from small schools.

A player may slide under scouts' radars for a variety of reasons. One is that the player might come from college conferences or small schools that aren't heavily scouted. It came as quite a surprise when the Mets took Nieuwenhuis in round three, since he came from the NAIA—the National Association of Intercollegiate Athletics. Many of the Mets' junior college selections, like Darrell Ceciliani, also fit in here. A second reason that a player might slip by unnoticed is if he's a senior. Seniors aren't usually thought of as high-profile talents since they are a year older and, perhaps more importantly, most of the good players get drafted as juniors. The Mets haven't shied away from these types. Satin, den Dekker, and 2010 selection Jeffrey Walters are all examples of senior signs, taken perhaps a couple rounds before most teams would consider drafting them. Rustich might also fit in here as a red-shirt junior. All teams do eventually draft seniors, but usually only after their younger brethren have been gobbled up.

6. He was definitely hamstrung by the draft budget.

Why did Terrasas so routinely go for senior signs? Simple: They have no bargaining leverage since returning to school isn't an option. No bargaining leverage means they'll sign cheaper, and there's little doubt that Terrasas didn't have all the resources at his disposal that he would have liked. But I don't think the lack of a huge budget is an excuse for not drafting well. You can certainly have a good draft without spending a lot of money, a sort of Moneyball approach to drafting. But there's also little doubt that having the cash to take who you want when you want is liberating, and it is a shame that Terrasas didn't always have that.

AND WHAT ABOUT THE FUTURE?

Frankly, I just don't know enough to make any concrete prognostications about the philosophies of new scouting director Chad MacDonald. He's never held the position before, and when asked about drafting philosophy in a press conference, all Sandy Alderson said was that he didn't think McDonald preferred any one type of draftee over another, at least in terms of college vs. high school or tools vs. skills.

I can make some conjectures based on the Diamondbacks' recent drafting history, which McDonald was a part of before becoming their head of international scouting. Generally the Diamondbacks preferred a more balanced attack, often supplementing their top ten picks with several high schoolers. They almost always get their picks signed, even getting creative in this regard if necessary. For instance, in 2010 they tried to think outside the box by over-drafting Barret Loux on a pre-draft deal in the hopes of signing several other high school talents. Loux didn't work out, but they did sign high school picks with their next two selections. On the whole, the Diamondbacks probably did skew a little more toward raw players with high upside, but not overwhelmingly so.

I do have one big piece of advice for the new scouting department: Know the organization you work for. All teams have different strengths in player development. For example, give the Dodgers a power arm from any prep school and they'll do their best to make a pitcher out of him. Yes, some players will succeed in any environment, but they are few. The vast majority will thrive with certain coaches and not with others. Maybe your staff is great at fixing a certain mechanical flaw. Maybe a particular coach can teach a kid to lay off balls down and away with great success. As of this printing, it does not appear as if the Mets will be making broad changes to their instructional staff, and we've seen that the team has done well with college hitters and control pitchers in the past. I'd interview the development staff and search for a reason why this might be the case. If it's true, it will be wise to adjust your draft strategy accordingly.

As in 2010, the Mets will again have a top-15 pick this year, as well as an extra sandwich pick as compensation for Pedro Feliciano's defection to the Bronx. For once, they won't be missing any of their picks. The best part? It's an outstanding draft for talent at the top, especially in the college ranks, so the Mets have a great opportunity to add a player or two with some combination of reliability and upside to their system. In the end, I really can't say for sure what I'm expecting next June. But with Alderson promising loosened purse strings and a new voice calling the shots, I do know this will be the most interesting draft the Mets have had in years.

CHAPTER THIRTEEN

REVIEWING THE 2010 METS MINORS

ROB CASTELLANO

With the explosion of prospect coverage in recent years—and interest in minor leaguers in general—whenever we discuss the merits of a team's farm system we automatically think in terms of individual players.

"How did the Mets' farm system fare in 2010, you ask? Well, let's see: Duda raked, Havens was hurt, Thole and Niese graduated...."

You know the routine. But the fact of the matter is that prospect watchers sometimes forget that, beyond all of the scouting reports and radar guns, there are actual baseball games being decided down on the farm every night. At this point it's almost a novel exercise to look at a system in terms of wins and losses, but that doesn't make it any less interesting or instructive.

So how did the Mets' farm system fare in 2010? Well, just like on the player-development side, 2010 was a good year for Mets affiliates. In terms of the seven U.S.-based affiliates, the overall winning percentage was 51%, a nice improvement over the 45% mark in 2009. Much of that ground was made up by the two top rungs—the Triple-A Buffalo Bisons and the Double-A Binghamton Mets—who both bounced back from historically miserable 2009 seasons. In addition, three Mets affiliates made playoff runs in 2010, including two that went all the way to the championship round. That's a marked improvement over 2009 when only one affiliate made the playoffs.

Despite going home without any championship hardware, the Mets' system did boast the affiliate with the highest regular-season winning percentage in all of minor league baseball: the Brooklyn Cyclones, who won 68% of their games. Mets teams had hitting streaks, homer streaks, exhilarating winning streaks, and incredible losing streaks. There were players suspended and there were managers suspended. There was a cycle, a (kind of) no-hitter, lots of guys who were cold, and others who were on fire. One guy literally set himself on fire (seriously). So for some more of the nitty-gritty from the 2010 New York Mets farm system, let's dive in and review each affiliate's 2010.

❖   ❖   ❖

BUFFALO BISONS, TRIPLE-A

Before a single game had even been played in 2010 there was cause for celebration in Buffalo. After all, 2009 was over. That season, Buffalo's first as an affiliate of the Mets, the parent organization's relationship with the city of Buffalo got off on the wrong foot. The Bisons nearly went into the record book for all the wrong reasons, as the team won only 56 games, the second-lowest total since the team's revival in 1979. Buffalo ownership was publicly peeved with the way that former Mets GM Omar Minaya seemed to ignore the team, filling the roster with minor league journeymen and other dreck. To his credit, Minaya made improving the Buffalo roster a priority that offseason, signing players like Russ Adams, Mike Jacobs, Mike Cervenak, Mike Hessman, Val Pascucci, Michael O'Connor, Luis Hernandez, and Bobby Livingston, all of whom contributed to making Buffalo a more entertaining club for the local fans. It was also fitting that Buffalo Baseball Hall of Famer Terry Collins, as minor league field coordinator, helped oversee the instruction for the handful of legitimate prospects that did pass through there.

The Bisons were good in 2010, finishing with a 76–68 record that placed them third in a competitive International League North Division which ultimately saw the Yankees' Scranton/Wilkes-Barre affiliate run away with the title. For the sixth straight season, the Mets' Triple-A affiliate was managed by Ken Oberkfell, who started that run as a Norfolk Tide, then followed the team to New Orleans then up to Buffalo. As for the team itself, the Bisons were yet another example of a system-wide trend in 2010: dynamic offense with big-time power backed by a lackluster pitching staff short on upper-tier talent. This formula worked for the first two-thirds of the season thanks to a lineup that scored runs in bunches just about every day, but after big league call-ups for Ike Davis, Josh Thole, and Chris Carter, and injuries to Hessman and Fernando Martinez, the Bisons fell out of contention late in the summer and eventually finished 11.5 games behind surging Scranton.

At its best, the Bisons' offense was a thing to behold. Powered by sluggers like Hessman, Carter, and Pascucci, there was no doubt that this was the premier offense in the International League (and perhaps among all minor leagues) for the lion's share of the season. And though they slowed after the mass promotions to the big club, guys like Nick

Evans and Lucas Duda jumped up and continued to pepper Oak Street with long balls, while Jesus Feliciano made a season-long run at the league batting title. When all was said and done, the Buffalo lineup ranked at or near the top in doubles, homers, runs, on-base percentage, slugging percentage, and batting average. The only thing they didn't do was run. Make no mistake, this was a three-run-bomb kind of club.

Unfortunately, they suffered from the same lack of impact pitching depth that afflicted the organization as a whole. And though 'tween-ers like Pat Misch and Dillon Gee held the fort admirably—with the aid of an early-season run by some egghead knuckleballer—in the end, the overall weakness of the staff was patently obvious. On-the-fence prospects like Mike Antonini (now with the Dodgers), Tobi Stoner, and Dylan Owen all struggled facing Triple-A hitters, and retreads like Ramon Ortiz didn't help much, either. The staff placed in the bottom third of the league in ERA, wins, WHIP, and a host of other pitching statistics. The one bright spot was the work of the bullpen, where—despite surprisingly poor results from Bobby Parnell—less-heralded pitchers like Mike O'Connor, Jose de la Torre, and Chad Cordero provided strong relief work.

BINGHAMTON METS, DOUBLE-A

As was the case with Buffalo, 2010 was a huge improvement over the B-Mets' historically bad 54–86 campaign of 2009, which sent manager Mako Oliveras packing to the Mexican League. In his place, longtime Met Tim Teufel made his Double-A managing debut after two seasons serving that role for High-A St. Lucie. In many ways, Binghamton's roster resembled St. Lucie's (and Buffalo's for that matter): It had a powerful offense and numerous position-player prospects, but a glaring lack of impact starting pitching ultimately crippled the team, leading to a final record of 66–76, and a 17-game deficit in the standings.

Business was good for the B-Mets' offense in 2010 despite some in-season turnover. The team boasted five hitters with 14 or more home runs, and it seemed that whenever one slugger left—either as a result of injury (in the case of Reese Havens and Zack Lutz) or due to a promotion—another one took his place to keep the Binghamton offense humming right along. When a middle-of-the-order spot opened up following the promotion of center fielder Kirk Nieuwenhuis to Buffalo, Sean Ratliff stepped right in to fill Captain Kirk's spot in center and at the plate. When Havens went down, Josh Satin answered the call. The same for Lutz and third baseman Eric Campbell. Ultimately, the B-Mets' offense ranked first in the Eastern League in doubles, homers, slugging, and OPS, and was second in the league in batting. As with Buffalo, Binghamton had a true Earl Weaver-style offense: Get on base, don't do anything foolish while there, then wait for a three-run home run.

The Binghamton pitching staff, just like Buffalo's, was the polar opposite of the offense, allowing run after run to score with no end in sight. It didn't matter who they plugged in because nothing seemed to work. Prospects like Brad Holt and Robert Carson were extremely disappointing, while middling starters like Dylan Owen—after a demotion from Buffalo—and Chris Schwinden seemed to meet their match at Double-A. The bullpen was just as bad. Intriguing offseason pickup Clint Everts was a disaster, and prospects like Roy Merritt and Eddie Kunz left a lot to be desired. All in all, the B-Mets' pitchers ranked second to last in hits, homers, ERA, WHIP, and saves. They were dead last in walks allowed. The pitching staff's struggles kept the team tethered to the .500 mark for most of the season before dragging them well below by season's end.

ST. LUCIE METS, HIGH-A

It was a rough season for the mini-Mets this year, as they finished 17.5 games behind first-place Charlotte and second to last in the Florida State League's South Division. Managed by Edgar Alfonzo—brother of former Met Edgardo—it wasn't a complete lack of talent that doomed the High-A Mets, but rather an unbalanced roster that prevented the club from getting on track. For much of the year they possessed a strong lineup, pacing the FSL in most offensive stats at the All-Star break. Guys like Stefan Welch, Josh Satin, and Jordany Valdespin carried the load for the first half, while call-ups Wilmer Flores and Kai Gronauer took the baton after the break. Unfortunately, the team's collective undisciplined approach at the plate (337 walks vs. 1,117 strikeouts) caught up to them and contributed to an extended period down the stretch where they averaged just 1.9 runs per game.

St. Lucie likewise suffered from the system's lack of pitching depth, perhaps more so than any other affiliate. The Mets' pitching staff was an abomination all season long, with starters Kyle Allen, Scott Moviel, and Jeurys Familia all underperforming, while midseason additions Brad Holt and Nick Carr just added gas to the flames. There were a couple of bright spots—the promotions of Brandon Moore and Jim Fuller from

Savannah, and a strong season from Eric Beaulac—but they were too few and far between. And it just gets worse when you look deeper into the numbers: St. Lucie brought up the rear in the FSL in ERA, WHIP, and walks, while also recording a league-low three shutouts (for comparison, the Tampa Yankees had a league-leading 19 shutouts).

Despite the atrocious pitching, St. Lucie managed to hang around .500 for much of the season. In fact, as late as July 19 the team was still in contention for a playoff spot, boasting a 51–44 record. However, their season was ultimately undone by a nightmarish 25-game stretch in late July and early August when the club went 2–23. The Mets dropped like a rock in the standings and never recovered. The lackluster pitching staff went from bad to flat-out embarrassing, as they allowed an average of 5.9 runs per game during that stretch.

SAVANNAH SAND GNATS, A

In the first half of 2010, the Sand Gnats were not very hospitable to their guests at Historic Grayson Stadium, rolling to a 24–11 mark at home. Powered by a terrific opening month from erstwhile Sand Gnat Wilmer Flores, Savannah pounded their way to an overall mark of 42–28, good for a .600 winning percentage and first place going into the South Atlantic League All-Star break. Flores's sensational performance—a .360 batting average with an OPS over 1.000—as well as a flurry of intentional walks, had many calling for his promotion to St. Lucie. But Flores went into a prolonged funk as May gave way to June, reminding Mets fans and scouts alike that the kid was still just 18 years old. However, outfielder Juan Lagares, a former shortstop prospect who had perhaps been rushed earlier in his career, helped anchor the offense with a stellar first half of his own, recharging his own waning prospect status.

The other big story of the first half was Savannah's incredible pitching. Starters Mark Cohoon, Brandon Moore, and Jim Fuller all sported ERAs below 3.00, with Armando Rodriguez and Collin McHugh not far behind. Even the bullpen was dominant—John Church, Darin Gorski, and Taylor Whitenton posted great numbers as they itched for a shot in the rotation. It seemed like every night some Savannah starter would pitch at least seven strong innings and be followed by great relief. Cohoon even managed an incredible stretch of three straight complete-game shutouts to end the first half. In fact, the Gnats' pitching was the true reason for their first-half success and ultimately led them to a SAL first-half title and a September playoff berth.

Unfortunately, the second-half Gnats were a victim of their prior success. A great deal of their top performers were promoted over the All-Star break and the team suffered mightily as a result. The lineup was far less fearsome without Flores and Lagares, now doing their thing in St. Lucie, and they were quickly joined by other offensive cogs like Kai Gronauer, Rafael Fernandez, and Wilfredo Tovar. To make matters worse, two of the remaining regulars, Cesar Puello and Jefry Marte, battled injuries for the remainder of the year, so late surges from Robbie Shields and newcomer Matt den Dekker were too little, too late.

The second-half struggles weren't limited to the offense. The once-mighty Gnats' pitching staff was just a shadow of its former self once Cohoon, Moore, and Fuller were promoted, and McHugh, Church, and Whitenton all faded once they moved into the rotation full-time. Before the break, Gnats pitchers allowed more than three runs just 24 times; in the second-half they did so 39 times. The team was obviously worse and it showed, as they posted a 33–36 record in the second half and were eventually swept by the Greenville Drive in the SAL best-of-three Championship Series.

But enough with frivolity. As for the truly important stuff, *ESPN The Magazine* recently selected Savannah's August 14, 2010, "Man on Fire" stunt—where daredevil Ted Batchelor rounded the bases fully ablaze—as the 2010 Pro Sports Promotion of the Year, no doubt a far sweeter victory than any league title could have been.

BROOKLYN CYCLONES, LOW-A

Where else could we begin but with the Cyclones' demonstrative, highly controversial—but also undeniably successful—manager, Wally Backman? Backman made his triumphant return to affiliated baseball with the Cyclones in 2010, his first such gig since he was briefly hired to be the Diamondbacks' manager in 2004. Backman lived up to fans' expectations as a character this season by relentlessly pushing his ultra-aggressive style and, of course, letting quite a few umpires know where they could stick it. Backman fit the Brooklyn attitude to a T, so it's almost a shame that he's moving up the organizational pecking order next season to manage Double-A Binghamton.

Even without Backman's antics, it was quite a memorable season for the Cyclones. From day one the Cyclones dominated the New York-Penn League, especially in the friendly confines of MCU Park, where they went an incredible 30–8 during the regular season. Brooklyn played a well-rounded style of baseball but was anchored by the team's monstrous offense, which led the NYPL in runs, average, OPS, total bases, and homers. The Cyclones' bats were on a record-setting pace until injuries struck around the All-Star break, claiming shortstop and leadoff hitter Rylan Sandoval for the remainder of the season, while also slowing cogs like Cory Vaughn and Darrell Ceciliani at various points. Though hitting was their strong suit, the Brooklyn pitching staff was nothing to scoff at, leading the circuit in both ERA and WHIP for the year. Starters Angel Cuan and Yohan Almonte posted ERAs around 2.00, while Cyclones closer Ryan Fraser established himself as an intriguing power arm by allowing just five earned runs all season. Unsurprisingly, Brooklyn led the NYPL in All-Stars with eight representatives.

Overall, the 'Clones posted a 51–24 record and a .680 winning percentage, the best mark among all US-based minor league teams in 2010. They finished the year twelve games ahead of the next closest team in the McNamara Division, sealing home-field advantage throughout the NYPL playoffs. Unfortunately, the Cyclones looked far less crisp in those playoffs than they had throughout the regular season, especially their starting pitching who posted a 5.52 playoff ERA. The only aspect of their game that held true throughout the playoffs was their penchant for poor defense. They did manage to win their semifinal matchup against Jamestown, but they ran out of magic in the championship, dropping the series 2–0 to the average-but-streaking Tri-City ValleyCats. Regardless of the final result, it was still a special summer in Coney Island.

KINGSPORT METS, ROOKIE

Managed by former Mets backstop Mike Difelice, the K-Mets were the cellar dwellers in the Appalachian League's Western Division in 2010, posting a 28–39 record for the season. The team just wasn't very good, suffering from a lack of impact talent apart from the Rodriguez boys, Aderlin and Javier. Even so, Kingsport was only a handful of games out of first place after their first full month of play, but a 10–19 August put a stop to that. Strangely, the K-Mets didn't seem to like playing at home, as they were 12–22 at Hunter Wright Stadium this season.

GULF COAST LEAGUE METS, ROOKIE

The GCL Mets were actually a pretty strong team, posting a 31–25 record and a .554 winning percentage, the best figures in the league for

a non-division winner. They finished the regular season six games behind the Marlins in the GCL East and earned a wild-card spot for their
effort, but they ultimately lost their one-game semifinal matchup with
the eventual GCL-champion Phillies. The Mets were managed for most
of the year by Sandy Alomar, Sr., but Alomar was quietly suspended in
the final week for an on-field dispute with his own pitching coach, Hec-
tor Berrios. Details have been sparse, but the organization has said—
despite reports to the contrary—that the conflict did not get physical.
Alomar was replaced by Terry Collins for that final week. It was an unfortunate way to end a successful season.

CHAPTER FOURTEEN

PROSPECT PROFILES AND PREDICTIONS

ROB CASTELLANO

2010 was a good year for the Mets' farm system. The successful graduation of three top prospects into everyday major leaguers is enough to consider the year a success. Ike Davis, Jon Niese, and Josh Thole combined to add more than seven wins to the big club and all look like mainstays for years to come. Before Davis, the last Mets player to receive Rookie of the Year votes was Kaz Matsui, who garnered just 1% of the 2004 vote. Until 2010, the last starting position player the Mets' system produced was David Wright. So, yeah, 2010 was a bumper crop for the organization. Beyond those three, Mets fans also got a peek at a few other homegrown talents that figure to contribute in the near future. Guys like Jenrry Mejia, Ruben Tejada, Dillon Gee, and Lucas Duda all flashed potential during their trials with the major league squad.

Looking at minor league team performance shows 2010 was also an improvement. Buffalo and Binghamton bounced back from awful 2009 seasons, while Savannah and Brooklyn both made the playoffs. Player development was more like a split decision. On the one hand, it was a good year to be a Mets hitting prospect. There were a handful of pleasant surprises, like Duda, Eric Campbell, and Justin Turner, while teenagers Wilmer Flores and Cesar Puello solidified their status as potential stars. On the other hand, pitchers didn't fare well. System-wide command issues saw top arms Brad Holt, Jeurys Familia, and Eric Niesen—to name just a few—struggle with walks, likely a heavy factor in the dismissal of pitching coordinator Rick Waits. Fortunately, the June draft brought Matt Harvey and Erik Goeddel, and they figure to help. And the emergence of a number of talented teens in the Gulf Coast League—Juan Urbina, Domingo Tapia, and Akeel Morris—bodes well for the distant future.

All told, the Mets' system looks better than it has in years. However, that is more a reflection of depth than star power. That's not the ideal from a farm system, especially one for a large-market club where replacement-level players often make up a small percentage of payroll.

But fans should be pleased that the system has finally started to produce useful players, with the likelihood of more on the way in 2011.

Now that we have a feel for the big picture, let's take a more in-depth look at the top Mets prospects heading into 2011. We've expanded the rankings to include players yet to appear in a professional game as well as include players who have exceeded major league rookie eligibility but are, for practical purposes, still prospects. Before profiling the organization's top 30 prospects, look at how some of them rank in key areas.

TOP 5 POWER HITTERS	TOP 5 WITH THE GLOVE
Aderlin Rodriguez, 3B	Wilfredo Tovar, SS
Fernando Martinez, OF	Matt den Dekker, CF
Lucas Duda, OF	Darrell Ceciliani, CF
Sean Ratliff, OF	Kai Gronauer, C
Cory Vaughn, OF	Javier Rodriguez, OF

TOP 5 LEFTY PITCHERS	TOP 5 RELIEVERS
Juan Urbina	Manny Alvarez, RHP
Mark Cohoon	Ryan Fraser, RHP
Robert Carson	Chad Sheppard, RHP
Zach Dotson	Nick Carr, RHP
Jim Fuller	Roy Merritt, LHP

TOP 5 ELECTRIC ARMS	TOP 5 SECONDARY STUFF
Jenrry Mejia, RHP	Dillon Gee, RHP
Matt Harvey, RHP	Mark Cohoon, LHP
Jeurys Familia, RHP	Jim Fuller, LHP
Erik Goeddel, RHP	Kyle Allen, RHP
Akeel Morris, RHP	Dylan Owen, RHP

TOP 5 SLEEPER PROSPECTS	TOP 5 MAKE-OR-BREAK SEASONS
Zach Dotson, LHP	Brad Holt, RHP
Wilfredo, Tavar, SS	Fernando Martinez, OF
Brian Harrison, 3B	Francisco Pena, C
Albert Cordero, C	Brant Rustich, RHP
A.J. Pinera, RHP	Javier Rodriguez, OF

1. JENRRY MEJIA

BAT/THROW: R/R				STARTING PITCHER						BORN: 10/11/89			
	G	IP	H	BB	K	BB/9	K/9	HR	ERA	FIP	BABIP	LOB%	LD%	GB%
2008 (A-)	11	56.2	42	23	52	3.7	8.3	4	3.49	3.55	.257	73%	NO DATA
2009 (AA)	10	44.1	44	23	47	4.7	9.5	2	4.47	3.49	.333	63%	11%	58%
2010 (AA)	6	27.1	19	14	26	4.6	8.6	0	1.32	2.83	.268	85%	16%	62%

What a strange, strange season 2010 was for the Mets' top prospect. It all began with the misguided bullpen foray at the behest of lame-duck manager Jerry Manuel. Middling results aside, the worst thing about Jenrry Mejia's time with the big club was his sporadic usage, as well as Manuel's insistence that Mejia limit the use of his secondary pitches. Both had detrimental effects on Mejia's development. In June, the Mets finally came to their senses and assigned Mejia to Binghamton, where he resumed work as a starter. Unfortunately, during that transition Mejia came down with shoulder stiffness and hit the minor league disabled list. He did come back to make a few more starts down the stretch—including three at the major league level—but once again succumbed to shoulder woes. All in all, Mejia's 2010 was a study in how to mishandle a pitching prospect.

Fortunately, it looks as if no permanent damage was done. Mejia's shoulder pain was not considered serious, and he was dominant in his nine minor league starts, including an eight-inning, five-hit, nine-strikeout performance in his first Triple-A game. Mejia still possesses the ceiling of a staff ace, thanks in large part to his mid-90s, hard sinking two-seam fastball, and still-developing 12-to-6 curve. His hard change-up lags behind as a third offering, which, along with his smaller stature, leads some to project Mejia as a future fireballing closer. But it would behoove the Mets at this point to slow him down and give him every chance to stick in the rotation. With a multitude of options at the back end of the big league staff, there is no reason to rush his development, though Terry Collins has indicated that he expects Mejia to be ready for the majors at some point in 2011.

Estimated Arrival In New York: Late 2011

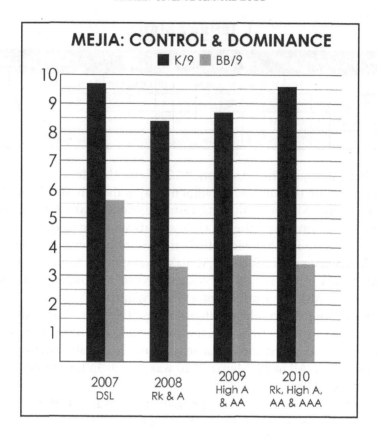

2. WILMER FLORES

BAT/THROW: R/R					SHORTSTOP						BORN: 08/06/91		
	G	PA	R	HR	RBI	BB%	K%	AVG	OBP	SLG	BABIP	wOBA	SB	SB%
2008 (Rk)	59	265	36	8	41	5%	11%	.310	.352	.490	.322	.375	2	67%
2009 (A)	125	528	44	3	36	4%	15%	.264	.305	.332	.301	.294	3	50%
2010 (A+)	67	290	32	4	40	3%	14%	.300	.324	.415	.336	.334	2	33%

Wilmer Flores had a strong year in 2010, acquitting himself at the plate in his first exposure to upper-level pitching in St. Lucie. He even improved his play at short, working hard on his agility and quickness. More importantly, he addressed the power and plate-discipline issues from his 2009 season.

His 2010 numbers are especially impressive when you consider that he spent half the season as an 18-year-old in the High-A Florida State

League, generally a pitcher-friendly environment where the average age is usually around 23 years old. What he has done at such a young age is pretty remarkable. One-time wunderkind Fernando Martinez is an interesting comparison. While he, too, once reaped praise as a future superstar, he was merely surviving as an extreme youngster, never flourishing. Flores, on the other hand, not only has age on his side but proved last year that he can flourish as well.

Despite lacking a plus-plus raw tool, his advanced hitting skills—particularly the ability to not just make contact but consistently make hard contact—are what give him the potential to be a special player. Carlos Beltran probably said it best during his rehab stint with St. Lucie: "When I was 19, I had no idea of the things [Flores] knows." The popular comparison to slugger and fellow-Venezuelan Miguel Cabrera probably isn't fair, but in a perfect world I can see Flores becoming a middle-of-the-order bat in the mold of Carlos Lee. The one thing probably keeping Flores out of the elite-prospect discussion is his defensive uncertainty.

Estimated Arrival In New York: 2013

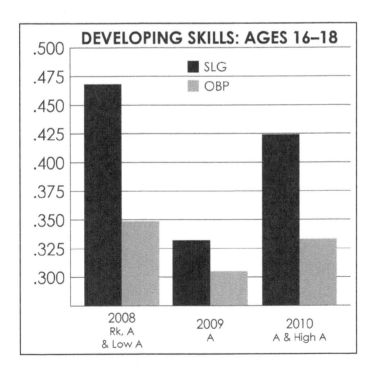

3. MATT HARVEY

Though he has yet to throw a pitch as a professional, the Mystic, Connecticut, product lands near the top of this list thanks to an exciting combination of physicality, raw stuff, and the potential to rise quickly. Originally drafted in 2007 by the Angels, Matt Harvey chose not to sign and instead went on to an uneven collegiate career at the University of North Carolina. A top talent out of high school, Harvey's first two seasons in college were erratic and somewhat disappointing. However, more consistent mechanics in 2010 helped him recapture the electric stuff he showed in high school, as he posted a solid 3.09 ERA and averaged more than a strikeout per inning while allowing just six home runs all season. What's more, he was back to working consistently in the mid-90s—often touching 98 mph—and, more importantly, holding that velocity late into games. Things peaked on a Friday night in April when Harvey wowed scouts with a complete-game, six-hit shutout against Clemson, striking out 15 and throwing a whopping 156 pitches. The most amazing part? Pitch number 156 clocked in at 96 mph.

The mid-90s fastball is Harvey's bread and butter, overpowering hitters and generating lots of swings-and-misses. He complements it with a two-seamer with heavy sink that works in the 91–93 mph range and produces weak contact and lots of ground balls. Harvey also possesses two major league-quality off-speed pitches: a tight, low-80s slider and a slower, hammer curve, both of which flash plus potential but need to be more consistent. Despite limited use during college, the Mets are encouraging Harvey to focus mainly on the curve. His changeup lags behind, mainly due to its lack of use as an amateur, but he has shown decent feel for the pitch. Perhaps his greatest weakness is his inability to consistently command his off-speed repertoire. Even so, Harvey's impressive mix of pitches paired with a perfect pitcher's build—6 feet 4 inches and 225 pounds—give him the ceiling of a top-of-the-rotation workhorse.

Estimated Arrival In New York: Late 2012

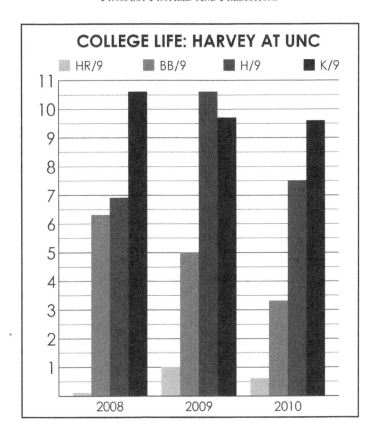

4. KIRK NIEUWENHUIS

BAT/THROW: L/R				CENTER FIELDER							BORN: 08/07/87			
	G	PA	R	HR	RBI	BB%	K%	AVG	OBP	SLG	BABIP	wOBA	SB	SB%
2008 (A-)	74	319	34	3	29	9%	25%	.277	.348	.396	.355	.343	11	61%
2009 (A+)	123	547	91	16	71	10%	25%	.274	.357	.467	.332	.383	16	80%
2010 (AA)	94	433	81	16	60	7%	24%	.289	.337	.510	.338	.370	13	65%

Another level, another strong line from the hard-hitting lefty who just keeps chugging away. In his first full season at Double-A, Kirk Nieuwenhuis garnered an Eastern League All-Star appearance, the Mets' Sterling Award for best Double-A position player, and a call up to Buffalo on August 5, all while posting a .370 wOBA, a mark right in line with his career average. "Captain Kirk" also continued to feature his trademark power-speed mix, knocking 18 home runs while stealing

13 bases, though he was caught seven times. Unfortunately, his high strikeout rate remained around his career norm, and his walks did come down a shade, a harbinger of a lower on-base percentage in the majors.

Many have expressed concerns about Nieuwenhuis's ability to man center field in the majors because of his linebacker-type build, so it's important for his prospect status that he played well defensively in center throughout 2010. If he needs to move to a corner outfield position, there will be more pressure on his bat to produce. To that point, he's shown good power to all fields since being drafted in 2008, but his line drive-oriented swing robs him of some home run potential. As a fielder, he has the speed and instincts to cover a lot of ground and features a great throwing arm. He likely profiles as an average-defense major league center fielder, at least for the first few years of his career. Don't be too worried about the struggles in his brief 30-game trial with the Bisons—Nieuwenhuis has shown a propensity to catch up after struggling early on.

Estimated Arrival In New York: Late 2011

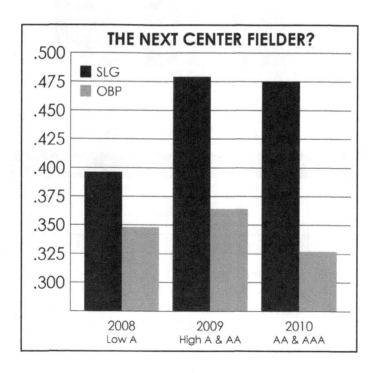

5. REESE HAVENS

BAT/THROW: L/R				SECOND BASEMAN								BORN: 10/20/86		
	G	PA	R	HR	RBI	BB%	K%	AVG	OBP	SLG	BABIP	wOBA	SB	SB%
2008 (A-)	23	97	13	3	11	11%	32%	.247	.340	.471	.327	.373	3	75%
2009 (A+)	97	430	53	14	52	13%	20%	.247	.361	.422	.272	.364	3	60%
2010 (AA)	18	75	12	6	12	8%	22%	.338	.400	.662	.362	.446	0	0%

Yet another season-ending injury for Reese Havens in 2010 marked a serious threat to the former shortstop's long-term prospects as a second baseman in the majors. Most frustrating is that the kid can hit when he's on the field. In fact, he looked like he was kicking off the breakout campaign many predicted for him when, in his first exposure to Double-A pitching, Havens teed off for six bombs in just 18 games and hit .338 with a .400 on-base percentage. Unfortunately, that was it. Havens went down with a re-aggravation of a prior oblique injury and missed the remainder of the season when the injury led to back issues. The idea of surgery was tossed around, but the organization ultimately felt the best course of action was for Havens to take the rest of the season—and winter—off.

As much as Mets fans like to project him starring at the keystone in Queens, Havens is at the point where he can no longer be penciled in to the Mets' future infield. That's not to say he can't or won't get there, but he has to prove he can stay healthy for an extended period before projecting him, let alone imagining him as a major league starter. He looks to have a major league bat with very good power to go along with a discerning eye at the plate, but Havens has played more than 23 games in a season just once in his three-year career. It isn't hard to picture Havens as an All-Star-level talent, but as impressive as his offensive tools are, they still need to develop.

Havens was advised to rest after the 2010 season so his back could heal. Upon arriving at spring training, Havens told reporters he had visited noted sports surgeon Dr. James Andrews over the winter. Rib surgery was performed to relieve lingering pressure on Havens's oblique, the original source of his back troubles. While early reports suggest Havens enters the season healthy and ready, chalk this up as another entry on his list of injury concerns.

Estimated Arrival In New York: 2012

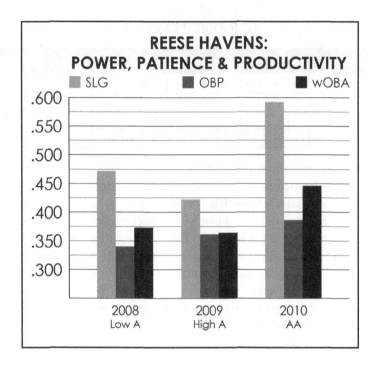

6. ADERLIN RODRIGUEZ

BAT/THROW: R/R				THIRD BASEMAN						BORN: 11/18/91			
	G	PA	R	HR	RBI	BB%	K%	AVG	OBP	SLG	BABIP	wOBA	SB	SB%
2009 (Rk)	17	72	5	1	10	13%	24%	.290	.389	.387	.370	.367	1	50%
2010 (Rk)	61	267	44	13	48	6%	17%	.312	.352	.556	.333	.400	3	75%

An injury-shortened pro debut in 2009 left evaluators with more questions about Aderlin Rodriguez than answers. In just 17 games with 72 plate appearances for the Gulf Coast League Mets, Rodriguez posted good numbers—notably a .290 batting average and a .389 OBP—but the sample size was too small for anyone to get a sense of what type of player Rodriguez may be.

Fortunately, Rodriguez was healthy in 2010 and emerged as one of the Mets' more intriguing prospects. He was the most talented player on the field in just about every game he played for Kingsport, despite being one of the youngest in the Appalachian League at 18.

Appearing in all but eight of the team's 69 games, Rodriguez put on a show. On the year, Rodriguez was second in the league in doubles, third in homers, and finished in the top five in slugging and OPS. This kid can flat-out hit for power. The natural loft in his swing, as well as impressive raw strength, produces the kind of pop rarely seen in players as young as he is. His performance was so strong that the team gave him a taste of the next level, allowing him to get some time with the A-level Savannah Sand Gnats, where he received 39 plate appearances in eight games.

Unfortunately, it's not all peaches and cream for Rodriguez: He lacks foot speed and he doesn't profile long term as a third baseman—it would be a surprise if he doesn't end up at first base. And for all his raw power, his plate discipline and secondary offensive skills leave much to be desired.

Put simply, his plus-plus power and advanced bat will have to carry him as a prospect since the other aspects of his game are all subpar. Nevertheless, he's one of few Mets prospects with the potential to be a monster at the plate.

Estimated Arrival In New York: 2013

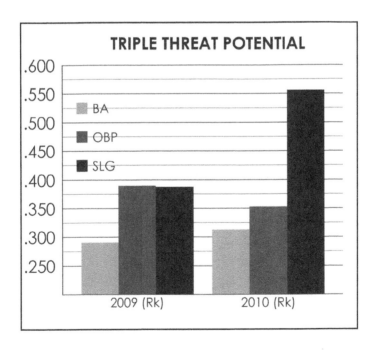

7. FERNANDO MARTINEZ

BAT/THROW: L/R				OUTFIELDER								BORN: 10/10/88	
	G	PA	R	HR	RBI	BB%	K%	AVG	OBP	SLG	BABIP	wOBA	SB	SB%
2008 (AA)	86	385	48	8	43	7%	21%	.287	.340	.432	.339	.346	6	75%
2009 (AAA)	45	190	24	8	28	6%	19%	.290	.337	.540	.316	.382	2	67%
2010 (AAA)	71	287	39	12	33	6%	25%	.253	.317	.455	.291	.339	1	100%

Martinez endured yet another injury-shorted season that saw him on the disabled list with a variety of hamstring and knee ailments. To make matters worse, he was diagnosed with chronic knee arthritis after going down in his first game of winter ball. When he was on the field last year he seemed rusty, which no doubt hurt his overall batting line.

Factoring that in, "F-Mart" looked about the same in Buffalo this past season as he did in 2009: solid, yet unspectacular, That isn't necessarily bad for a 21-year-old at the highest level of the minors, but all of the missed games from injuries have stunted his development. For the fifth straight season since he reached full-season baseball, Martinez failed to reach the 100-game plateau. For some perspective, Kirk Nieuwenhuis has played in 123, 131, and 124 games in his first three seasons. What's more, Martinez has totalled just 349 professional games since signing in 2005. Nieuwenhuis has 329 since being drafted in 2008. To add insult to injury, the previous front office often promoted him to higher levels before he was probably ready.

Once projected as a strong all-around hitter and a center fielder with good speed, Martinez now looks like a low-OBP lefty slugger with corner-outfield range. The best-case scenario for him may be to become a low-OBP version of J.D. Drew. Hopefully, things will get back on track for the once-touted youngster.

He's only 22 and continues to put up strong power numbers at Triple-A—a .202 ISO in 2010—but it's hard to see him bouncing back to an elite level. Unfortunately, the damage from injuries and the Mets' irresponsible handling of him may have done irreparable harm. His biggest advocates are gone due to the change in the Mets' front office, so 2011 looks like a make-or-break season for Martinez.

Estimated Arrival In New York: Mid-2011

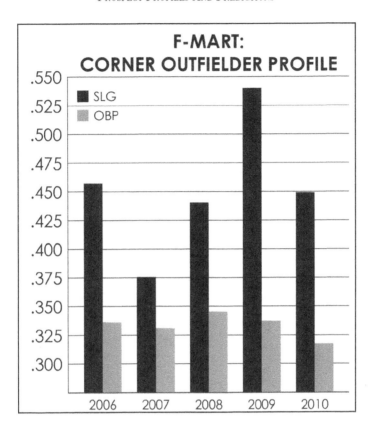

8. Cesar Puello

Bat/Throw: R/R				Right Fielder								Born: 04/01/91	
	G	PA	R	HR	RBI	BB%	K%	AVG	OBP	SLG	BABIP	wOBA	SB	SB%
2008 (Rk)	40	163	24	1	17	3%	21%	.305	.350	.364	.378	.345	13	72%
2009 (Rk)	49	221	37	5	23	5%	26%	.296	.373	.423	.379	.372	15	75%
2010 (A)	109	469	80	1	34	7%	20%	.292	.375	.359	.363	.360	45	82%

Few Mets prospects boosted their stock in 2010 more than Cesar Puello. He opened the year overmatched by full-season pitching, hitting just .234 with no home runs through May. Then the coaches stepped in to rebuild his stance and his swing. Where his old swing lent itself to spraying the ball to all fields, the Mets decided Puello would be better suited focusing on hitting for power. They moved him back from the plate and made mechanical adjustments to his swing, thus making it easier for Puello to pull the ball. He went on to bat .336 the rest of the summer, showing tremendous contact ability and much more pop in the tough offensive environment for right-handed power that is William Grayson Stadium.

For a guy with a bigger build, Puello also demonstrated tremendous speed this season—45 steals in 55 attempts—and good defensive ability, including a strong and accurate arm in right field. Rumor has it that he played a bit of center in the instructional league this fall, a change which, if permanent, would boost his value tremendously.

In terms of his tools, scouts love Puello because he does it all: He can hit, run, field, and, despite the low homer total, his size and strength suggest decent power will come. Eventually, his size will probably cut down on his stolen bases, but if things go right for Puello in 2011, it's easy to see him challenging for the top spot in the entire system by this time next year. The big issue holding back his ranking now is the wariness of a right field prospect who hit just one home run in 2010.

Estimated Arrival In New York: 2013

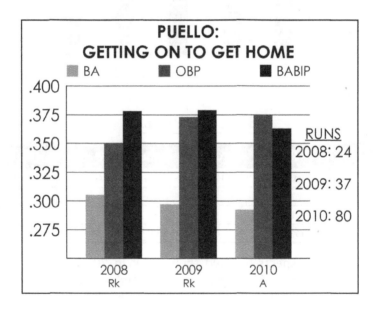

9. ZACH LUTZ

BAT/THROW: R/R				THIRD BASEMAN								BORN: 06/03/86		
	G	PA	R	HR	RBI	BB%	K%	AVG	OBP	SLG	BABIP	wOBA	SB	SB%
2008 (A-)	24	86	9	3	12	16%	17%	.333	.442	.514	.368	.428	0	0%
2009 (A+)	99	415	46	11	62	12%	20%	.284	.381	.441	.327	.380	1	50%
2010 (AA)	61	263	42	17	42	13%	28%	.289	.389	.578	.331	.420	0	0%

Zach Lutz has had nearly as many problems staying healthy as Fernando Martinez and Reese Havens. 2010 was no different, as he suffered another foot injury which cost him over two months of the season. The big difference with Lutz is that, unlike Havens, he still played a good portion of the season and, more importantly—unlike Martinez—he keeps improving at each level.

His 17-homer barrage in 61 games with Binghamton produced an eye-popping .289 ISO, tops among prospects in the Eastern League. Factor in his 13% walk rate, and Lutz's combination of power and patience continues to impress. Some even believe Lutz possesses one of the best offensive mixes in the system. His defense, while unspectacular, is serviceable thanks to his athleticism. Fielding, more than any part of his game, has probably suffered the most due to the time he has missed with injuries.

The biggest problem for Lutz, besides being injury-prone, is that the Mets aren't likely to need a third baseman for the foreseeable future. And the situations at first base and in the outfield are also crowded, so a position switch wouldn't help him. It's highly unlikely that Lutz could successfully make the switch to second base, so there's a good chance the Mets take their time with him. If the right deal comes along, it wouldn't be surprising to see him moved. Either way, putting aside Lutz's health, he is a strong bet to be a solid, everyday third baseman in the majors.

Estimated Arrival In New York: Late 2011

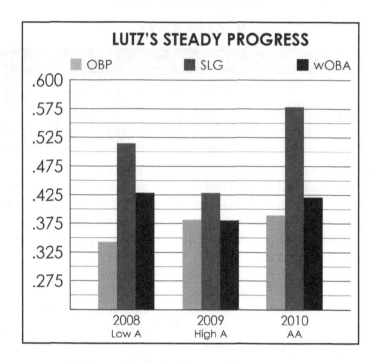

10. LUCAS DUDA

BAT/THROW: L/R				LEFT FIELDER								BORN: 02/03/86		
	G	PA	R	HR	RBI	BB%	K%	AVG	OBP	SLG	BABIP	wOBA	SB	SB%
2008 (A+)	133	559	58	11	66	12%	27%	.263	.358	.398	.335	.345	2	22%
2009 (AA)	110	467	49	9	53	13%	23%	.281	.380	.428	.340	.368	2	50%
2010 (AAA)	70	298	44	17	53	10%	22%	.314	.389	.610	.346	.424	0	N/A

Lucas Duda was a revelation in 2010, the most pleasant surprise in the Mets' system. By season's end Duda was a Double-A All-Star, the Buffalo Bisons' MVP, and the organization's Triple-A Sterling Award winner as the level's top position player. From the time he was promoted to Buffalo on June 14, he had more extra-base hits than any other hitter in Triple-A. The 23-year-old left fielder came into the season as a guy with a solid bat but was labeled by many as organizational filler due to his lack of power. That changed in a big way in 2010 as he knocked 27 homers, including four at the big league level. At one point he even rode an astounding five-game homer streak while in Buffalo, only the fifth Bison to do so in the franchise's 125-year history.

The late-blooming power was a welcome surprise for Duda who, as far back as his days at USC, had been regarded as a lumbering lefty with a penchant for contact but not enough power for a first baseman or left fielder. What's more, his strikeout-to-walk ratio also improved tremendously this past season. He still exhibited heavy platoon splits—just a .244 average vs. lefties—but Duda has gone from being a so-so prospect to a definite major league asset. Depending on how he handles lefties in the bigs, Duda's future is somewhere between being a solid, power-hitting left fielder to being the lefty-side of a platoon split.

Estimated Arrival In New York: Mid-2011

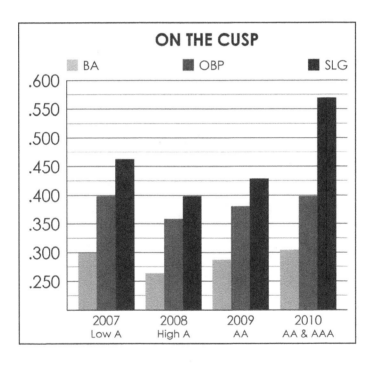

11. JUAN URBINA

BAT/THROW: L/L		STARTING PITCHER										BORN: 05/31/93	
	G	IP	H	BB	K	BB/9	K/9	HR	ERA	FIP	BABIP	LOB%	LD%	GB%
2010 (Rk)	11	48.1	54	14	38	2.6	7.1	5	5.03	4.15	.322	62%	NO DATA

For a brief taste of Juan Urbina's 2010 season, check out these earned-run totals from his final nine starts, not including his last appearance which was purposely limited: 1, 7, 1, 5, 1, 4, 0, 5, 2. It was a roller coaster debut for Urbina, who took the kind of lumps expected of any 17-year-old in pro ball.

The good news is that Urbina—son of former big leaguer Ugeth Urbina—also flashed the potential that has scouts excited about his future. The lanky lefty touched 90–91 mph with his heater and showed signs of a strong breaking ball to go along with a well-developed changeup. Physically, he's still filling out his long, 6-foot-2-inch frame. Scouts and organizational folks alike are unanimously impressed by his advanced feel for pitching. And don't let the ERA fool you: For a kid who was the same age as a junior in high school, this was a promising season.

It should be fun to watch the trio of young lefties in Urbina, Steven Matz, and Zach Dotson over the next few years. Urbina likely has the highest ceiling of the three, with many projecting him as a special lefty. But the operative word here is "project," as Urbina is a long, long way from Queens and much could still go wrong.

Estimated Arrival In New York: 2014

12. DARRELL CECILIANI

BAT/THROW: L/L				CENTER FIELDER								BORN: 06/22/90		
	G	PA	R	HR	RBI	BB%	K%	AVG	OBP	SLG	BABIP	wOBA	SB	SB%
2009 (Rk)	42	176	29	2	13	7%	20%	.234	.313	.310	.280	.310	14	88%
2010 (A-)	68	303	56	2	35	8%	21%	.351	.410	.531	.430	.417	21	60%

After a somewhat inauspicious pro debut in 2009 with Kingsport, Darrell Ceciliani established himself as one of the top outfield prospects in the Mets' farm system this past season. The 2009 fourth-rounder set Brooklyn records for batting average, hits, and triples on his way to a New York-Penn League batting title and an organizational Sterling Award as the top position player in Low-A. He sported a .410 OBP, was third in the league in total bases and extra-base hits, and played excellent defense all year. He topped it all off by batting .474 during the postseason. Perhaps even more impressive was that he accomplished all this as the youngest player on the team.

He isn't without flaws, though. His 18.5% strikeout rate needs improvement, he would help his stock a bit by walking more, and a 60%

stolen base rate—14 times caught stealing in 35 attempts—isn't good for someone with his speed. Defensively, while Ceciliani has the glove to project as a center fielder, he does have a below-average arm.

Ultimately, developing his gap-to-gap power into home run pop will probably determine whether he improves his prospect status. Either way, Ceciliani showed the ability and tools this past season to solidify himself as a top prospect. There's a bit of an outfield logjam in the Mets' lower levels, but a 2011 jump to High-A St. Lucie for Ceciliani would certainly be justified. The frequent Jacoby Ellsbury comparisons may seem too easy since they're both left-handed center fielders from Northwest Oregon, but that's an accurate ceiling for Ceciliani at this point.

Estimated Arrival In New York: 2013

13. JEURYS FAMILIA

BAT/THROW: R/R					STARTING PITCHER						BORN: 10/10/89		
	G	IP	H	BB	K	BB/9	K/9	HR	ERA	FIP	BABIP	LOB%	LD%	GB%
2008 (Rk)	11	51.2	46	13	38	2.3	6.6	2	2.79	3.16	.275	71%	NO DATA	
2009 (A)	24	134.0	109	46	109	3.1	7.3	3	2.69	3.16	.273	73%	13%	58%
2010 (A+)	24	121.0	117	74	137	5.5	10.2	7	5.58	3.89	.341	61%	15%	47%

After a seemingly disappointing season in 2010, a reasonable argument can be made that Jeurys Familia shouldn't appear so high on this list. There was a bit not to like about his 2010 campaign, especially the out-of-control walk rate—he walked nearly twice as many batters this year as he did last year while pitching 13 fewer innings. He also allowed seven homers in 2010, two more than the previous two seasons combined. There is an explanation for all the walks, and perhaps even the homers: According to Familia himself, he was encouraged by coaches to throw more changeups this season, walks be damned.

Even if you don't buy that explanation, there are still some good reasons to be optimistic about Familia's future. For starters, his strikeout rate surged in 2010—he whiffed more than a batter an inning, a considerable improvement over 2009. He also improved his ground ball rate, which, along with the increased strike outs, helped drive down his FIP to 3.89, a number far more palatable than his 5.58 ERA. That large discrepancy was driven by a handful of simple factors. He was surrounded by terrible infield defense featuring not-really-a-shortstop Wilmer Flores, an out-of-position second baseman in Michael Fisher, and Richard Lucas with 21 errors at third. That defense, along with some old-fashioned bad luck, led to an unsustainably high BABIP of .350, compared to a career mark around .290. Finally, he had an uncharacteristically high home run rate. If you figure all of those factors will return to more expected levels next season, coupled with reports that Familia's velocity climbed up to 96–97 mph to go along with increased diving action as the year progressed, you've got yourself a pretty good bet for a breakout season—just a year later than we were all expecting. Familia's long-term role will depend entirely on the development of his secondary stuff—some figure he will eventually land at the back end of the bullpen—but with an electric arm like his, the Mets will give him every opportunity to stick as a starter.

Estimated Arrival In New York: 2013

14. CORY VAUGHN

BAT/THROW: R/R				RIGHT FIELDER						BORN: 05/01/89			
	G	PA	R	HR	RBI	BB%	K%	AVG	OBP	SLG	BABIP	wOBA	SB	SB%
2010 (A-)	72	313	45	14	56	11%	24%	.307	.396	.557	.347	.429	12	71%

Cory Vaughn was nothing short of spectacular in his pro debut this past year, showing real potential as a middle-of-the-order run producer. After being drafted in the fourth round out of San Diego State, Vaughn signed quickly and got right to hitting as the Cyclones' cleanup man. Like Ceciliani, Vaughn's name was all over the New York-Penn League's offensive leader boards. He led the league in slugging and OPS while finishing in the top three in homers, extra-base hits, doubles, and RBI. He also showcased his all-around athletic ability, stealing twelve bases and covering center field in a pinch. But what really surprised those who had seen him in college was his improved plate discipline. Vaughn attributed the striking improvement at the dish to regular playing time, something he didn't always receive while playing for Tony Gwynn at San Diego State.

It's not all good news for Vaughn, though. His strikeout rate and walk rate significantly worsened after the All-Star break—just 13 walks and 31 strikeouts over his final 30 games, compared to 21 and 29 in 38 games before that—further bolstering critics' claims that he was a toolsy-yet-flawed college player beating up on inferior competition. A promotion to High-A next spring should serve as a litmus test for Vaughn.

Estimated Arrival In New York: Late 2012

15. SEAN RATLIFF

BAT/THROW: L/L				OUTFIELDER								BORN: 02/24/87	
	G	PA	R	HR	RBI	BB%	K%	AVG	OBP	SLG	BABIP	wOBA	SB	SB%
2008 (A-)	59	225	32	7	22	8%	33%	.229	.300	.388	.305	.312	1	25%
2009 (A)	122	509	64	15	68	6%	28%	.265	.312	.451	.332	.343	11	65%
2010 (AA)	73	311	48	16	50	7%	26%	.317	.371	.562	.372	.404	1	33%

Sean Ratliff is a somewhat divisive Mets prospect because his 2010 season was one of extremes. The 2007 fourth-rounder performed like a star, getting off to a quick start in St. Lucie and, upon promotion to Binghamton, taking the Eastern League by storm as possibly its best offensive player from that point on. Just 12 more games under his belt would have ranked Ratliff second in the Eastern League in OPS, and as a center fielder no less. Ratliff also jumped from a career average against lefties in the low .200s to a .333 mark against them in 2010.

In contrast to all those positives is Ratliff's strikeout total. The kid swings and misses. A lot. Pair that with his low walk rate, and many question whether or not his on-base skills and big swing will translate to the majors. It's also pretty clear at this point that Ratliff's future is in a corner outfield position, not as a center fielder.

Ratliff is reminiscent of Detroit's Brennan Boesch, another tall, skinny lefty with prodigious power and a high strikeout rate who was taken in the early rounds out of the Pac-10. Like Boesch, Ratliff isn't likely to hit much above .250, but he could produce double-digit home run power from day one while playing plus defense as a corner outfielder. For that reason, Ratliff is probably undervalued in Mets prospect circles and could be a solid contributor to the club by the end of 2011, though a more likely arrival is probably a little later.

Estimated Arrival In New York: 2012

16. ERIK GOEDDEL

BAT/THROW: R/R		RELIEF PITCHER											BORN: 12/20/88
	G	IP	H	BB	K	BB/9	K/9	HR	ERA	FIP	BABIP	LOB%	LD%	GB%
2010 (Rk)	1	1.0	1	0	1	0.0	9.0	0	0.00	1.20	.333	100%	NO DATA

Yes, Erik Goeddel pitched just a single inning in 2010, but he's worth mentioning here because he's the most intriguing arm drafted by the Mets in 2010. The UCLA product was a shocking 24th-round signing for the Mets, who uncharacteristically paid way over slot for someone with first-round talent who had dropped due to signability concerns. While Matt Harvey probably trumps Goeddel on pure stuff, Goeddel features his own impressive arsenal, in particular a low-90s fastball that touches 95. Where Goeddel gains an edge over Harvey is in command—it's not nearly the question mark for Goeddel that it is for Harvey. Add in a sharp slider and a developing changeup with good fade, and you're looking at an appealing pitching prospect.

Arm injuries plagued him in high school and early in college—resulting in Tommy John surgery—but he now seems to be hitting his stride, which means there might be even more to come from his slender frame. Scouts continue to question whether his arm can hold up as a starter—in addition to the past elbow surgery, he was shut down due to shoulder soreness this summer—but even in late relief, Goeddel could become a steal for the Mets. How quickly he moves will depend a lot on his long-term role as well as if he can avoid becoming the next Brant Rustich, the Mets' last highly-touted pitcher from UCLA with a big arm and an even bigger injury history.

Estimated Arrival In New York: 2013

17. DILLON GEE

BAT/THROW: R/R		STARTING PITCHER											BORN: 04/28/86
	G	IP	H	BB	K	BB/9	K/9	HR	ERA	FIP	BABIP	LOB%	LD%	GB%
2008 (A+)	21	127.1	117	19	94	1.3	6.6	6	3.25	3.00	.291	70%	13%	39%
2009 (AAA)	9	48.1	47	16	42	3.0	7.8	5	4.10	4.11	.298	75%	20%	40%
2010 (AAA)	28	161.1	174	41	165	2.3	9.2	23	4.96	4.01	.332	67%	18%	44%

It was a funny year for Dillon Gee, who probably had his worst statistical season as a professional but emerged as a solid, if unspectacular, back-of-the-rotation option for the Mets. Gee's 2010 season was all the more impressive when you consider he came back from a labrum injury suffered early in 2009 that many thought would require invasive surgery. Eventually, Gee's efforts would earn him Buffalo's Comeback Player of the Year honor as well as the Mets' Sterling Award as the top Triple-A pitcher.

In one respect, Gee was dominant in 2010, setting the Bisons' all-time strikeout record. Using pinpoint control of a five-pitch arsenal—including a low-90s heater and a 12-to-6 curve—he led both Triple-A leagues in punch-outs. He struck out seven or more batters in 10 of his starts, all while posting a walk rate around 2.0 per nine innings. Unfortunately, Gee's kryptonite was once again the long ball, as he ranked among the International League leaders with 23 bombs allowed. Some look at this figure as unsustainable bad luck, others see a tendency toward giving up hard contact. In either case, Gee is coming to the right home ballpark in order to cut down on the home runs. And though he likely pitched over his head during his impressive five-start debut last September—his 2.18 ERA is stunning—if he can limit the big flies he figures to be a solid and inexpensive Brian Bannister-type fifth-starter. At the least, he should be good long-relief option.

Estimated Arrival In New York: Mid-2011

18. RUBEN TEJADA

Bat/Throw: R/R						MIDDLE INFIELDER						Born: 10/27/89		
	G	PA	R	HR	RBI	BB%	K%	AVG	OBP	SLG	BABIP	wOBA	SB	SB%
2008 (High A)	131	555	55	2	37	7%	16%	.229	.293	.296	.265	.277	8	62%
2009 (AA)	134	553	59	5	46	7%	12%	.289	.351	.381	.319	.346	19	86%
2010 (AAA)	65	244	25	1	16	6%	17%	.280	.329	.344	.328	.295	1	25%

Like Mejia, Ruben Tejada was in over his head in 2010, thrust into a major league role well before he was ready. In fact, Tejada spent most of the season as the second-youngest player in the National League, and it showed as he struggled to keep his batting average above the Mendoza Line. In July and August, Tejada twice threatened to bat below .100 for the month. Even worse, the speed of the game, coupled with a move to second base from his natural shortstop position, had the usually sure-handed infielder looking shaky on defense, too.

As poster boy for the Minaya regime's misguided rushing of Latin prospects, 2010 was the icing on the cake for Tejada, who hadn't played at an age-appropriate level since his time in the Gulf Coast League at age 17 back in 2007. The good news is that the Mets' new brain trust has indicated that Tejada will begin 2011 in Triple-A Buffalo for seasoning, and his timetable will slow down considerably. Just 21, Tejada has plenty of time to develop the solid contact skills and plate discipline he showed throughout the minors, as well as the great defense he displayed at shortstop and second base. All in all, 2011 should be a chance for Tejada to catch his breath and refocus on building his foundation as a solid middle infielder. Long term, his lack of pop and average speed probably limit his role as an everyday player, but his glove work, versatility, and contact bat could make him a useful defense-oriented middle infielder in the mold of Asdrubal Cabrera.

Estimated Arrival In New York: 2012

19. BRAD HOLT

BAT/THROW: R/R				STARTING PITCHER						BORN: 10/13/86			
	G	IP	H	BB	K	BB/9	K/9	HR	ERA	FIP	BABIP	LOB%	LD%	GB%
2008 (A-)	14	72.1	43	33	96	4.1	11.9	3	1.87	2.62	.258	82%	NO DATA	
2009 (AA)	11	58.0	58	23	45	3.6	7.0	9	6.21	5.01	.293	59%	13%	36%
2010 (A+)	14	65.0	68	56	62	7.8	8.6	4	7.48	5.32	.344	61%	13%	33%

In short, Brad Holt was a disaster in 2010, and there were warning signs during the second half of 2009 that many overlooked. Now the Mets have a cloud of uncertainty where their top pitching prospect used to be, and Holt's future is up in the air. Holt's problem in 2010 was an extreme lack of command, the rudiments of which could be seen throughout 2009. In fact, his stint with St. Lucie in 2009 was the only time he posted a walk rate below 3.0 at any level, including college. It's beginning to look as if the good Holt we saw in 2009 was the exception, while the bad Holt we saw in 2010 was a return to form.

If there's a bright side for Holt it's that, despite his regularly unspectacular walk rates, his control was never quite so bad as it was in 2010. So is this just a bump in the road or the beginning of the end? It's likely that Holt can no longer be projected as a top-of-the-rotation starter, but it's probably too soon to relegate him to middle-relief fodder just yet. Scouts maintain that his stuff is still there. The dominant fastball is still touching the mid-90s with the same downward tilt, and his secondary stuff is still improving. Even if you don't buy into his breaking stuff, when he's able to spot the fastball he's capable of missing bats, a quality he has exhibited at every level. In that regard, it's not out of the question that he could grow into a mid-rotation starter, but it's more likely that he'll be a late-inning reliever. Of course, he'll have to get his command under control first if he expects to have any kind of future in baseball.

Estimated Arrival In New York: Late 2012

20. MARK COHOON

BAT/THROW: L/L					STARTING PITCHER						BORN: 09/15/87		
	G	IP	H	BB	K	BB/9	K/9	HR	ERA	FIP	BABIP	LOB%	LD%	GB%
2008 (A)	7	33.0	29	18	21	4.9	5.7	2	3.82	4.53	.267	69%	18%	38%
2009 (A-)	14	92.0	69	20	70	2.0	6.8	4	2.15	3.03	.252	77%	NO DATA	
2010 (AA)	13	71.0	74	15	56	1.9	7.1	5	4.18	3.47	.318	62%	10%	41%

Last year was a good year for 22-year-old Mark Cohoon, who really solidified his status as a legitimate pitching prospect. The soft-tossing lefty destroyed the South Atlantic League in the first half, finishing his stay there with a record three straight complete-game shutouts. The Mets responded to this dominance by challenging Cohoon with a promotion to Binghamton, skipping over High-A St. Lucie. Cohoon scuffled at first—he had a 7.09 ERA in July—but seemed to right the ship and pitched to a 1.65 ERA the rest of the way.

Cohoon is your classic crafty lefty. Not blessed with much fastball velocity—he rarely tops 88 mph—he is a master at mixing pitches and hitting his spots on both sides of the plate. He features a strong curveball-changeup mix and he's adept at cutting the fastball for more run. He's a cerebral pitcher, one who gets raves for his mound presence, and his pickoff move is an effective weapon. However, because of his low velocity, Cohoon must maximize every tool to succeed as a major league starter. At this point, it's difficult to peg him as more than a future fifth starter, but on the bright side, he's already close to that ceiling.

Estimated Arrival In New York: 2011

21. STEVEN MATZ, LHP

Steven Matz was the Mets' first selection in the 2009 draft, 72nd overall out of nearby Ward-Melville High School. As an athletic, 6-foot-2-inch lefty with a good build and the ability to hit 94 mph before age 20, Matz immediately became one of the better arms in the system. Matz signed late and didn't appear in any games in 2009, then during extended spring training in 2010 he felt a twinge in his elbow which required season-ending Tommy John surgery. Long-term, Matz is still a projectable lefty with lots of talent and a ceiling as a mid-rotation starter. Chances are, however, he won't get his pro career underway until the spring of 2012, and even then he'll be behind in his development. You might see him catch on with a short-season team late this summer if rehab goes well.

Estimated Arrival In New York: 2015

22. ZACH DOTSON, LHP

Despite just four career pro appearances with the Gulf Coast League Mets, Zach Dotson still ranks pretty high on this list heading into 2011. His 2010 season was cut short by a PED suspension, but the performance enhancer he was caught taking is usually used as a decongestant or as a weight-loss supplement. Like Steven Matz and Juan Urbina, Dotson is a lefty with the kind of size, stuff, and youth which project as potentially successful. Former Mets scouting director Rudy Terrasas said, "His fastball has as good a life as I've ever seen... and I've been scouting for 27 years." Urbina may be the class of the group, thanks to his age, but Dotson belongs right there alongside Matz when discussing talented young lefties in this system.

Estimated Arrival In New York: 2014

23. ALBERT CORDERO, C

A relative unknown coming into the season, Albert Cordero put himself on the prospect map with a strong batting line as a teenage catching prospect. He'd always shown a solid bat in his prior seasons with the Mets' Venezuelan Summer League team, and according to 2010 Kingsport Manager Mike Difelice, he shows enough potential defensively to start behind the plate at the highest levels. Currently he's a work in progress as a catcher, but he did exhibit a strong arm and soft hands in 2010. Teenage catchers with his kind of batting power are always fun to watch.

Estimated Arrival In New York: 2014

24. ROBERT CARSON, LHP

Robert Carson received one of the more surprising promotions this season, as the Mets pushed the 21-year-old up to Binghamton after middling results in his first season at High-A St. Lucie. Unfortunately, the big lefty made the organization look bad, getting rocked for the better part of three months. Either way, he's still an intriguing arm thanks to his size and velocity—he works around 93–94 mph—and his nearly overhand delivery creates excellent downward tilt, resulting in lots of ground balls. Long term, Carson probably lacks sufficiently consistent secondary offerings to stay in the rotation, but he could well become an excellent late-relief option if he shores up his fastball command.

Estimated Arrival In New York: Late 2012

25. JEFRY MARTE, 3B

Jefry Marte received mixed reviews in 2010. His plate discipline improved by leaps and bounds as he doubled his walk rate and brought down his strikeout rate, all while flashing more signs of dynamic power. On the down side, even with his defensive improvements Marte still made 23 errors in 82 games. He also suffered from hamstring issues that ended his season in late July. What's more, while he continues to demonstrate excellent bat speed and good pull-side power, for a prospect who was touted for his pop, you'd like to see him put up something better than a .136 ISO. In some ways, Aderlin Rodriguez may be the prospect many thought Marte could become when he put up a .532 SLG as a sixteen-year-old in 2008.

Estimated Arrival In New York: 2014

26. Wilfredo Tovar, SS

With nearly all of the attention on the other teenage shortstops from Venezuela, Wifredo Tovar quietly starred for three separate Mets affiliates in 2010 and put his name firmly on the team's prospect landscape. Tovar's profile is like the yin to Wilmer Flores's yang. He has enough glove to stay at short long term thanks to excellent hands, instincts, and speed, but his bat may not play at the highest levels. Despite a total lack of power, Tovar showed solid contact ability for someone matched up against far older competition. He'll never be a slugger, but his incredibly advanced feel for the shortstop position may have us looking at Rey Ordonez, part two.

Estimated Arrival In New York: 2013

27. Matt den Dekker, CF

Following a superb senior season with the Florida Gators, Matt den Dekker rewarded the organization for selecting him in the fifth round this past June by flying out of the gates with the Sand Gnats. He batted .413 in August with an impressive 11 doubles and immediately established himself as one of the best defensive center fielders in the system. Though he cooled off a bit in September, this is someone with plus speed playing stellar defense at a premium position, all while posting a .407 wOBA in his pro debut. Whether he can turn those doubles into homers at the higher levels will likely determine whether or not he'll ever make it to the majors. Either way, he demonstrated enough in his brief debut to solidify his floor as an Endy Chavez-type fourth outfielder.

Estimated Arrival In New York: 2013

28. Jordany Valdespin, 2B

A favorite of the Minaya administration, Jordany Valdespin is one of the more unusual prospects in the Mets' system. He's athletic, fast, and has surprising strength for someone his size (5 feet 10 inches, 150 pounds). He elicits praise from scouts for his "major league actions" in the middle infield and his excellent bat speed at the plate. The problem is that in other areas the 23-year-old looks downright awful. In the field, out-of-control play leads to unnecessary errors. At the dish, the lefty-swinger has little plate discipline and difficulty with quality breaking pitches. To top it all off, he has shown a lack of maturity which has led to a number of suspensions. Valdespin looks to have the raw tools to play at the higher levels—a .355 average in the Arizona Fall League—but his flaws require attention before he can be considered a potential everyday big leaguer.

Estimated Arrival In New York: 2012

29. Akeel Morris, RHP

The knock on Akeel Morris at draft time was the level of competition he'd faced in his native St. Thomas. He answered that question and more once he hit the field with the Gulf Coast League Mets. The 2010 tenth-rounder immediately showed why many consider his ceiling to be one of the highest of any pitcher from the Mets' 2010 draft class. The 17-year-old righty flashed electric stuff, regularly working in the low-90s, and has the makings of a hard-breaking curve. Expect him to add a couple more ticks to that fastball as he fills out his wiry 6-foot-1-inch frame. Like fellow teenager Juan Urbina, Morris has a long way to go, but he's already highly regarded within the organization and could see his stock skyrocket in 2011 if he has another strong season.

Estimated Arrival In New York: 2014

30. Armando Rodriguez, RHP

Armando Rodriguez was superb for the Sand Gnats in 2010 as their most consistent starter from day one until their last game in the South Atlantic League championship. Overshadowed in the first half by a trio of more dominant Savannah starters, Rodriguez overpowered SAL hitters all season with his low-90s heater and developing slurve. He also kept the ball in the park, allowing just five homers all season, only one of which came in 73 innings after the All-Star break. You may remember that Omar Minaya famously called him "another Mejia," but that's not a fair comparison. Mejia had just turned 20 and spent a bit of 2010 time in the majors, while Rodriguez will turn 23 before he even thinks of Double-A. With good, not great, velocity, middling breaking stuff, and strong fastball command, it's far more likely he'll contribute in the majors as a power reliever rather than as a starter.

Estimated Arrival In New York: Late 2012

Players Who Just Missed The Top 30 Prospects List

DOMINGO TAPIA, RHP

Mets officials were impressed with the teenager's pro debut, particularly his hard-sinking, two-seam fastball which led to an excellent ground ball rate. He also showed superb control and a developing changeup. As a well-built, 6-foot-4-inch 18-year-old, Domingo Tapia figures to add velocity to a fastball that already touches 94 mph. He has the kind of potential to shoot up this list next year

BRIAN HARRISON, 3B

After slipping in the draft due to durability concerns while in college, the Mets nabbed Brian Harrison in the 13th round this past June. During his only collegiate campaign with 200 or more at-bats, the toolsy Harrison posted 12 bombs and a strikeout-to-walk ratio of nearly 1:1. He brought those tendencies to professional ball, hitting seven homers with a .900 OPS in just 35 games with Brooklyn. Injuries popped up again, however, and his season ended early due to a shoulder strain. Harrison has the physical tools and offensive ability to make some noise, but he needs to stay healthy.

MANUEL ALVAREZ, RHP

The 25-year-old Alvarez burst onto the prospect scene with a stellar 2010 season. He ran through St. Lucie without allowing a run and went well into the summer months with Binghamton before he allowed his first homer. By the time he reached Buffalo, Alvarez had blown past his previous high in innings and, despite running out of gas, still featured the pinpoint command that made him so successful. The big-bodied righty spots his low-90s fastball and surprisingly good curve extremely well to both sides of the plate. A Mets reliever with excellent command is indeed an unusual creature, which is probably why Alvarez will likely get a shot at some point in 2011.

KAI GRONAUER, C

2010 was a big year for the German national, as he put himself on the map enough to earn a winter assignment to the star-studded Arizona Fall League. Aside from a solid, if unspectacular, offensive profile, scouts have lauded Kai Gronauer's ability behind the plate. Demonstrating good agility and footwork, a strong, accurate arm, and advanced game-calling, it's easy to picture Gronauer as a successful role player in the majors. At 23, Gronauer isn't exactly young, but 2010 was only his third pro season and, like most European players, he is significantly less experienced than most North and South American ballplayers.

PART 5: BEYOND THE CHALK

CHAPTER FIFTEEN

THE UNSUNG SUPERSTAR

JOE POSNANSKI

I've been asked by the good folks at Amazin' Avenue to make the case for one of my favorite players, Carlos Beltran. This would normally be an easy and fun thing to do. Trouble is, I am looking over his last couple of years with the Mets and realizing that it is difficult, if not impossible, to make much of a case for someone who has only played 145 games over two seasons. Injuries, especially nagging injuries that never quite seem to heal or that bleed into each other, tend to end all arguments. I cannot tell you that Beltran will be his old self in 2011. I don't know how his knee and body will hold up. I don't know if he has what's left to play center field. He's going to be 34 in April, and he has not played a full season since back in 2008, and I don't know exactly what the Mets are trying to accomplish in 2011 either. So, this whole thing is kind of muddled. It's hard to write about a player who isn't there.

I will tell you that even before the recent injury issues, Carlos Beltran was well on his way to being the strangest combination of unappreciated and hyped player of his era... maybe any era. He came by it honestly. From even before the day he arrived in Kansas City in 1998, people seemed to think he was squandering something. He was selected by the Royals in the second round in the 1995 draft, which seems plenty high, but not for a player of his talent. He was a switch-hitting center fielder with great speed and power potential and he had that rare talent of making everything look too easy. Those are the sorts of players who go No. 1 overall in the draft—think Josh Hamilton. When DiMaggio flashed that talent, people called it grace. For some reason, when Beltran flashed that talent, people called him a malingerer. Scouts doubted him for fuzzy reasons that had more to do with the way he looked than the way he played. Those doubts have followed him all his career.

"It's strange, he's got all the talent in the world, but he doesn't seem to like baseball," one scout told me. This was four years after the Royals had taken him in that second round, and in the middle of what turned out to be his Rookie of the Year season. Beltran was not a great player as a rookie. He led the American League in outs, for instance. But he did great things. That's how it seemed to go with the guy. The Royals, who were in one of their sporadic "let the kids play" phases, had called up the 22-year-old Beltran and told him, "Your only job is to catch the ball. Don't even worry about hitting. We don't care if you hit .200. Your job is to play defense."

Unshackled by any expectations, Beltran became the first rookie since Fred Lynn in his MVP season of 1975 to score and drive in more than 100 runs. Beltran hit 22 homers, he stole 27 bases, he played superior defense in center field. It really was quite a show. A lot of it was the context of the time—despite all that, he only posted a 99 OPS+ because he didn't walk and because offense was out of control in 1999 and because Kauffman Stadium was a big-time hitter's ballpark in those years before they moved the fences back. Beltran was not a great player yet. But he was already mesmerizing to watch.

Only people in Kansas City didn't always see it like that. Beltran had a strange second season which included—and this might have foreshadowed his strange knee-surgery dispute with the Mets—a bizarre fight with the Royals where he refused to report to the team's training facility to rehab an injury. The Royals never really understood what principle Beltran was standing for, and they fined him, and then the fine was challenged by Scott Boras, and it was all very odd. But from 2001–2003, Beltran scored and drove in 100 runs each season, and he made spectacular plays in center field, and he hit with good power, and he stole bases at a percentage unmatched in baseball history. Those three seasons, he stole 107 bases and was caught 12 times, a 90% clip.

Over his career—and I like to go to his Baseball-Reference page every so often just to see this—you can see that Carlos Beltran has stolen 289 bases in his career. He has been caught 39 times. It's so amazing it looks like a misprint.

But even Beltran's almost supernatural stolen base efficiency was kind of held against him. One line of thought was he didn't try to steal enough, that he only tried to steal a base when he knew he would make it. Nobody could really explain why this was a bad strategy, but it was part of a much larger vision of Beltran not pushing the limits of his talent. He hit 24–29 homers per year when people were sure he could hit 30. He stole 30–40 bases when people were sure he could steal 50. He was so smooth and fluid running down fly balls in the alleys that people were sure he wasn't going all out. There are people who watched Beltran play every day in those early years who, even now, will swear up and down that he was not a great defensive player because he got bad jumps and took bad angles for the ball. I also watched him just about every day, either live or on television, and thought he was remarkable as he chased down balls that seemed unreachable. But that's just how it goes with the guy—Beltran is like one of those Magic Eye puzzles. People see different things. Some don't see anything at all.

In 2004, the Royals traded him to Houston in what turned out to be one of several regrettable star-for-prospects deals made by Kansas City in the decade. It turned out pretty well for Houston. In 90 regular-season games and 12 playoff games, Beltran seemed almost to say, "OK, you want to see how good I can be? Here you go." In those 90 regular-season games, he hit 23 home runs. He stole 28 bases without being caught. He scored 70 runs. In the postseason, he put on a show unlike anything that anyone had ever seen—in 12 games he hit .435 with eight homers, six steals (without being caught), scored 21 runs, and drove in 14 more.

I will always remember someone coming up to me during those play-off games and saying: "But you didn't know he was *this* good." And I said: "Yeah, actually, I did."

But you know all this already. After that was when the Mets gave him the gargantuan deal and put him in center field and watched him put up his miserable 2005 season. The one thing that baseball person after baseball person told me after Beltran signed with the Mets was that he was not suited for New York. Beltran is a quiet guy, doesn't like the spotlight, doesn't like heavy responsibility, isn't a leader. That sort of stuff. The general feeling was that Beltran should have signed with Houston, a good market without tabloids where fans had fallen hard for him in just half a season. If you are a ballplayer looking for a nice, quiet place where you can feel comfortable and make some money, you don't hire Scott Boras to be your agent. Boras is the guy you hire when you want to break the bank. Beltran broke the bank with the Mets. Then he had a bad season in 2005 and the doubters nodded. He couldn't handle New York.

In 2006, then, he had what I honestly believe is the best season in New York Mets history. Oh, there are plenty of great seasons to argue about—Cleon Jones's 1969, Darryl Strawberry's 1987, John Olerud's surprising and massive 1998, a couple of David Wright's best seasons, and so on. But Beltran in 2006 had the year that would not look out of place on Willie Mays's Baseball-Reference page. He hit 41 homers, had 80 extra-base hits, scored 127 runs, drove in 116 runs, walked 95 times, stole 18 of 21 bases, and played brilliant defense in center field. He finished fourth in the MVP voting in large part, I think, because MVP voters do not take positional value into play as much as they should—he finished behind three first baseman (of which, in my opinion, only Albert Pujols had the better year). Beltran was spectacularly good, a point missed for three reasons, I think:

1. As mentioned, I don't think people take position into account as much as they should. For a center fielder—and a brilliant defensive center fielder at that—to put up those numbers is rare.

2. Beltran has a few things working against him. He's not a high average hitter—he only hit .275 in 2006—and people can't help but consider batting average no matter how many times it has been shown to be a flawed statistic. He put up his numbers at old Shea Stadium, a lousy hitter's park, especially for Beltran (he hit only .224 with 15 homers at Shea; he hit .317/.406/.683 with 26 homers away from the old Queens rock pile).

3. He watched strike three go by to end the National League Championship Series.

The last of these particularly irked Mets fans, I think, because it so neatly fit into the enduring image of Beltran as a guy who doesn't try as hard as he might. Beltran went on to have seasons that were similar but not quite as good in 2007 and 2008. Basically, his home run totals dropped, and he walked a few times less. Other than that, it was about the same. In 2008, for the sixth time in his career, he scored and drove in 100 runs and stole at least 20 bases. I admit, it's not the most compelling statistical combination in the world, but only Barry Bonds (with seven such seasons) has done it more. In 2009, he seemed on his way to his best season—he was hitting .336/.425/.527—when he got hurt. And he has been hurt on and off ever since.

Which brings us back to the beginning. What does Carlos Beltran have left? I don't know. Nobody knows. But it's a good bet that people will underestimate him. The thing that has bothered me most about the Beltran criticism through the years is that he has found himself being measured against an opponent he cannot defeat: his better self. Beltran throughout his career has had the gift—and the curse—of gracefulness. It never looks hard for him. It is hard for him, because playing baseball that well is hard for anyone. It has wrecked his knees, his quads, sparked dizzy spells, and so on. But it doesn't look hard, which means it looks easy, which means he should be even better. That seems to be the enduring Carlos Beltran headline: "He should have been even better."

It seems that people too easily forget how good he has actually been.

CHAPTER SIXTEEN

LEVITTOWN

SAM PAGE

People always ask how I became a Mets fan growing up in Tennessee. I've developed a few quick stock answers, the best being: "My dad is from New York." That statement is technically true. The implication, in the context of the question, is not. In the mind of the inquiring party, it probably conjures the image of a proud dad eagerly bringing his son to his first Mets game. Really, I took my dad to my first Mets game. My father likely would have been content for me to grow up never hearing the name Tom Seaver. I'm not being totally disingenuous, though. My dad being from New York does have something to do with how I became a Mets fan.

During the summer of 1998, like every summer, we visited my grandparents in Levittown, New York. Unadorned and barn-house red, my grandparents' house occupied the same 750 square feet it always had. The hippies and beatniks that had once bemoaned houses like it would probably now praise the little box of ticky-tacky. By 1998, the neighborhood immortalized in American history text books as the ultimate symbol of post-war conformity now typified a new suburban aesthetic—competitive excess. Every year the houses of Levittown get bigger and pastel-pinker, until the white picket fences that used to keep dogs in lawns are the trimmings of aluminum siding. In 2050, when the neighborhood merges into a single shopping mall, eminent domain will allow my grandparents' house be torn down and replaced with an inflatable Santa.

In 1998, though, the time warp was fully intact. The oven, dishwasher, and stove were bright plastic turquoise with faded white numbers on analog controls. The refrigerator bore magnets predicting success for the Islanders in the '87–'88 and '88–'89 seasons. Predating the invention of the ice dispenser, it hummed with a cadence that had undoubtedly influenced the invention of the ambient music genre. The toaster may or may not have been there since the time of the moon landing. If archaeologists in some futuristic human civilization ever found this kitchen buried deep in the Earth, they might conclude the Cuban Missile Crisis hadn't been averted.

And though my grandparents occupied the last original-looking unit in town, they were technically its second residents. They had missed the wave of G.I.'s who had come home from World War II and moved their families east in the late forties and early fifties. Both of my grandparents belonged to an obscure demographic of Americans born during the absolute worst of the Great Depression. Just as my dad was a "baby boomer" born during a year of sharp birth-rate decline and I am a "digital native" born without a personal computer in the house, my grandparents had moved to Levittown after it had been settled, after the Korean War. They were of a generation in between, the generation of Ken Kesey: "I was too young to be a beatnik, and too old to be a hippie"—but the perfect age to be a Mets fan. My grandmother had played (and supposedly bested) Willie Mays in stickball on the streets of New York City. My grandfather had climbed fences to watch Pee Wee Reese's Dodgers. The Mets came just in time for them to pass New York's proud National League tradition on to their kids.

My dad was eight during the summer of '69, which meant the summer of Koosman and Jones, not the Summer of Love. While his older brother tried (unsuccessfully) to sneak off to Woodstock, the rest of his family watched the Amazin' Mets sneak past the Cubs into first place. In the summer of 1998, I was seven and knew baseball was played with a red-stitched white ball. And despite only visiting for a few weeks each year, I knew the pace of life in my grandparents' house. Every night, we ate dinner and afterward I would go upstairs to bed while the preceding branches of the family tree huddled around the television. I watched from the stairs one particular summer night as my grandmother took the throne, a green corduroy La-Z-Boy recliner, and my father and grandfather sat across from her on the couch. This seating arrangement was set and, along with the expressions of their faces, clearly indicated that the men watched at the pleasure of my grandmother. Before finishing the trip upstairs I glanced at the TV. There was a shape I recognized as a baseball diamond with some names written on it. One looked like "Pizza." I remember thinking, "I like pizza."

My room was one of two bedrooms in the house, the one my dad had once shared with his older brothers. The room was just big enough to fit its three pieces of furniture—a queen-sized bed, a dresser, and an art desk where my grandfather designed model boats. The walls were beige and the ceiling, mimicking the shape of the roof, shrunk the room the farther you got from the door. In addition to the furniture was a crucifix on the wall, a lamp, and a radio on the dresser. The radio, though also old-looking, broke with the décor of the house by about 50 years. It was made to look like those giant receivers people owned before TVs, arched on top with a large, tan speaker below the dials. Only seven, even I knew it was fake with a cassette deck in the back, holding some quit-smoking instructional pep talk.

Unable to sleep, I sat looking out the window. The night washed out the neighborhood. Only the glow of a single gas lamp two blocks away shone through the darkness. From that distance the lamp didn't really illuminate, it just vaguely marked the distance. It glowed amber—not the reassuring yellow of the sun or a light bulb, but not quite menacing red. It might as well have been another planet. I imagined this street-light as an impartial observer, a constant for 50 years as the neighbor-hood around it changed. A nuclear bomb could have hit that night—the one that buries my grandparents' kitchen to confuse future historians—and that lamp would probably survive, gazing disinterested and orange on the rubble. The thought of the streetlamp never changing consumed me. I imagined my dad as a kid, sitting on the same bed, looking out the same window, with just the same faint light looking back. I imagined him sitting next to my grandfather on the couch, 30 years ago, watching the TV after dinner. What could be worth watching at the same time in that same spot every single night for that long? I felt a tinge—false nostalgia for my life not yet lived, a creeping fear that the damn streetlight was going to outlive us all.

So I turned on the radio to break the silence and grounded myself in July 1998. I only knew one station in New York, the only numbers my grandmother would dial on every car and clock radio—660. The first voice to come out of the set sounded vintage in the way the radio tried to look. Hearing Howie Rose for the first time, I thought the sun would come up and Levittown would look like 1947 again.

The aesthetic of broadcasting gets overlooked in the age of "Fire Joe Morgan," with fans allying with a given announcer's ideology. Making a 6–1 Islanders blowout loss in front of 4,000 fans at the Colosseum sound like an episode of *The War of the Worlds*, however, is no simple feat. In that moment, Howie Rose was a much-needed reminder that some things never change but for the better; they are timeless. Rose's voice is timeless. It's a voice that could say, "It's hit deep to left center...

this one has a chance... home run! Mike Piazza! And the Mets lead, 3–1!" and make you forget that it was September 21, 2001, and believe the world would still be here on Saturday.

The second voice I heard didn't sound quite as trained I think there's at least a large, silent minority of Mets fans that really know what they're talking about, fans who feel the team's successes most earnestly because they love the team and its history and can wait. Not the nuts who call in to WFAN to argue with Mike Francesa every time the Mets drop a series. No, these fans carry the proper bemused sense of humor to root for their team, even at its very worst. Before I knew this type of fan, I knew Gary Cohen was one. The two biggest sports broadcasting clichés are "they bring the game to you" or "they make you feel like you're there." Gary Cohen certainly had no business bringing the game to me that night—unless the Mets wanted to pray before the rosary or draw some boat blueprints—and I had no conception of Shea Stadium in July with which to imagine myself there. Cohen merely spoke the subconscious inner monologue of the informed Mets fan sitting at Shea, with the din of the crowd behind him. His ability to articulate what Mets fans are seeing without losing any of the associated emotion is unparalleled. Gary Cohen can say, "Back goes Chavez... near the wall... leaping... and... he made the catch!" and I know it means as much to him as it does to me, even though I can only say "WOOOOO!"

I don't remember who scored the Mets' run that inning, or who had the RBI. For some reason I remember it as Ventura and Alfonzo, but that's probably wishful thinking. I do remember, though, hearing Gary Cohen's call and feeling his excitement, knowing that it was the excitement my grandmother and so many like her felt in that moment. I ran down the stairs.

"They did good. They scored!"

"Yea, they did," my grandmother chuckled, beaming. I took my seat on the couch.

CHAPTER SEVENTEEN

ROOKIE IN THE PRESS BOX

ERIC SIMON

Though he has spent just one season on the Mets' beat, Andy Mc-Cullough has quickly distinguished himself from his clubhouse colleagues by supplementing traditional sports reporting with more advanced statistical analysis, an exceedingly rare combination on the local sports scene. Andy sat down with me for a phone interview in January, during which we discussed all things baseball: the state of beat reporting in emerging media, the role Twitter plays in modern sports coverage, and his place in the Mets' press box pecking order.

❖   ❖   ❖

Eric Simon: Talk a bit about your background, specifically as it pertains to writing and baseball.

Andy McCullough: I grew up in Philadelphia, so I really wasn't a baseball fan because the Phillies were awful when I was seven or eight and starting to pay attention to sports. They were going through the post-'93 lull, and they were just so boring and bad every year that I never got into watching them, and so I was only really an Eagles fan, but that sort of faded in college at Syracuse when I decided I wanted to be a journalist. I was smart enough to get a degree in newspaper journalism, which is pretty much like U.S. mint at this point as far as value goes, but I started working at the school paper, *The Daily Orange*, when I was a sophomore and I did features and sports. There's no baseball team at Syracuse, so I covered men's lacrosse and football, and I was a sports columnist my senior year and managing editor of the newspaper, so that's really where the writing aspect came into play for me.

So how did you end up at *The Star-Ledger* covering baseball, considering you hadn't been interested in the sport for a dozen years or so?

I kind of failed my way upwards at the *Ledger* [laughs]. When I say that I wasn't interested in baseball, I wasn't so much a fan of the Phillies, but I had always been a fan of writing about the game, if that makes sense. Writing about the game interested me more than the actual game, because I had been so attuned to the idea in football that every game is so important, and baseball, when you're 15 or 16 and you don't really care about the team, it seems kind of staid and boring. But I had grown up reading Roger Angell, who wrote for so long in *The New Yorker*, and that was how I learned part of the history of the game, and I read *Moneyball* when it came out, and the idea of on-base percentage always stuck with me.

As far as the *Ledger* goes, I had interned at a couple of other papers, including one in suburban Philadelphia and at *The Columbus Dispatch* after my junior year, and when I graduated from Syracuse I had an internship at the *Ledger* with Matt Gelb, we were the two sports interns. He went off to work at the *Philadelphia Inquirer* at the end of the summer, and I got offered a job at the *Ledger*. I did college enterprise for about a year: I covered the Rutgers women's basketball team and I did features on schools in the area like Monmouth and Ryder, I covered wrestling and lacrosse. Then, when the Yankees were in the playoffs, I was with them in '09, and that was my first real experience with everyday baseball stuff, and that carried over a little bit into the next season.

When we started out in 2010, I was our third baseball writer, with Marc Carig, our Yankees beat writer, and Brian Costa, our Mets writer, so I was doing college enterprise stuff Monday through Thursday and whoever was home between the Yankees and Mets from Friday through Sunday. That went on for about six weeks before Brian got the opportunity to go cover the Yankees for *The Wall Street Journal*, and I talked my way into getting a chance to try out for the Mets job. It was kind of short notice, because the *Journal* was just starting up its baseball beat coverage and trying to hit the ground running, so we didn't have a lot of time to figure out who was going to cover the team those first couple weeks. So my boss told me to go cover the Mets, and that it would be something of a tryout while they continued to search for a full-time beat writer, and he'd be conducting interviews with candidates while I was gone. My interview for the position would be my work, I guess. They were happy with the stuff that I did, so I kind of lucked into the job.

I would never pretend that I was prepared to be less than a year out of college and covering a beat. It may be more a statement about where newspapers are right now, because of the manpower and the way the economy has hurt newspapers. Unfortunately, instead of having someone experienced, *The Star-Ledger* readers have to deal with me learning on the job [laughs]. I'm just trying to learn as much as I can every day to do it and that may be where the interest in advanced statistics comes from in that I'm not going to sit here and pretend at age 23, after stopping playing competitive baseball at age 12, that I understand a ton about the game from just looking at it, so I have to rely on some frame of reference, and if that's going to be Bill James and the guys on FanGraphs and the guys on Baseball Prospectus, I think that's probably a decent place to start as far as just trying to get information about the game.

What were your early experiences covering the beat? Specifically, getting to know the other writers as well as the Mets players.

I would say across the board everyone was unbelievably nice and helpful, and these guys have been doing it for a long time. Dave Lennon [of *Newsday*] and Steve Popper [of *The Bergen Record*] have been invaluable in their tips and being able to see what those guys do every day, how they train their bodies in order to get through the grind. Everyone was nice, and that was great. It helped that Tony DiComo, who covers the team for MLB.com, is only a couple years older than I, so he has become a friend. And Mike Sielski, who covered the team for *The Wall Street Journal*, he was a guy who I had grown up reading in suburban Philadelphia—he and I actually went to the same high school, though he graduated ten years earlier than I—but he quickly became a friend. There was never a problem fitting in with the writers. It's not like I showed up in Milwaukee on May 28 and we were all partying every night, but it was pretty easy to get along with people, and they knew who I was from filling in for about a year or so and spending some time in spring training.

With the players, that's the hard part, and not just with the players, because you literally have to introduce yourself to everyone. You have to introduce yourself to the players, the coaches, clubhouse people, front office people, everyone, and it's the middle of May and they don't know if you're a new face who's just going to be there for a day, they don't understand that you're one of the beat writers, that you're one of those nine or ten guys that they're going to see all the time. And that just takes time. You have to be there, you have to be asking questions, and so it was kind of like you go up and you just introduce yourself and try to strike up a conversation with 25 guys and 10 to 15 other folks and just try and talk to them, and you can't do it all at once. I don't think

I introduced myself to Ike Davis until I had been on the beat for three weeks, for whatever reason. I had stories to write, I had other guys to talk to, the manager was speaking. So that was kind of the hard part, starting from scratch with everyone, and no one else was starting from scratch. Everyone had a head start, and in the case of guys like Adam Rubin [of ESPN.com], Popper, and Lennon, they've been doing this for five or seven years. Adam especially. Adam has known these guys since they were minor leaguers, so they know who he is, and that's why he has good relationships with them.

To what extent is it difficult to write negative pieces about players who you know you're going to see the next day or the day after and who'll probably know that you've written those things?

I think you just have to be fair. You can't just write that someone is a bad baseball player. You have to explain—and this is where the use of statistics helps—you have to explain what it is that they're doing that might not be good. In Jeff Francoeur's case it might be his on-base percentage. If you were writing a story about, say, Jon Niese's month of September, you can just write about all of the runs he gave up. Players aren't stupid. They know when they're playing poorly. Mike Pelfrey knew how horrible his month of July was. It wasn't like he didn't know he had a 10.00 ERA. He knew he was pitching poorly. He was getting lit up every time he went out there, so it's pretty easy when you're writing something negative about a player on the field.

The one guy who was interesting to talk to about that was K-Rod, because there was a time around the midway point where he was starting to have these long innings and he was throwing a lot of pitches. He was someone you could talk to and get more answers than most players. So it's pretty easy to write something critical about a player, if only because they know what the issue is a lot of the time. And if they don't know what the issue is, the pitching coach does, or the hitting coach does, or their teammates have seen him do it before. It wasn't a secret what was wrong with Oliver Perez last year. He had no velocity and no control. It's not like if you wrote a story about how Ollie had no velocity and no control that he would come up and shake his fists in your face. The day before you were talking to him about it and about why it's a challenge and what he's doing to get through it. I think to be that high level an athlete you have to be pretty self-aware of your mechanics, of what you're doing, and how you're feeling, and I think these guys had a pretty good idea. I never had a problem with writing anything negative about someone and them having an issue.

So you're saying it shouldn't come as a surprise to them when they've been playing terribly.

Right, these guys know.

Describe a typical day on the Mets beat.

If it's a night game you try to wake up by like seven or eight. The Mets are very kind, and they collect all of the previous night's clips, and they'll send them in an e-mail, so you can read those and just make sure there isn't any news or anything that didn't go out on Twitter the night before. A lot of times I'll just have some interviews on my tape recorder that I never had a chance to transcribe, so I'll spend the morning transcribing and sending out e-mails, making phone calls to high school coaches, agents, other executives, just people I might need to talk to. Sometimes I'll only make one or two, and sometimes I'll be chained to the phone trying to get in touch with people.

The clubhouse opens around 3:30, so I try to be at the park by 2:00 or 2:30, just to get set up. If it's the first stop at a park, I make sure the Internet works and that my computer is going to be fine, that the sight lines are all right, just get situated. Sometimes I'll scribble down questions for guys I need to talk to, just make a mental checklist of things I need to get done. Then when the clubhouse opens, it's pretty much a free-for-all. You walk around and talk to the players, pull guys aside for a minute or two, just basically get your work done. The manager speaks to the press for 10 or 15 minutes, then it's back into the clubhouse. By 5:30 or 6:00, they're closing up, and you head upstairs [to the press box] and you write your early stuff. In my case, last year it was just getting stuff online, the notes and the pregame stuff, and then the game starts and you go from there.

The whole time during the game you're tweeting and things, picking up stuff for Twitter later, maybe cataloging stuff that I might want to come back to later. You know, guys I might want to talk to, questions I might want to ask. I keep MLB Gameday open so I can see the pitch type and the pitch break, that kind of stuff, just so I can have an idea of what's going on. Then by the fifth or sixth or seventh innings, you start writing your running stuff so you can have that ready to go after the final out, so you kind of spend the last three innings with your head down writing. Sometimes it's easy, and you can just make sure no one blows a save, and your story holds up. Then you file the story and head downstairs to hear the manager talk again, then it's back to the clubhouse to talk to the players. Then you go and write for a half-hour to an hour and a half, and then it's time to do it all again the next day. It can be a grind, as you might imagine.

What's the *Ledger's* approach to Twitter and other forms of social media? Obviously a lot of beat writers and other writers who cover the Mets and the Yankees on a daily basis are on Twitter. It's sort of become the big thing. To what extent does *The Star-Ledger* encourage that or push you guys in that direction? Do they have any rules or is it just, "Go out there and try to make yourself more popular?"

We went through some phases. There was one point where we were live-tweeting games. I'm tweeting things like, "A double for Wright," which was just too much. That was the policy, I guess, and we kind of realized that it was a waste of our time.

One time I did accidentally re-tweet a Buzz Bissinger thing with the f-word. I just totally forgot I wasn't able to do that. So I got slightly wrist-slapped for being a dope. But, mostly, there's no real rules; just don't be an idiot. Be professional. If you have a joke, make sure it's funny. That's my own personal rule, which I try to adhere to as much as I can.

If you can make obscure music references, definitely do it.

Right, right. If you can reference the '90s, bands you like, pro wrestling. I went through a *90210* phase. I like it in that there can be instant feedback. If there's something that's wrong, there are plenty of people that will chime in and tell you that you were wrong. It's very, very nice for all these nice people to immediately say that you are wrong about something. Which can be good, but when it's a typo it's annoying.

But I like it. It's something I wasn't really crazy about initially, because I thought it was really just a self-serving thing, two or three years ago, I guess. But now I think it's great. I'm on Twitter all day long because that's where news gets dropped first. Mostly it's just fun. I follow a lot of baseball people, and I also follow a lot of guys from *SLAM Magazine*, because they're all really funny. They tweet about basketball. It's funny.

But it's good—good to have reader interaction. And it's good for sources of information, too.

The fact that information can transmit so quickly—whether it's

something in the locker room or at the game or a news release, it goes from a beat writer to Twitter to an independent news outlet like Amazin' Avenue—does that take value away from being on the front lines of covering the team as a beat writer? To a large extent, it makes it unnecessary to be at the game. From my own perspective, I don't have to be at a Mets game to get most of the value that you would get from having been there. And even things in the locker room, whether quotes or stuff like that, even that gets filtered very quickly to everyone out there, whether they're consuming it for their own information or if they're consuming it because they're writing their own take on things. To what extent is that something you think about or that gets talked about? What's the perception of independent coverage of the team compared to people who are actually at the games covering the team every day?

Being there every day, you're in control of the questions. Even if you can't control the answers, because a lot of the questions are the same every night—trying to get the routine stuff, you can get a lot of similar answers, so it does appear as if the same sort of stuff gets said every night—but being there you find the stories that you couldn't find elsewhere. You find the people who are involved in these people's lives, who have an impact on them and have an influence, who they wouldn't be talking about normally. That's not a lot of the stuff that gets reported.

But it still remains to be seen how we will do this job. How beat writers do their job. Lord knows I'm not qualified to answer this, but I know there is discussion of what's important for beat writers to do, should you be doing this and doing that. I know I'm going to be there every day. I want to write memorable stories. I want to write stories that people can talk about, that they wouldn't find out about if they're just paying attention to Twitter or the stock stuff that comes out after the games.

You're absolutely right: Who gets credit for breaking the news is a lot different than it used to be. I'm probably going to butcher the exact attribution on this—I'm pretty sure it was in '04—*Newsday* was the first newspaper to break that Alex Rodriguez was either in talks or had been traded to the Yankees. They were first on that. That sort of stuff doesn't happen as much anymore, unless it's with, say, a major investigation, the way the *Times* does sometimes with the steroids [issue]. At the Winter Meetings, I'm pretty sure that Peter Abraham [of *The Boston Globe*] broke the Carl Crawford signing. But there might have been someone a minute and a half before him who tweeted it. You know what I mean?

But it doesn't mean that that skill—him being able to break that news—is any less valuable or shouldn't be applauded. It was fantastic. And that's what his job is and he did it. But the credit sometimes get muddled, because there's so many people trying to do it.

I just know, personally, I'm not that good at it. I'm trying to get better. Lord knows I'm trying to get better. But I haven't been around the game long enough to have the relationships to do what some of these other guys can do. So, I try to get the different sort of stories, the prototypical feature type of stuff. I feel like that's what I can find and maybe do well. I don't know. I know it's hard.

The type of connections, personal relationships, that somebody like Jon Heyman or Ken Rosenthal have—they've been around the game for a long time—they're invaluable. When he's got a good number of baseball GMs and front office executives on text message or on e-mail, those are avenues that someone who hasn't been around long enough won't have. It means you're always playing catch-up with that sort of thing. Or you take a different approach, like you were saying.

One of the things we don't see as fans is the coverage of the personal side of the players. A lot of them don't make it known: They have their baseball lives and they have their personal lives, and they do keep them separate. We can scrutinize their on-field accomplishments all day long, but getting a feel for what these guys are actually like off the field? We don't really know what they're like. As a fan, it's a lot easier to root for a guy who's a good guy and an interesting person, rather than a guy who's kind of surly or seems disinterested, etc.

I think that's what, as beat writers, we can always give. Is it easier to talk to the 25th man on the roster than a superstar? Theoretically, but, you know, Jose Reyes is very easy to talk to. There's always the potential to connect with a player and be able to find something new about him that fans wouldn't read otherwise. Stuff you couldn't just tell from looking at how he plays every night.

There are other things we don't see that go into performance, whether it's things like nagging injuries or something bothering him off the field. These are people. They have things that affect them, apart from the skill set that applies to baseball. Those things

don't show up on FanGraphs or Baseball-Reference. But if a guy had a baby, and the baby was sick, a death in the family, or any of these non-baseball things which affect somebody on a day-to-day basis and drag you down emotionally, it's inevitable that it would seep into what you do every day.

Right, right. Like with Pelfrey in July, to come back to him. I looked at his numbers for a long time to try to figure out what the difference was, and, really, everyone said he had no confidence in his fastball. He couldn't throw his sinker. He didn't trust himself. He didn't do this, he wasn't throwing inside as much as he could. It just seemed like there was a big muddle of information that he needed to sift though and get back to being simple. Sometimes I think the numbers, without a doubt, make things clear. And sometimes they make it seem more confusing. I'm not good enough to really discern what the difference is, yet.

I think it's a great point. If you look, thanks to FanGraphs and some of these other sites, we know how often he throws one pitch versus another. So when you look at 2009 versus 2010, and you found that he was throwing his splitter less, or throwing his sinker less, all you can look at and guess is, "Oh, well, he just changed his repertoire. Or he lost confidence." But we don't really know. It could just be an aberration, or it could be that he was working on it and wasn't confident. And there might be some other thing. Those are the sorts of things that are beyond the box score, that we don't really know. It doesn't change his performance, but it does change the formula, and it's at least an explanation as to why something is happening, instead of drawing immediate conclusions like, "He's on a decline." There are other factors that contribute to it that we may or may not even know.

Exactly.

What's your favorite thing about covering the Mets? Or maybe it's just about writing in general. Obviously, the grind of it is, perhaps, the least favorite part. But what do you love? What gets you up in the morning to go do this?

It's hard to say what you like. Having the respect of your peers. I've enjoyed being in the ballpark. Having interesting conversations with players and talking to them about whatever. I remember during the ALCS I had a five- or ten-minute talk with C.J. Wilson from the Rangers, about Felix Hernandez and advanced statistics. It was fascinating. It was very interesting to hear someone who plays the game, who still seems attuned to stuff, that I could talk to about FIP [Fielding-Independent Pitching], and he knew what I was talking about. It's interesting to have conversations like that during the day. It's an interesting form of work, more than anything else. There's not really one thing that I enjoy doing the most, but I certainly wouldn't say that I dislike the job at all. This job is fantastic.

It's an opportunity to interact with people who are better at their particular thing than anyone else in the world. They're baseball players. Most of them are multimillionaires. But they've excelled like no one else. There are 700–800 professional Major League Baseball players, and you get to talk to a couple dozen of them every day. There's probably a lot to learn there. I don't know to what extent that interests you, but to pick the brains of such people... It's different than if you were to work with a team of, say, advanced evolutionary biologists who have this vast amount of knowledge about a particular thing. Whereas a lot of these guys, they work hard, but some of them happened to have been born excellent at baseball. It's not an easy thing to impart—"Here's why I'm so good at baseball"—but it's got to be interesting to be in the room with so many talented guys.

I could not imagine—with how many players there are, how many guys wash out, and how the draft is such a crapshoot, I think you have to be pretty focused and pretty driven to reach the major leagues, unless you're some sort of bonus-baby type who makes the majors immediately after being drafted out of college. I think the difficult part in drawing it out is that a lot of these guys are very singleminded and very focused on not having discussions on the process, so much as the nuts and bolts of doing it. Sometimes the philosophy behind it all can be a little difficult to draw out. That's not with everyone. There might be some guys who seem like that, but they like being guarded, which is fine. But for a lot of them, it's such a difficult, frustrating game that it's best to keep it simple and not try to analyze it too much. That can be a challenge [as a writer].

Do you get a hard time from the other beat writers who aren't really into stats? Are you the stat nerd among Mets beat writers?

Oh, yeah. Without a doubt. Slide rule jokes. "What's David Wright's

FIP?" But these guys aren't dumb. They're professional journalists who are doing a difficult job at high-level places. I mean, you never say someone who covers the New York Mets for a major paper in New York [City] is a dumb person. They just do it to mess with me.

I don't know what it is. I mean, I bring it on myself, because I'm the jerk-off in the conversation who brings up a guy's OBP for no reason, just to do it, to be a smart-ass. I like to be the smartest guy in the room. Unfortunately, that's a personality trait that I have. But, yeah, the guys joke around, but I thinks it's all good-natured. I'm certainly not bullied. I'm 6 foot 3, 220 pounds.

Physically, David Lennon's not going to push you around.

Dave's an intimidating guy [laughing]. Yeah, David is shorter than I.

Do we philosophically differ sometimes on what's important? Sure. But I don't think it would be a wise thing to have everyone agree on what makes a good baseball team and what are the most important things. I haven't seen enough baseball to pretend that I know more than those guys covering it, that I have a better idea of how to put a team together than Omar, all those sorts of things.

I can always rely on the things people smarter than me are saying, the Bill Jameses, the Joe Posnanskis, Tom Tangos, all those sort of guys. But, yeah, [the other reporters] joke around, but it's all in good fun. And I bring it on myself most of the time, I'd say.

Do any of the other beat writers express any interest in statistical analysis? I'm trying to get a sense of whether they think it's only for nerds, if they think there's some value to the statistics, or if they're just not interested in them.

Without a doubt, August and September were long, slow months, and we definitely had legitimate conversations about statistics. I think what some of the guys would say, what the question was, is, "Why do I need this stat when I have that statistic?" If you look at a guy's RBI, batting average, or home runs, it seems like it gives you a pretty good idea of what he does. Theoretically. And the whole WAR thing is difficult. And UZR. The metrics weird me out a little. I'm not as quick to jump to defend them.

To be fair, there are a lot of problems with advanced defensive statistics in general. There are certainly plenty of reasons to have reservations about a lot of it, but to have a conversation about why

batting average is good but on-base percentage is better, or that RBI aren't good for knowing what kind of run producer a guys is, etc. Home runs are still good. Still awesome.

Maybe it's fighting an uphill battle with guys who have been there forever. If they're not interested in it, that's okay. If the question is, "Why should I look at on-base percentage instead of batting average?" then...

It's not so much that. Everyone understands the importance of it. FIP is without a doubt the biggest one. FIP is the one where I get the most razzing, because it sounds silly. One time a writer said to me when we were talking about batted balls in play—I was trying to explain that the average for a pitcher is about .300—he said, "What about Tom Glavine? Glavine knew if he put a ball here it could do that." To which I said, [laughing] "Uh, I don't know. I read it in a book."

It's hard. Guys can bring up exceptions to every rule. That makes it difficult sometimes. But FIP is the one that without a doubt I get the most [hard time] for. Maybe it's just because I'm on FanGraphs so often, but it's one of the stats I use the most for looking at what a pitcher should have done and his actual value. At the same time, is FIP that valuable with a guy like R.A. Dickey? Is it as valuable with Pelfrey and [Tim] Hudson, who are extreme sinkerballers? That's stuff I'm sure folks know, but I need to keep researching to find the answers.

Right. There's a big difference between knowing something and being able to explain it.

If you're trying to get lost in the game, it's all fantastic. If you're trying to explain something to someone in 35 seconds, when they're in the middle of their day and they're taking time out to try and show interest in this stuff, it can be hard.

So, yeah, [other writers] definitely talk about it. A lot of times it's a joke, but there have definitely been times when guys were like, "What did you put in that story? Why would you use that?"

Similarly, I know Marc Carig, our Yankees writer, had written about this on his blog once, about the difficulty of explaining [this stuff]. I had this issue writing about Chris Young the other day, and thanks to Bill Baer [of CrashburnAlley.com] on Twitter who pointed out that PETCO Park just crushed lefty hitters. You couldn't hit a home run if you're a lefty. And Chris Young is a righty fly ball pitcher. So [Baer] pointed out the park factors for PETCO and Citi Field, how even though they're both barns, PETCO is much, much tougher on lefty power hitters. And I wondered, "Do I waste 40 words explaining that?" or do I just write that PETCO destroys lefty hitters? That is the difficulty of explaining it. Do I spend a sentence talking about a guy's wOBA or do I just put in OPS and hope that people know what it is?

A friend of mine who covers another team for another paper says his editors tell him, "Don't even use OPS." So I can understand, without a doubt, why people would be reticent to use advanced metrics, because they're difficult to explain. That's one of the things that Ken Davidoff does so fantastically; with an economy of language, he can explain statistics and why they matter, and be very quick about it. He gets that out of the way, so he doesn't have to waste time going over the jargon. But that's a difficult thing, to be able to do that. That's not something I've mastered.

I think with Davidoff it helps that he's a columnist, so it's not always his job to explain what happens with, for instance, a particular game. If he needed to, he could take extra time to explain why FIP is important. But I can certainly appreciate that skill he has. On Amazin' Avenue, all we do is write about baseball. We can do a thousand-word post explaining why we think something like wOBA is important, but that's not something you can do at a newspaper that's relying on you to cover the team while writing something interesting that most people will understand, and not waste 300 words explaining something to readers.

Right. Like I said, that's why I can understand why some writers on the beat aren't as interested in advanced metrics as I am. I can totally understand why, because their bosses may not be interested and the readers may not be. I've never done a poll, say, of how many guys know what OPS is, but it's funny: I put Valdespin's OPS on Twitter, that he had a .547 OPS in 28 games, and one guy was like, "What the heck does that mean?" I told him that Valdespin wasn't good for 28 games. But even then, you have to find a blend of the advanced and the basic statistics that pleases everyone. That's difficult. If you were to stick with RBI, home runs, ERA, saves—all that sort of stuff—I think you'd please the majority of the people. But since I know this [advanced] information exits, I'd like to understand it.

I can understand how for a lot of other writers who cover the team,

trying to delve into these advanced statistics is only going to make more work for themselves, not just in the work they would need to do to learn more, but also in trying to convey that to readers. Whether or not that's something their editors would even encourage, it sounds like that would be an impediment to them doing their job. It's extra information that doesn't allow them to better communicate to readers, at least the vast majority of readers.

Is it better to spend an hour on a FanGraphs piece in the morning, or is it better to be on the phone talking to people? You know what I mean? You have to make that choice. If people don't call me back, I'll just spend the time on FanGraphs.

That's what I do, because I want to have all the information, and I have the flexibility to talk about that [advanced stuff]. Nobody's paying me to make sure that I get the story, let alone work in some of these arguably esoteric stats that most people probably aren't interested in.

Exactly.

It seems like the perception of the front office has transitioned from one that wasn't quick to embrace statistical analysis to one that certainly is. There have been books written about their interest in statistical analysis. Do you expect that might change the way the team is covered? Maybe it doesn't, but from our perspective at Amazin' Avenue, it's a sea change because we've gone from questioning a lot of things which didn't line up with a more objective, evidence-based way of looking at things to now where we've got a group running the front office which you know is going to take all the information they have and consider it.

It's all based on the context, the context of what Sandy Alderson's goal is this year versus the context of what Omar Minaya's goals were last offseason. They're so phenomenally different that you have to grade them appropriately. If Omar comes off that [2009] season and spends no money, that would have been like throwing up a white flag and saying, "What I had been doing, the way we had been going about building this team, was wrong. We need to blow it up." That would signal, maybe, "I'm not the right guy for this." He had to do something.

But this year, Sandy Alderson gets a grace period. The things that Omar had done in the past couple of years were from when the grace period had ended, so he wasn't allowed, as much, to make mistakes, even though there were obvious mistakes—contract signings that went poorly, trades that might not have been the best ideas, etc. But you look at this offseason, they've certainly figured out what the market inefficiency was: It seems like it's pitchers coming off arm injuries. Capuano and Buchholz had Tommy John surgery. Chris Young has obviously had injury problems. Taylor Tankersley had arm problems. [Boof] Bonser is coming off injury problems. So they very clearly found what the inefficiency was in this bloated market, and they were going to get guys who were coming off arm troubles, injuries, things like that, and roll the dice. They've got $10 million or whatever to spend, so they grab ten lottery tickets and see what happens.

Yeah, it's pretty consistent with what Alderson said early on when he took the job. He said he's not going to have a lot of money to spend, but that he needs to find guys who, if things break right, can provide a lot of value. He certainly seems to have found some of those guys. A lot of them probably aren't going to work out, but if things happen to go well—Capuano stays healthy all year, the same for Chris Young, etc.—you've got guys who are going to be pretty good pitchers, and they won't have been paid much money at all.

Right. You'd have an okay rotation if Jon Niese progresses a little bit—that will be interesting to watch—and if Pelf is able to get his sinker back. You'd have an okay rotation, and that's not bad considering how things were. I think one of the funny things is that, coming into this, everyone said, "This is *Moneyball*, but with money." Not for a little while. It's just *Moneyball*. They have a lot of money committed to a lot of guys, even after this year, depending on what happens. There's K-Rod's option, guys who are going to get raises year by year through arbitration, they're going to have to figure out what to do with Reyes.

It's going to be interesting to see how they navigate all this, and how they're able to figure out the financials of it. That's the one thing, I guess, that's pretty easy for me, as far as covering the team, to understand their philosophies. For Sandy to come out and say he's reticent to give long-term extensions to aging players, that makes total sense to me because I read a piece at Baseball Prospectus about peaks. I have an idea of when a guy peaks when he has a certain skill set. And I'm sure they have that information available, too. With the previous regime, maybe that wasn't as prevalent. Or maybe they just decided to ignore it. I don't know.

But I don't think the coverage of the team will be different. I just think they might make moves that make a little more sense to different people. Some of Omar's moves might have made sense to some fans. They needed a big bat, so last offseason they went and got a big bat [Jason Bay]. If you're thinking in that sort of way, maybe that move made sense.

I don't think any of this will really change how I do my job, but it will certainly be interesting to see how they deal with the dilemmas set up by this roster.

Maybe it gives you an advantage in covering the team, because you're already familiar with why they might make some of these decisions, why they might implement some of these organizational philosophies that might not be so obvious to, say, someone who is covering the team from a more traditional angle.

Maybe. But I'm not that talented. Maybe. But likely not. I'm still the 23-year-old guy who's too busy tweeting about pro wrestling to pay attention to the baseball game.

CHAPTER EIGHTEEN

The Mets Legacy Initiative

Greg Prince and Jason Fry

It's fitting that a franchise known for engineering so many transcendent come-from-behind victories through the years—from down 3–0 to Baltimore in 1969, 3–0 to Houston, 5–3 to Boston in 1986, and 8–1 to Atlanta in 2000, to name a few famous examples—came from behind in 2010 to score a pretty big win. The one we're thinking of, however, didn't show up on the Citi Field scoreboard. Instead, it happened all around Citi Field.

The 2010 Comeback Player of the Year in Queens may have been New York Mets history, or, more specifically, its presence in the home of the New York Mets. It rebounded from 2009 better than Oliver Perez did, that's for sure.

There's no need to rehash what a barren disappointment Citi Field was upon its opening when it came to telling the Mets' story. No need to recall how the trifecta of Brooklyn Dodgers influences—architectural theme, grand entranceway, and the first club you ran into up the first escalator—was about three times as great as those features that paid homage to the New York Mets (never mind the myopic, Giants-free portrayal of the Mets' National League ancestry). There was a little Metsishness around the edges of Citi Field, but its muted quality left patrons screaming for more.

The Mets listened. Scream loud enough, long enough, and sincerely enough, they eventually will. In 2010, Citi Field's Mets quotient was raised exponentially, from Nearly Nothing to Fairly Amazin'.

- The Mets Hall of Fame and Museum opened just inside the Jackie Robinson Rotunda, revealing itself to be a pleasingly light and airy space that still managed to be delightfully dense with stare-worthy Metsamabilia and a series of engaging, interactive exhibits.

- The plaque wall of said space was enhanced in August by four new faces, chosen wisely by a revamped Hall of Fame selection committee in January. For too long, the Mets Hall of Fame existed primarily as a media guide page. With the negligently delayed induction of Frank Cashen, Davey Johnson, Dwight Gooden, and Darryl Strawberry, it sprung to life as it never had even at beloved Shea (where the Hall was limited to sculpted heads hidden from general view in the Diamond Club lobby).

- The pedestrian walkway by which foot traffic flows beyond right-center field was respectfully dedicated as the Shea Bridge, with an image of Bill Shea's stadium affixed on both sides. Considering how the Mets cobbled together strained options like "Miracle Mile Bridge," "You Gotta Believe Bridge," and "Amazin' Alley" in a 2009 fan questionnaire, it was a triumph of taste and appropriateness that Mr. Shea received his due.

- The geographically correct VIP entrances of '09—First Base, Third Base, and Left Field—rose and shone in 2010 as Hodges, Seaver, and Stengel. Towering mosaics greeted entrants and passers-by, and if you were lucky enough to make your way through their portals, you saw some great archival items celebrating the three numerically retired Mets legends.

- On the first- and third-base sides of the Field Level, two rows of vintage Topps cards showing Mets from across the team's decades gave anyone who'd ever opened a wax pack something to wax nostalgic over.

- The Ebbets Club, with its faintly executed Dodgers theme, was remade as the Champions Club, honoring 1969 and 1986 at the expense of 1955.

- The players took the field for every single game to a recording of "Meet The Mets," but not just any recording—it was Jane Jarvis, as recorded for posterity in 1996, and it remained timeless in 2010.

- The Home Run Apple, in its lovably anachronistic magic top hat, emerged from the obscurity of the Bullpen Plaza to helm a reinvigorated Mets Plaza. Get off the 7 train, you see the Apple. Waiting to meet somebody? You hang by the Apple. You have a camera phone, you take a picture of the Apple.

- The lampposts that dot Mets Plaza and ring the stadium were adorned with banners of current and classic Mets, memorable players from every era. If not every Met was so honored, a surprising cross-section of them made the cut. For example, Marvelous Marv Throneberry was spotted flying in tandem with Cliff Floyd in the players' parking lot, just a few rows from 2000 NLCS MVP Mike Hampton and not far off, either, from 1980 Gold Glove second baseman Doug Flynn. Whether the 2010 Mets gave them a second glance en route to their Lincolns and Lexuses is up for debate, but fans who caught a glimpse from the World's Fare food court certainly felt fulfilled.

- The commemorative brick "fanwalk," the one certifiable hit of 2009—where Mets fans' personally etched tributes to their beloved team—was augmented by a series of greatest-moments ground-level plaques. True, one initially misplaced the decision from Game 7 of the 1986 World Series (almost understandably crediting Sid Fernandez with the 'W' that went on Roger McDowell's ledger), but in the spirit of Year Two of Citi Field, the mistake was fixed, and a brighter day continued to dawn.

All of these installations were elegantly executed and laudable. Taken together, the Metsification of Citi Field represented a great leap forward and an Endy leap upward. One might even say it was, per Neil Armstrong, one giant leap for mankind, but with the owner's Dodger fixation still deeply embedded in the foundation of the park, we won't go nuts.

All told, 2010 was a great step toward preserving the legacy of the New York Mets, but it was a first step. We need further steps. Why?

Because we need to preserve that legacy. We need to embellish it, burnish it, and make it ubiquitous where it lives. While the Mets reside in the hearts of every one of its millions of enthusiasts, the focal point of that attachment is Citi Field. That's where it needs to flourish, where it must continue to gain attention and grab traction. That is where it must nourish the psyche and the heart of every Mets fan. The Mets legacy is what we hold onto when the Mets' present is wanting and what we strive to build upon when the Mets' future couldn't be more inviting. It's what we pass along to the next generation, what we pass back and forth to each other.

So let's not just dabble in Mets history. Let's, as if channeling Judge Reinhold in *Fast Times At Ridgemont High*, learn it, live it, and know it. Let's envelop Citi Field in it. Let's forcefully and thoroughly nurture an indelible half-century of Mets baseball. Let's consider what some of our next steps could be and should be.

And, as always, Let's Go Mets. That is the fans' cry. If we don't dwell on these matters, who will? Certainly, as the screaming of 2009 and the results of 2010 illustrated, not the Mets—not unless we nudge them in the right direction. So let us begin nudging.

RETIRE A NUMBER OR TWO

This is indeed going to require some thought, as retiring numbers is the highest honor a team can bestow. And based on the dialogue taking place online, it's one of the most emotional issues for Mets fans.

We can agree the Mets have been rather stringent in permanently taking numbers out of circulation. They retired #37 for Casey Stengel in 1965, #14 for Gil Hodges in 1973, and #41 for Tom Seaver in 1988 (with Jackie Robinson's #42 joining them on an MLB-wide scale, at Shea, in 1997). Stengel was so honored for having essentially invented the Mets mystique in 1962 (it wasn't for losing 120 games out of the box). Hodges was the certified miracle worker lost too young in 1972. The real standard here is Seaver, universally understood to be the greatest Met ever.

That makes the question, who is worthy of joining Tom?

There are no agreed-upon specifications for what gets a player's number retired, though some teams have tried. The Red Sox, for instance, reserve consideration for members of the Hall of Fame whose Boston tenure was at least 10 years.

When you break it down, qualifications for having a number retired usually fall into one or more of four components. First is statistics. If a player's numbers don't make you whistle, or at least nod appreciatively, we can move on.

The stats discussion often turns into one about longevity. There's not necessarily something magical about 10 years, but a player has to have worn the uniform for a baseball generation, whatever that is exactly.

Titles matter, too. We naturally celebrate players we remember throwing gloves into the stratosphere or leaping into catchers' arms after the last out of a World Series.

And then there's the X factor, which might actually be the most important of all. Does a mere mention of the player evoke something deep in the fan's heart? Does intoning his name cause fans to reflexively rise up from their seats in a pregame ceremony?

And what do you do if a player ticks some but not all of these boxes?

There are potential Met numerical retirees who have longevity but not stats: Ed Kranepool, Bud Harrelson, John Franco, and Lee Mazzilli all had tenures of at least a decade, and three World Series rings among them, but their stats are either pedestrian or saves.

Then there are the players whose candidacies are the reverse. These are statistically strong Mets with other accomplishments, but whose longevity raise questions: Edgardo Alfonzo, Gary Carter, Keith Hernandez, and Mike Piazza were gone before a decade was out.

And then there are players who seem to tick most or all of the boxes, yet who may not quite have that X factor we're looking for when retiring a number.

If there is an advantage to the Mets' lack of retired numbers it's that we can consider some other teams' retirees for lessons to be learned. There are teams whose handling of retired numbers elicits an immediate nod of agreement and those that leave you scratching your head.

In the former camp, we can put the Braves. Dale Murphy, Warren Spahn, Greg Maddux, Phil Niekro, Eddie Mathews, Hank Aaron, and Tom Glavine make for a solid list, even if Mets fans might want to spraypaint an asterisk on that last name. And the Orioles' pantheon should elicit an approving nod: Earl Weaver, Brooks Robinson, Cal Ripken Jr., Frank Robinson, Jim Palmer, Eddie Murray. You and I probably could have come up with that list, which is a sign that Baltimore did well.

On the other hand, the Padres have four homegrown retired numbers: Steve Garvey, Tony Gwynn, Dave Winfield, and Randy Jones. Gwynn is beyond reproach, but Garvey played 14 years in L.A. and five in San Diego; Winfield only stayed for eight years, and Jones didn't win 100 games wearing the Padres' taco colors. One must allow for local customs and quirks—Garvey did hit a huge home run to help secure the Pads' 1984 pennant—but still, it can get a little eccentric out there.

Did a cameo by Tampa-native Wade Boggs, accented by his 3,000th hit, justify that no Tampa Bay Ray ever wear #12 again? Does the earnest sentimentality that drove the Marlins to retire Joe DiMaggio's #5 in honor of their first team president Carl Barger and his childhood idol after Barger died in 1992—four months before the Fish had played a single game—quite add up? And can we excoriate the Nationals for unretiring the Expos' numbers? Bringing back digits worn by Gary Carter, Andre Dawson, Rusty Staub, and Tim Raines is the baseball equivalent of desecrating a grave.

If the Mets wish to consider the mixed signals a flurry of number retirements sends, they need look no further than their 1962 expansion brethren. The Astros have nine retired numbers of their own, and they're an odd mix of the underwhelming, sentimental, and tragic. They've honored Jimmy Wynn and Jose Cruz, good but not great players. They've given Mike Scott and his 110 regular-season Astros wins (plus the two NLCS victories in which he confounded the 1986 Mets) a place on the wall. They've hung up Nolan Ryan's digits, also retired by the Angels and Rangers. They've honored Don Wilson, a good pitcher who committed suicide, and Jim Umbricht, an original Colt .45 who made a courageous return from cancer, then died at 33. More recent picks Jeff Bagwell, Craig Biggio and Larry Dierker are a lot harder to argue with. Overall, though, it seems the Astros' generosity has diluted the intended impact.

With those warnings ringing in our ears, let's look at seven Mets who might qualify for retired-number status and their cases according to our four admittedly non-scientific criteria:

Tug McGraw, #45

Statistics: Not so good anymore. 85 saves is pretty devalued by now.
Longevity: On the edge at nine years
Title: Yes. Plus, he was the heart and soul of a team that almost won another.
X Factor: High. Beloved during his time as a Met, mourned since his untimely death in 2004 at 59.

Jerry Koosman, #36

Statistics: Good. Koosman is third on the franchise list in wins and strikeouts and second in starts. He won 140 games, posted a 3.09 ERA as a Met, and had four wins in the postseason.
Longevity: 12 years
Title: Yes, plus his jackknifed leap into Jerry Grote's arms is an iconic Mets snapshot.
X Factor: Medium. Fairly or not, Koosman stands in the shadow of Tom Seaver in retirement, just as he did when they were teammates—a complementary ace to the Franchise.

Darryl Strawberry, #18

Statistics: Superb. Straw still sits atop the Mets record book for homers, RBI, and runs, and he's fourth in steals. He had three 100-RBI seasons and held the single-season home run and RBI records for years.

Longevity: A bit lacking at eight years, and further hurt by a nasty contract dispute that took him to L.A.

Title: Yes.

X Factor: Medium. Straw was persona non grata for a while after his departure, undone by his off-field troubles and seeming insistence on saying stupid things. But he has been accepted back into the fold, forgiven for never living up to his sky-high potential, and embraced as a crazy-uncle-type who turns up to reminisce about '86 and say mildly controversial things.

Keith Hernandez, #17

Statistics: A bit thin. Keith collected 939 hits as a Met, and drove in 97 RBI in his best season.

Longevity: At seven years, also a little thin

Title: Yes.

X Factor: Off the charts. Hernandez was adored not just as an '86 Met, but as the quintessential New Yorker—an immigrant who was shocked to find himself in the city but came to realize it was a perfect match. His capsule biography—tightly wound, slightly unhinged, familiar with the far side of midnight, and successful despite all that—is one at least a million young New Yorkers would love to claim as their own. His myth has only grown since his departure, first with his appearance on *Seinfeld*, and then with his mix of cerebral analysis, world-weary despair, and goofy unpredictability alongside Gary Cohen and Ron Darling in the broadcast booth.

Dwight Gooden, #16

Statistics: Solid. Doc is second among Mets pitchers in wins and strikeouts, third in starts, won 157 games as a Met, and it seems certain no Mets starter will ever approach the heights he reached in that spellbinding 1985 season.

Longevity: 11 star-crossed years

Title: Yes

X Factor: Medium. Mets fans have never turned against Doc despite the many, many times he's disappointed them. But for all that, neither the team nor the fan base seems to trust him to stay out of trouble. Sadly, it's hard to blame them.

Howard Johnson, #20

Statistics: Better than you think. HoJo racked up 997 hits as a Met and recorded three 30–30 campaigns. He's third in homers, fourth in runs and RBI, third in steals, and fifth in games played.

Longevity: On the cusp at nine years

Title: Yes

X Factor: Low. A part-time player in '85 and '86, HoJo eventually stepped out of the shadow of Keith and Gary to record his best season as the Mets collapsed, then struggled through two subpar seasons.

Mike Piazza, #31

Statistics: Excellent. Piazza is second in homers and third in RBI, hit 30 or more homers four times, and still holds a share of the single-season RBI record.

Longevity: A bit short at eight years

Title: No. (Stupid Kenny Rogers.)

X Factor: High. Piazza brought star power back to the Mets, was chosen to appear with Seaver as a franchise bookend for the closing of Shea and the opening of Citi Field, and he has been rapturously greeted whenever he's returned.

So what are our conclusions?

Painful as it is to say, McGraw flunks the stats and longevity criteria. John Franco, generally not considered a candidate for a retired number, easily bests him in both departments. HoJo dramatically fails the X factor test, and Gooden's chronic troubles remove him from contention there as well. Strawberry also feels like a miss, weighed down by the memory of off-field troubles, a perceived inability to fulfill his potential, and the imminent eclipse of his records by David Wright.

That leaves us with Koosman, Hernandez, and Piazza.

Retiring Koosman's number, frankly, would feel more like an act of historical correction than consecration, as the lefty was constantly pushed out of the spotlight by Seaver's oversized accomplishments and charisma. And so now we have two: Hernandez and Piazza.

Saying yes to #31 and #17 would be well-received moves for the

Mets, with ceremonies for Mike and Keith packing Citi Field with well-wishers. But do Hernandez and Piazza merit that, or would they be Citi Field versions of Jose Cruz since neither played a decade with the Mets? Keith is long on highlight plays and goodwill, but short on stats. Mike was the best player on a team that never won a World Series, a Hall of Famer who might well be inducted as a Dodger.

Franchises ought to be restrained in taking numbers out of circulation, making such decisions with a certain confidence that they're in it for the long haul, that ultimately their histories will be studded with new franchise players, titles, and great moments. They should make decisions with an eye toward future players who will play for more than a decade, own the team record books, get to douse a commissioner or two with champagne, and wear a hometown cap into Cooperstown—or at least do nearly all of those things and supply some indefinable but instantly recognizable something beyond that.

And even if #36, #31, and #17 remain unretired, the Mets could keep them under wraps for all but the most deserving players. Piazza's #31 hasn't been worn since he left town, and that's the way it should be. Keith's #17, on the other hand, graced the backs of such immortals as Jeff McKnight, Jason Anderson, and David Newhan. And Koosman's #36 adorned Tito Navarro, Jeff Tam, and Henry Owens, among others.

Those numbers should be handed out rarely, if at all. The same is true for #8, #16, #18, and other digits Mets fans reflexively associate with an obvious icon, like Mookie's #1.

Such a course of action wouldn't be unique to the Mets. The Tigers haven't retired #1 (Lou Whitaker), #3 (Alan Trammell), or #47 (Jack Morris), but they also haven't issued those numbers to anyone since parting ways with those players.

Notably, however, the Mets have been judicious in one case of re-issuing a number: Willie Mays's autumnal turn as a Met may not justify retiring #24, but reserving it for the likes of Rickey Henderson pays homage to the Say Hey Kid and deepens the reservoir of team lore. So, too, does knowing that #24 was assigned to Kelvin Torve and then quickly repossessed. But that's for another year's annual.

BRING BACK THE BANNER DAY DOUBLEHEADER

Few things proclaim "Mets!" more loudly than Banner Day. It's been absent from Flushing for 15 years, yet it's still spoken of with reverence and yearning. And why not? It was a Mets fan invention, birthed in

1963 when M. Donald Grant, tired of fighting the power of the people, co-opted it and told those bearing bedsheets at the Polo Grounds that their messages were not just welcome, they were welcome on the field between games of a doubleheader. The tradition took root instantly and flourished at Shea. Dick Young, moonlighting as scriptwriter, referred to Banner Day in the team's 1968 highlight film as the Mets' "soul" promotion.

Think about that: Banner Day was so beloved an institution that even the two most loathed villains in Mets history were all for it.

Planned doubleheaders faded from the Mets' schedule (and everybody else's) by the late 1980s. Banner Day hung on until the mid-90s as a pre-game ritual. Mets fans, no matter how bad the Mets were in a given season, still participated. But then it went away altogether. Not at all forgotten, but undoubtedly gone.

So bring it back. Bring it back as it was in its Shea heyday, as a between-games festival of commitment and creativity. Bring back the Banner Day Doubleheader. To do that, you need to make a single allowance once a year: Schedule just one twin bill.

It can be done. It's being done in Oakland this year—not a banner day, but a day with two baseball games for the price of one that has nothing to do with making up a rainout. For the A's, it's a promotion aimed at boosting attendance. They got everybody on board (aka the Players Association), and it's coming in July.

For the Mets, it needn't come from a perspective of desperation, but celebration. 2012 is the 50th anniversary of the New York Mets. What a perfect occasion to at least once bring back the banners between games. View it as an exception to the rules that govern revenue-driven thinking (though properly promoted, it's a sellout, for sure). Secure an exemption in the spirit of the Red Sox hosting a Patriots' Day game every year at eleven o'clock in the morning. If it works, consider it the baseball equivalent of the Lions and Cowboys playing home games every Thanksgiving and make it sacrosanct. From there, form a line and send the banners on parade.

Banner Day is carved into the soul of Mets fans. More soul is exactly what this franchise needs. Bring it back.

PLANT THE APPLE SEED TRAIL

The Home Run Apple that sits in Mets Plaza (as well as its larger, less visible successor just over the 408 sign inside Citi Field) represents the New York in the New York Mets—you know, the Big Apple. The Mets exist because the apple didn't fall far from the New York National League tree, planted jointly by blood rivals and Mets godfathers, the New York Giants and the Brooklyn Dodgers.

In a practical sense, the Mets are here because those teams aren't, but in an equally tangible—and spiritual—sense, the Mets are here because those teams were here. The blue is from Brooklyn. The orange made its way from Manhattan. Mr. Met has serious bloodlines.

Now that we're feeling confident and secure that the Mets' history is first and foremost at Citi Field, we can fill in the backstory a little. Let's surround the apple, which is the focal point of the Plaza, by dedicating an Apple Seed Trail. On each planter in Mets Plaza, affix a small identifier to honor a great pre-Mets New York National Leaguer. Divide them equally among Giants and Dodgers, if you want. One for Mel Ott, say. Another for Zach Wheat. Christy Mathewson here. Dolph Camilli there. Monte Irvin on the right. Pee Wee Reese on the left.

New York National League baseball lives at Citi Field. Let's make it a home for the entire family.

DEDICATE THE WILLIE MAYS CONCOURSE

Of course there will never be full and fair historical equivalency between the presentation of Giants and Dodgers as Mets influences as long as Citi Field strongly resembles the ghost of Ebbets Field, and the greatest Dodger of them all, Jackie Robinson, is titleholder to its Rotunda. Apparently, that's an immutable aspect of life under Wilpon. But that doesn't mean something can't be done to close the history gap.

If we have the Jackie Robinson Rotunda on one end of Citi Field, let's bring the Willie Mays Concourse to the other end—specifically the bustling area beyond deep center field (the position Willie made famous). Border that region of Citi Field, the one that features Shake Shack, with two banners. On one, show a young Willie Mays lighting up baseball in a black cap with orange "NY." For the other, have a mature Willie Mays returning to the city where it all began, now in a blue cap but with that familiar "NY" in orange.

Position them correctly and it will evoke a sense of center field at the Polo Grounds—the first home of the Mets—where two sets of bleachers flanked an enormous green batter's eye. (And, hey, if you can build in a stickball batting cage somewhere nearby, all the better.)

Is a player who batted .238 in not quite two seasons as a Met worth that kind of fuss? In a word, yes. He was Willie Mays. He was a Met precisely because nobody inspired more fuss and more love among baseball fans. Ours was his final uniform, and our ballpark was the setting of one of the most riveting farewell speeches baseball has ever heard ("Willie, say goodbye to America"). There's a reason uniform No. 24 has usually been unissued all these years since 1973: Willie Mays wore it. The number was his and so was New York. To this day, we remember.

For an added bonus, hold a ceremony in early May to dedicate (or at least announce) the Willie Mays Concourse. His other team, the Giants, will be in town on the eve of the Say Hey Kid's 80th birthday.

TAKE THE COOPERSTOWN STROLL

As of this writing, eleven players who have earned induction into the National Baseball Hall of Fame spent part of their careers playing for the New York Mets. It's mostly a trivia question that gets updated on those January afternoons when a new enshrinee with Mets ties is announced. Let's make it more than trivia.

Take the space between the Seaver and Stengel VIP entrances and etch in stone the Cooperstown Stroll, with a marker representing each Met who is in the Hall of Fame, no matter how much (Tom Seaver, Gary Carter) or how little (Warren Spahn, Roberto Alomar) of their immortality was earned in blue and orange. If their Cooperstown plaque includes "NEW YORK (N.L.)" from 1962 onward, that's part of Mets history, and the Mets should take a step to own it. When fans are making their way inside the stadium, they can take their own steps and see who was Fame-ous for their favorite team.

Be prepared, though. Leave room for future Hall of Famers who have at least some shading of blue and orange to them, whether it's a ton (Mike Piazza), a taste (Pedro Martinez) or even a lingering bad taste (Tom Glavine). And keep one space in reserve for David Wright... we sure hope.

TREAT EVERYONE LIKE A VIP

Every Mets fan should see the treasures on display within the Stengel, Seaver, and Hodges gates, but generally you're not welcome through those entrances unless you're a big shot with the right tickets. Stop that silliness. The Mets don't have to make a big deal out of it; we understand the need to regulate flow. But if someone who's not holding a ticket for one of the swankier sections of Citi Field wants to come in through

Hodges so he can be immersed in the majesty of Gil, don't give him a hard time. Search his bag, pat him down, scan his ticket, give him a moment to pay homage, then direct him to the Promenade once he's on the elevator. Same for Seaver, same for Stengel.

It's a small thing, but it would have a great effect. It lets a dad tell his son or daughter, "That's the man who led our team to its first world championship." It makes everybody a little more of a Mets legacy expert. It further fills the souls of fans with Mets history. Those are good things.

HAND MR. SEAVER THE BALL

When the Mets prepare to take the field to Jane Jarvis's organ on April 8, the first ball of the season should be thrown out by Tom Seaver. When they are ready to play their first home game of 2012, the first ball of the season should be thrown out by Tom Seaver. Come 2013, this ceremonial task needs to be put in the capable of hands of Tom Seaver.

Tom Seaver throwing out the first ball to start every Mets season would be a Terrific tradition. The more Tom Seaver at Citi Field, the better. Granted, he's a full-time Californian these days, but he makes a couple of trips back east annually and serves as a diligent, if low-profile, Mets Ambassador. Raise that profile. He's the best thing we've ever had. Keep him going. Make Opening Day = Tom Seaver. Make every Mets Hall of Fame induction day = Tom Seaver. Even if the new inductees weren't his teammates, they are by definition some of the greatest Mets ever. Tom Seaver is the greatest Met ever. Nobody is more fitting to give a laying on of ceremonial hands.

Tom was not part of the 2010 induction of Cashen, Johnson, Gooden, and Strawberry. He should have been. He should be on hand for any occasion we deem sacred, including the first home game of every Mets playoff series (sooner, rather than later, one hopes).

And if possible, each of us individually should interject his name into every conversation about great pitching. For example, when someone starts comparing Stephen Strasburg to Walter Johnson or Bob Gibson or (God forbid) Roger Clemens, you say, "If he's lucky, he'll have a career like Tom Seaver." When someone else, for whatever reason, brings up Greg Maddux or Sandy Koufax, you say "Tom Seaver." For someone who was as dominant for as long as Seaver was, his name doesn't come up nearly enough outside Mets circles.

At the very least, let's keep his face visibly in our midst.

ERECT A STATUE ALREADY

Seaver's pitching motion is the most logical candidate. "Meet me at The Knee," you'll tell friends. And there are others who deserve bronzing. How about the Jerrys, Koosman and Grote, embracing at the mound, with Ed Charles racing to start the party after winning the World Series in 1969? Wouldn't that look nice on one side of Citi Field? Or how about Jesse Orosco, down to both knees, glove about to head skyward, Gary Carter charging hard to begin the 1986 dog pile on the other side of the park? Two championships, two fitting commemorations. "Meet me by the Kooz" or "See you at Jesse." They've got a nice ring to them, just like the ones those players earned in their day.

One wonders if the Mets just don't feel worthy of establishing these sorts of monuments to themselves. There's no reason to feel that way. The Giants have statues outside AT&T Park. The Braves have several greeting their fans at Turner Field. Bob Feller is the touchstone outside Progressive Field. Each of those teams has fewer world championships in the past 50 years than the Mets. No need for the Mets to be shy in putting themselves out there. It's not about the Mets. It's about their fans, their memories, and giving them something to literally and figuratively point to as their own.

NAME MORE STUFF

Can't do anything about Citi Field. Somebody paid a massive chunk of change, and $20 million per year is too substantial an amount to eschew in the name of idealism (we admit sheepishly and cynically). But you can work with sponsors elsewhere inside the Ballpark Not Known As Shea.

Shake Shack is already a tradition unto itself, so let's resist the temptation to call it Shea Shack. But what about talking to Danny Meyer's restaurant group and making the most natural connection in Metsopotamia: re-christen Blue Smoke as Rusty's Blue Smoke, and provide Le Grand Orange a perch from which to greet his many fans (with all employees wearing those classic Rusty's visors from 1986's Rusty Staub Day, if not necessarily the orange wigs). What about signing Keith Hernandez and re-branding Mex's Taqueria? Instead of Box Frites, let's line up for a box of Franco Frites.

There are more possibilities. The Acela Club doesn't mean anything to anybody. But how about the Stork Club (presented by Acela)? The Stork Club was one of New York's most legendary postwar nightspots.

A generation later, George "The Stork" Theodore became one of New York's most iconic Mets utility men. Make that theme-free club into one honoring the everyman in all of us. Make the Stork the official greeter. Put his picture up over the bar. Maybe even extend the theme and offer drinks like the Super Joe Scotch & Soda or the Hot Rod Rum Punch. Lower the price just a tad, though, so the everyman in all of us can afford to partake.

And why is there a Caesars Club when Seaver's Club (presented by Caesars) would sound so much better? Or, to keep the classic New York theme going, the 41 Club by Caesars as a Queens answer to 21? The Mets need to indulge these corporate sponsors while acknowledging their core constituency is Mets fans.

Make everything about the ballpark as Metsian as possible rather than simply giving attendees the feeling Citi Field is one big commercial.

Turn the Hershey's Dunk Tank into Hershey's Krane Pool. Cut Ed in on the deal for use of his name. Put Cascarino's in business with Joe Pignatano's and give us Piggy's Pizza, a special pie made with the kinds of tomatoes Joe used to grow in the bullpen. Can McFadden's turn itself into Murph's By McFadden's (and alternate great play-by-play calls with a little "L.A. Woman" or "Takin' Care of Business" over its speakers)? How about the Promenade food court being transformed into Mrs. Payson's Place? And can't Carvel reintroduce the Strawberry sundae?

There are all kinds of possibilities. Start making them happen.

Do Better Bobbleheads

Bobblehead giveaway 2010: Jason Bay. The fun factor was akin to receiving a piece of wood. Bay could have been hitting at his Pirate/Red Sox best and the Jason Bay bobblehead would have been as boring as the season he was putting together. The same could be said for many of the expressionless "Last Guy We Signed" or "Star We're Sucking Up To" bobbleheads the Mets have given away in recent years.

Meanwhile, this is a franchise with some of the most colorful characters the game has ever known, certainly some of the most visually evocative. So how about a Casey Stengel bobblehead (add a voice chip and hear why his Metsies are "Amazin', Amazin', Amazin'"). A bobblehead day for Yogi Berra, in his 1973 Mets finery, wouldn't be over until it was over. Or Tug McGraw in an era-specific-closer's fireman's helmet. Or John Franco showing off his trademark Sanitation Department tee shirt (it could be given away to help promote recycling). Hand out two different Rustys: one evoking the 1972 Staub, the other the robust early '80s pinch-hitter.

Cleon Jones going to one knee with the final out of the World Series; Lee Mazzilli, skintight uniform; Robin Ventura, hand up, shooing Todd Pratt from tackling him shy of second base; Turk Wendell about to slam the rosin bag; Jose Reyes in his traditional winter knit cap—it all beats the blank stare of bobbleBay.

Induct Mets Hall Of Famers Annually

The Mets waited eight years after honoring Tommie Agee in 2002 before finally bestowing kudos on the Ignored Four in 2010. Since Cashen, Johnson, Gooden, and Strawberry all should have been Mets Hall of Famers much sooner, we can infer there are others who have been kept waiting too long.

Guys like Edgardo Alfonzo, Craig Swan, Howard Johnson, David Cone, John Franco, Sid Fernandez, Lee Mazzilli, Jesse Orosco, Al Leiter, Wally Backman, Jon Matlack, Todd Hundley, Ron Darling, Felix Millan, Ron Hunt, Mike Piazza, Bobby Valentine... you get the idea. There are dozens of worthy candidates for the selection committee that now boasts Howie Rose, Gary Cohen, Al Jackson, and Marty Noble to consider (they might even consider Rose, Cohen, and Jackson at some point). In 2011, the all-time Mets roster will have surpassed 900 players. Terry Collins will be our 20th manager. When you throw in key coaches—just ask Tom Seaver what Rube Walker meant to his career—and other important personnel, it's hard to argue that this process should be moving forward with such Magadan-like speed.

As we approach the Mets' 50th year, it's inconceivable there aren't more than the current 25 individuals worthy of recognition within the team's Hall of Fame.

Gather The Alumni In One Place

Now and then during the 2010 season, if you were paying close attention, you noticed there was an entity called Mets Alumni. Dutifully, the Mets sent a few former players at a time into the community to assist in charitable works. It was a nice thing, but it ran under the radar. This is because the Mets insist on scattering their old-timers here and there instead of gathering them together once a year for some kind of day. You know, like an Old Timers Day.

The Mets didn't invent Old Timers Day the way they came up with

Banner Day, but they did maintain a satisfying tradition with it from their inception (an expansion team built on the Dodgers/Giants legacy had no problem holding an Old Timers Day) into the 1990s. Then it disappeared. We have a theory, and it has something to do with the team nearby that did invent Old Timers Day. But we, the Mets fans, don't care that our alumni (we won't call them "old-timers" if that elicits comparisons which make Mets management insecure) weren't necessarily World Series winners or pennant participants. We just want to see many of them together. On the field. Once a year. If you have a sure-fire theme, like a 1986 reunion, great. If not, invent one. And 2012, the 50th anniversary? Make that the greatest gathering of Mets alumni ever. Not dozens of alumni. Hundreds. Print 42,000 special commemorative programs. Nobody would dream of putting one on eBay.

We're about to turn 50. We're worth it.

STOCK THE TEAM STORE WITH SOME THOUGHT

SNY may operate independently of the Mets, but the team and its network can put their resources together and produce a deluxe set of the *Mets Yearbook* series. Sell uncut versions at the ballpark. Add bonus material. We've recorded every episode, and we'd still buy every one of them. Same goes for *Mets Classics*. (Oh, and as much as we adore them, how about leaning on SNY to air something besides the Matt Franco and Dave Mlicki Subway Series games once in a while?).

The Citi Field stores could also do a little better in the publications department, which, to date, is nonexistent. There are plenty of fine Mets books out there. Expose your fans to them. It also wouldn't hurt to set up a kiosk with actual Mets collectibles. You know, baseball cards, yearbooks, scorecards from years gone by. Mets lovers are in the mood for Mets stuff when they're at a Mets game. Give them every chance to make those purchases. There will still be plenty of space left to display the discount "FRANCOEUR 12" tee shirts and what have you.

DRESS UP IN VINTAGE CLOTHING

One weekend a year, perhaps in sync with the alumni event, wear a retro uniform. Turn back the clock on those unis. Just for the hell of it. Because it's fun. It gives us something to talk about, something to remember from our mental attic of nostalgia. Because you can sell replicas.

And get creative. Dare to be the Mercury Mets one more time. Try on those navy blues from 1982–84. Wear the 1987 road script at home. Or do as you did in 2009 and conjure a Mets uniform that never was, like the "NY" that was a (rare) homage of sorts to the early-20th century Giants.

Don't worry about looking a little silly. You're the Mets. We'll love you no matter what.

CLEARLY IDENTIFY THE BROADCAST BOOTHS

You have to be on the inside to see that Citi Field, like Shea, is home to the Bob Murphy Radio Booth and the Ralph Kiner Television Booth. Add an identifier on the outside that can be seen from the seats.

One of the nicest, quiet things the Mets do after every home win is announce the "happy recap." That's great for fans who had an ear open to Murph's signature phrase from 1962–2003. Give those who have only heard about Murph after the fact a little cheat sheet. Make his name prominent. And maybe one of the many hideaways on the Citi grid can be christened Kiner's Korner.

DECORATE THE BULLPEN PLAZA PROPERLY

Except for the seven postseason banners, the Bullpen Plaza is a rather cold outpost. Do it up a little. How about some blue and orange speckles in the style of 1964 Shea? How about a couple of neon men from more recent Shea? That place has potential to be our rec room. Right now it's just an unfinished basement.

MAKE PEACE WITH BOBBY V

We don't want anybody with strong historical ties to the Mets to feel unwelcome at Citi Field. And while we know Bobby Valentine can make himself at home anywhere on the planet, it's obviously been frosty between our last World Series manager and the organization he led there. So figure out a reason to give Bobby an award—the tenth anniversary of his yeoman work on behalf of 9/11 families seems perfect— and invite him back as an honored guest one night. He doesn't have to be given the key to the manager's office, but he's too significant a piece of the Mets story to be glossed over.

OPEN THE DOORS TO WINTER FANFEST

Why don't the Mets have a fanfest anyway? They've always kind of halfwayed it. For a few years they'd send the players en masse around the city. Lately they have a few at a time come to New York in the winter cold and make scattered appearances. A winter fanfest with alumni and merchandise and Mets cheer would lift everybody's cold-weather outlook and, quite likely—wait for it—sell some more tickets.

METSIFY THE CITI FIELD TOUR

The Citi Field tour, inaugurated in 2010, is a great way for fans to set foot on the field, to sit in the Mets dugout for a few minutes, to glimpse where the players suit up and shoot pool. What it isn't so great at is giving those who take the tour any sense of what makes the Mets a special franchise. No talk about 1962. Or '69. Or '73. Or 1999. No time devoted to explaining the oversized baseball cards on the Empire Level. No pointing to first base and telling the tale of how one October night a ground ball skipped through somebody's legs. No equating the Citi Field mound of Johan Santana to the predecessor mound of Tom Seaver and Doc Gooden where there's now a parking lot.

The tour gives you a glimpse of luxury suites and clubs the hoi polloi are usually shooed from. There's got to be more to the ballpark experience than Big Shot Envy. Make it more about the Mets, less about what the rest of us are missing out on.

BUILD A WALL FOR ALL

Mets team history isn't all about Seavers and Piazzas and Reyeses. There are Schmelzes and Puigs and Rustecks in our past, too. And they ought to have a place in team commemorations besides the agate type in media guides.

Take one of the wide-open spaces in Citi Field and build a wall—one with a place for every Met. Dress that part of the building—it could be along a wall on the outside or inside a concourse, as Citi Field has no shortage of brick—in pale marble, about four-or five-feet high. On it, carve the name of every man to go into the record books as a New York Met.

Organize the players by year. Start, for the benefit of the historical record, with the 1961 expansion draft, listing the players in order of their selection. This means the first name encountered will be that of Hobie Landrith, and the last of those pre-Original Mets for our wall will be the serendipitously named Lee Walls, who never actually played for the team. (He was traded, along with $100,000, to the Dodgers for

Charlie Neal and Willard Hunter.) There's a great trivia question, and we've barely gotten started.

From there, you unveil the 45-strong Class of 1962, followed by the 22 members of the Class of '63, until you have all 895 names (plus Walls) and counting finely engraved. That is, until you have more after 2011, and more, still, after 2012. You get the idea. You could go alphabetically within each year, or organize the Mets via strict chronology. You could indicate All-Stars and award winners, or not—our preference, being simple souls, would be for a small loving cup next to the names of the members of the two World Series championship rosters.

But these are details. Let's stick to the big picture.

Imagine fans lined up to find their favorite players, with neophytes assisted by the knowledgeable. Buddy Harrelson? He's Class of '65. Piazza? Class of '98. People would bring pencils and paper and make rubbings—like Maya Lin's Vietnam Veterans Memorial, only much less depressing. Over time, shiny spots would appear next to Seaver and Tug and Willie and Pedro, evidence of thousands of appreciative hands. Traditions might arise—perhaps one day we'll tap Tom Terrific's name for luck before a big game. From David Wright to Dave Liddell, each and every Met would be immortal, part of the unbroken line stretching from Hobie Landrith to a destination as yet unknown, and celebrated with a tribute that would be envied and copied.

And so we say (pending any changes to ownership), "Mister Wilpon, build up this wall!"

Win Another World Series Soon

Nothing will further the legacy nearly as effectively as extending the list that so far starts with 1969 and ends with 1986. The tapestry that is Mets baseball can always use new and outstanding stitches. But that's something out of the immediate control of Mets management. Everything else here is doable.

In words borrowed from "Let's Go Mets," the peppy team song that echoed all over New York a quarter-century ago: Make it happen.

PART 6: RETROSPECTIVES

CHAPTER NINETEEN

OVERSHADOWED AND OVERLOOKED

ALEX NELSON

Question: Who is the best pitcher in baseball history to own a losing record over his career? The question is something of a novelty, but after watching guys like Felix Hernandez, Tim Lincecum, and Zack Greinke take home Cy Young hardware with unappealing won-lost records, we might also be more willing as baseball fans to appreciate value beyond those surface numbers that were glorified in the past. It stands to reason that some pitchers might not have received their due. As to the question at hand, there's no perfect answer, of course, but the best place to turn is Wins Above Replacement (WAR), a quick-and-easy statistic designed to determine how much value, measured in wins, a player added to his team. In the case of pitchers, factors he can directly control are used in the calculation, like walks, strikeouts, and home runs. Here are the top five pitchers, as measured by WAR, with career winning percentages south of .500:

LOSING-RECORD PITCHERS: WAR LEADERS		
PITCHER	WAR	W-L%
Bob Friend	48.9	.461
Bobo Newsom	45.9	.487
Tom Candiotti	41.0	.479
Murry Dickson	38.9	.487
Jon Matlack	38.7	.498

Well, that's a good place to start, but the top of the list is skewed toward guys like Bob Friend who weren't necessarily great pitchers but did pitch well enough for a long time, mostly for bad teams. Let's try again, this time sorting based on the best ERA among pitchers with a losing record. However, if we leave it at that we'll be stuck with a bunch of relievers whose role, by its very nature, puts them in a far better position to lose games than to win them. So we'll insert a 1,200-inning threshold with the qualification that a pitcher had to start 60% of his games. And instead of using ordinary ERA, we'll use ERA+, which takes a player's ERA, adjusts it for home park, and then compares it to the league average. An ERA+ of 110 indicates an ERA 10% better than the league average, and an ERA+ of 90 represents an ERA 10% worse than average. A 100 ERA+ would be average.

LOSING-RECORD PITCHERS: ERA+ LEADERS		
PITCHER	ERA+	IP
Jim Scott	121	1892.0
Thornton Lee	119	2331.0
Frank Sullivan	116	1732.0
Jon Matlack	114	2363.0
Johnny Niggeling	114	1250.2

Just one name appears on both lists: Jon Matlack. And it should be noted that if you use a more stringent criteria to define what a starting pitcher is—where 75% of his appearances are starts—then Matlack jumps to the top of this second list. For a pitcher with Matlack's short career, that 114 ERA+ is not an elite mark by any stretch of the imagination. He's certainly not Hall of Fame material. But it does suggest a pitcher who was a lot better than he's frequently remembered to have been.

Matlack, of course, is well known to Mets fans. Well, I take that back. He is known to Mets fans, though perhaps not especially well known. One Mets fan I recently spoke to confused Matlack for Andy Griffith— the actor who played the title character on TV's *Matlock*. But ask most Mets fans what they know about Matlack and you might hear a few things about the 1972 Rookie of the Year Award or how he was the number-three starter on a couple of great 1970s-era Mets rotations. Or maybe even how he served up Roberto Clemente's 3,000th hit. But for most Mets fans, that's where the story of Jon Matlack begins and ends. He deserves much better.

Shakespeare said some men were born great, others achieved greatness, and others had greatness thrust upon them. Joseph Heller said the same thing about mediocrity. But unlike greatness or mediocrity, no one is born underrated. A man can only perfect the art of being underrated through achievement and allowing his audience to thrust its attention elsewhere. All modern major league players begin as local phenoms outshining their teammates and competition, and most of them are highly regarded by scouts up until they hit the majors. But without performance at that top level, a player cannot deserve to be called underrated. And without an utter lack of public attention, the quality will always elude him.

Matlack was no different. He was a star pitcher at Henderson High School in East Chester, Pennsylvania. Thanks in large part to Matlack's contributions, the team was superb, even winning 40 straight games at one point. The talent in their star southpaw was obvious to anyone who saw him pitch.

One of the great myths about pitching is that you need three average or better pitches to make it as a starter. It's a lie. Plenty of pitchers make it with just two. Steve Carlton was very much a two-pitch pitcher, fastball-slider. Ditto for Randy Johnson. Hideo Nomo? Fastball-forkball. Fernando Valenzuela? Fastball-screwball. Dwight Gooden? Fastball-curve. This is not to say that extra pitches in the arsenal don't help, especially as a player enters his twilight. But if you have a good fastball and a great off-speed pitch, you don't necessarily need anything else. Of course, lots of young pitchers have those two things and a great many of them don't make it to the majors. So what separates the ones who become big leaguers from the ones who don't? Most of the time it's simply the ability to throw the off-speed pitch for strikes, particularly if that pitch is a breaking ball. Once a pitcher is able to bend a ball traveling far outside such that it catches the corner of the plate, or move a ball traveling right down the middle of the plate out of the strike zone—to turn a ball into a strike, a strike into a ball—then he's wrested control of the strike zone away from the batter. That is usually the difference between a true two-pitch pitcher and one who needs to look into becoming a three-pitch pitcher.

All of which is a roundabout way of saying that if I were a scout watching a young Jon Matlack, I'd be salivating. He stood 6 feet 4 inches and weighed 200 pounds, so while he didn't have a ton of room to fill out his frame, he still had the opportunity to add a little bit of strength. The fastball was very good, regularly hitting the low-90s, and the hard curve made evaluators' jaws drop. He threw with his left hand, always a plus. But best of all, Matlack had that edge: he could spot that big breaking ball wherever he wanted. The changeup would be a complete non-factor for most of Matlack's career, but with his control, that fastball, and that curve, he didn't need anything else. "Usually, you sign an arm and wait for the poise," Phillies farm director Paul Owens said. "[Matlack] was as polished a boy as I've seen in a long time. He [looked] like he could step right in and pitch in a high classification."[1]

His high school competition in Pennsylvania was overmatched from day one. His coach, Charlie Perrone, put Matlack on the varsity team as a sophomore and later reflected, "He has never pitched more than a three-hitter for me."[2] In high school, Matlack went 22–1, threw five no-hitters, one perfect game, and 14 one-hitters. The one game he lost? He struck out 16. Despite all that, Matlack wasn't the first pick in 1967—the Yankees took first baseman Ron Blomberg instead—and he fell to the Mets at fourth overall, much to the consternation of several teams picking below them. For the Mets, drafting Matlack was easy. The hard part was getting him signed.

The amateur draft was still in its infancy in 1967 (the first draft was held just two years prior), and there was a silly rule on the books: Any player on an American Legion team could not sign until after his season ended, something that seems ridiculous in retrospect. Major League Baseball did this to appease the nervous American Legion, who worried that the draft would rob the organization of its best players midseason. It prevented Matlack from negotiating a deal and signing quickly, something he wanted to do. His father was suffering from intestinal cancer and the family could have really used the money. Most pitchers couldn't negotiate until July, but Matlack's team made the playoffs, further holding things up until late August when he was finally able to sign with the Mets.

❖   ❖   ❖

Matlack was briefly sent to Double-A Williamsport to close out 1967, mostly because Williamsport was close to home, but he began his minor league career in earnest at Class-A Raleigh-Durham of the Carolina League in 1968. He was as good as advertised, going 13–6 with a 2.76 ERA and striking out an impressive 188 batters in 173 innings while walking just 66. Matlack had passed his first test as a prospect with flying colors.

---

1. *Baseball America*, Aug. 1967, p. 74.
2. Ibid.

The Mets felt comfortable enough with his progress that they had Matlack skip Double-A entirely to pitch at Triple-A Tidewater in 1969. While the Mets were off winning their first championship, Matlack was getting his first taste of adversity as a baseball player. His walk rate held steady, but the strikeout rate withered away, from nearly 10.0 per nine inning to a meager 5.0. His ERA rose to 4.14. It wasn't the end of the world; he was still only 19 years old with just one full season of experience under his belt, pitching against hitters four and five years his senior.

He returned to Tidewater in 1970 and this time around the strikeout rate improved. Unfortunately, his trademark control took a step backward. After walking 66 batters in 176 innings the year before, Matlack walked 90 in 183 innings in 1970, while the ERA stayed the same. Matlack was repeating the level, so it was perfectly reasonable for the Mets to begin to question his ability. Ideally, you'd hope to see a stronger performance in a top prospect repeating a level. On the other hand, he was striking out more hitters, a strong indication that he was being more aggressive with his curveball.

In 1971, Matlack returned to Tidewater for the third straight season and this time he improved across the board. The strikeout rate rose again. His walk rate was even lower than it had been at Raleigh-Durham. But the ERA didn't budge a whole lot due to what we now recognize as a fairly high batting average on balls in play (BABIP). That probably had more to do with shoddy glove work behind him at Tidewater than any deficiency on Matlack's part. The Mets called him up for the first time on July 11, 1971 to pitch the second game of a doubleheader against the Reds after Jerry Koosman went on the disabled list with "tightness in his left side." Before the game, catcher Jerry Grote strode to the mound and asked Matlack if he was nervous. When Matlack answered in the affirmative, Grote assured him that things would be okay: "Look, don't give 'em any runs, and I guarantee you a tie."[3] Grote lied. Matlack gave up two runs in seven strong innings and still got his no-decision. Unfortunately, he had a few weak outings after that and was sent down once Koosman's left side healed in mid-August.

It seemed like Mets farm director Joe McDonald might have been fooled by the subtleties of Matlack's performance in Triple-A and by his so-so stretch as Koosman's replacement. In an interview with Peter

---

3. *Baseball America*, Aug. 1997, p. 81.

Gammons in September 1971,[4] he commented that Matlack "still might make it, but time's running short." It was an odd statement since Matlack was just 21. Whatever he meant, it wasn't a vote of confidence from one of the organization's highest ranking officials. The team recalled Matlack a second time to make one September start against the Pirates. He pitched great, holding the Bucs to just one run over eight innings of work, though he failed to pick up his first career win since the Mets needed 15 innings to score a second run. It was to become a familiar theme in Matlack's career.

The next spring, after a winter of pitching in Puerto Rico, Matlack knew he had a good chance of making the team out of spring training. He pitched well but at no point was he told he had been added to the roster. Instead, he watched the clubhouse dwindle little by little, and on the final day of spring training, he counted the uniforms left sitting in the lockers. Twenty-five. Then Matlack looked around and quickly counted the men in the room changing. Twenty-four. He was the twenty-fifth. The whole time, Gil Hodges stood in the doorway, a ghost of a smile sitting on his face as he watched the wheels turning in Matlack's brain as he tried to count the moving players. Finally, he walked to his office and, as he passed Matlack, said, "That's right, kid. You made it."[5] Hodges died on a West Palm Beach golf course just a couple days later.

❖   ❖   ❖

The best seasons by a Mets rookie, according to WAR:

ALL-TIME ROOKIE METS: WAR LEADERS		
PLAYER	YEAR	WAR
Jerry Koosman	1968	6.8
Jon Matlack	1972	6.7
Tom Seaver	1967	6.4
Dwight Gooden	1984	5.4
Ron Darling	1985	4.4

Jon Matlack was very, very good in 1972. He was also just 22 years old, which was the best news of all for the Mets. The Mets had a crowd-

---

4. *Baseball America*, Sep. 1971, p. 55.
5. nydailynews.com/sports/baseball/mets/2008/11/29/2008-11-29_where_are_they_now_exmet_jon_matlack_can.html (http://nydn.us/11MID)

ed pitching staff—Nolan Ryan had just been traded away, but Tom Seaver, Koosman, Gary Gentry, Buzz Capra, and Jim McAndrew were still around—so Matlack opened the year in the bullpen. By the end of April he was back in the rotation once new manager Yogi Berra decided he needed a fifth starter. Matlack was an instant success. In his first start, against the Dodgers on April 28, Matlack went the distance while allowing just one run. He faced the Dodgers again on May 10 and threw a second complete game. The next time out he pitched into the ninth inning. He threw another complete game after that, and two starts later he tossed his first career shutout in a game against the Phillies. Matlack went 6–0 with a 1.99 ERA and four complete games in his first seven starts. He wasn't striking hitters out, but he wasn't allowing walks or home runs either.

In his next outing he threw a clunker. The wheels could have come off after that, but instead Matlack might actually have been better than he was at the start of the season. Over his final 24 starts, Matlack's strike-out ratio climbed from 4.6 per nine innings to 6.7, while his walk rate and ERA held steady. The only thing that worsened was his run support, so despite a 2.24 ERA over those 24 starts, Matlack only went 9–9.

In another season, Matlack might have had a strong argument for more than just the Rookie of the Year Award—which he won easily over Giants catcher Dave Rader (.640 OPS) and teammate John Milner (.762 OPS)—but for the Cy Young also. Unfortunately, Steve Carlton had the best year of his career, earning 27 of his team's 59 wins with a sub-2.00 ERA to take the prize unanimously. Matlack finished third in Pitcher WAR, fourth in ERA and ERA+, seventh in FIP, 10th in strikeouts, sixth in shutouts, and seventh in home run rate. But he was tied for last in Cy Young votes with zero. At 15–10, he just didn't have the wins. As for the award he did win, years later Matlack would be modest: "Maybe if you looked around the league there weren't enough rookies who did well, so there really wasn't a whole lot of competition."[6] While he was right about it being a weak year for rookies, it does not change how historic Matlack's season was. Only 14 rookie pitchers since 1901 have had a WAR as high as his, and of those 14, eight debuted during the dead-ball era. It was one of the six best rookie pitching performances since 1915.

If Matlack's rookie season was great, his sophomore campaign was merely very good, although it did have a sweeter ending. Much like his second season in Triple-A, he improved his strikeout rate—he crossed

---

6. *Baseball Digest*, Aug. 1997, p. 83.

the 200-strikeout threshold while doing so—at the expense of his walk rate. His ERA rose all the way to 3.20. What was most impressive about Matlack's 1973 season, however, was his resilience and toughness. On May 8, Matlack was hit in the left temple by a line drive off the bat of the Braves' Marty Perez. He was back on the mound in 11 days. He threw a one-hitter a month later. And after struggling for the first three months of the season, Matlack had a 2.57 ERA and struck out 128 batters over 140 innings from June 30 onward. The ERA placed him sixth in the NL over that time period, and the strikeout rate paced the league. It was admirable how well he adapted after finding adversity for the first time in his major league career.

In the 1973 NLCS Matlack pitched the game of his career. The Reds that year, as in most other years, had an extremely potent offense: Johnny Bench, Joe Morgan, Pete Rose, Tony Perez, plus useful offensive players like Ken Griffey, Davey Concepcion, and Dan Driessen. It was the definition of imposing. But for all the Reds' firepower, the only man to get a hit against Matlack in Game 2 was Andy Kosco, a veteran journeyman enjoying the last productive season of his career as a pinch-hitter for the Reds. The Mets won in five, and Matlack was given the Game 1 start in the World Series against the A's.

"The World Series was anticlimactic." Matlack would later say. "There was such tension and pressure in the [NLCS] that the series was almost matter-of-fact by comparison."[7] Felix Millan committed an error that led to two unearned runs in the opener, although most of the embarrassment stuck with Matlack: Both runs came off the bat of opposing pitcher Ken Holtzman, who doubled after Matlack fell behind in the count. The Mets lost the game 2–1. He rebounded to win Game 4 almost singlehandedly, 1–0, throwing eight great innings, and was given the nod to start Game 7. Many thought Berra should have started George Stone in Game 6 and pitched Seaver on full rest in Game 7, but Matlack was the hot hand and Berra wanted his aces to pitch as many games as possible. In interviews after the game, Matlack thought that he had pitched well—especially against Bert Campaneris, who swung at a terrible pitch and somehow knocked it over the wall for his third home run of the Series—but that the A's just came alive all at once. "The first two innings, I was getting away with mistakes, but in the third, they didn't miss any mistakes."[8] The A's won 5–2.

---

7. Peter Golenbock, *Amazin'*, p. 314.
8. *Baseball Digest*, Jan. 1974, p. 30.

No matter the final outcome, Matlack did his job in 1973, both in the regular season and in the playoffs. The best was still yet to come.

❖   ❖   ❖

The top NL pitchers in 1974, based on WAR:

1974 NL PITCHING WAR LEADERS		
PITCHER	TEAM	WAR
Jon Matlack	New York Mets	8.6
Phil Niekro	Atlanta Braves	7.5
Jim Barr	San Francisco Giants	6.2
Tom Seaver	New York Mets	5.7
Buzz Capra	Atlanta Braves	5.2
Lynn McGlothen	St. Louis Cardinals	5.2
Andy Messersmith	Los Angeles Dodgers	5.2

Matlack was a perfectionist in the way he dressed and the way he worked out and the way he pitched. I can still picture his motion, bringing his arms up in front of him, just far enough that he could see through the vee in the bottom of his two hands, and that's the way he pitched. He didn't have an overpowering fastball—not as hard as Seaver and myself, but he was still in the 90s, and he had an excellent curveball and real good control. Putting that all together, Jon was tough to hit.[9]

Jerry Koosman said that about Matlack in Peter Golenbock's *Amazin'*, and it sums up the kind of pitcher Matlack was. When he was at his best, when the curve was breaking just right and there were no hangers, hitters didn't stand a chance. Matlack was so precise with his location that an opposing hitter would have no idea where to expect the ball to go, even if he knew what pitch was coming. Batters might as well have been blindfolded. And in 1974, hangers were few and far between.

There were several reasons for Matlack's success. For one, he stopped giving up home runs. He was normally stingy in that regard, but he only allowed eight in 265 innings that season. That rate was the third-best in all of baseball. The 265 innings ranked seventh in the NL, and his 195

---

9. Peter Golenbock, *Amazin',* p. 314.

strikeouts put him fourth. He also placed in the top ten in walk rate and finished second in strikeout-to-walk ratio. His 2.41 ERA was 49% better than the league average. He threw 14 complete games and he led baseball with seven shutouts. Between his dominance and his durability, Matlack was certainly the best pitcher in the NL. But his record stood at just 13–15 and he did not receive a Cy Young vote.

The Mets in '74 scored 3.53 runs per game. Only the Padres scored fewer, and just one other team was below four runs per game. Worse, the Mets averaged just 3.15 runs in Matlack's 34 starts. In September Matlack made seven starts, averaged more than eight innings a start, and had a 1.74 ERA. His record was 2–5. The team lost twice by a score of 2–1 and twice by a score of 3–2. Shutouts secured the month's two victories. Had Matlack played for the Dodgers or the Reds that season and pitched just as well, it's easy to imagine him winning 25–28 games and taking home the Cy Young Award that went to Dodgers reliever Mike Marshall.

From 1972 through 1974, Jon Matlack had a 2.64 ERA, good for sixth in baseball over that time frame. He was tenth in strikeouts, third in home run rate, fifth in shutouts, sixth in WAR. Matlack was certainly one of the ten best pitchers in the game, and possibly one of the six or seven best. Heading into 1975, his career record stood at 42–44.

❖   ❖   ❖

Matlack was never as good again, but he was arguably the best number-three starter in the game. His ERA rose to 3.38 in 1975—for the first time, home runs had become a small problem for Matlack—but his FIP stayed low at 2.87 thanks to the league's third best strikeout-to-walk ratio. The highlight of the season may have come when he was co-MVP of the All-Star Game. He threw two scoreless innings and struck out four.

In 1976 Matlack received Cy Young votes for the first and only time of his career, finishing sixth in the balloting. He went 17–10 with a 2.95 ERA while throwing 262 innings. Despite the national recognition, it wasn't nearly his best season. His strikeout rate dropped for the fourth straight season, plummeting well under 6.0 per nine innings, and his home run rate never regressed to its pre-1975 levels. On the bright side, Matlack's control was as good as it had ever been, and he once again took the NL shutout crown. It was still a fine season, but the drop in strikeouts was a clear warning sign.

By Opening Day 1977, Matlack had thrown 1,279 big league innings plus another 689 minor league innings. He was consistently among the league leaders in complete games, and you can only expect a pitcher to stay healthy for so long with that kind of workload. Not everyone is as durable as Nolan Ryan. Matlack's shoulder started to give out in 1977 and his performance suffered as a result. He went 7–15 with a 4.14 ERA and was shelved for most of September. Privately, Matlack wasn't doing anything to endear himself to ownership, either.

After Tom Seaver was traded in June, Matlack made it clear to Joe McDonald, now the general manager, that he wanted to see the Mets make moves to bolster the team's major league roster. If the team wasn't willing to do that, he'd prefer to be elsewhere. Before the December 1977 winter meetings, McDonald and manager Joe Torre called up Matlack and asked if he still wanted to be traded. Matlack affirmed that his preference was to stay with a winner in New York, but he could read their disappointment: They were looking for an excuse to trade him. Matlack, like Seaver and Koosman, was always known for his preparation before games. Now, he readied himself for bad news. During the meetings, McDonald, Torre, and Rangers owner Brad Corbett began working on a deal for John Milner. Eventually Ted Turner and a delegation from the Pirates joined in on the negotiations. After eight hours of talks, the teams finalized a four-team, eleven-player deal which sent Matlack to the Rangers. He would later quip, "You [needed] an atlas to follow the trade."[10] The Mets gave up Matlack and Milner and received former All-Star Willie Montanez and outfielders Tom Grieve and Ken Henderson.

The trade was a disaster for the Mets. Montanez started for the Mets at first base in 1978 and posted an OPS of .712. Grieve batted .208. Henderson was traded away in May after hitting just .227. Matlack would go on to have one of his best seasons, pitching to a 2.27 ERA despite bad team defense behind him. He wasn't throwing as hard anymore, but he had successfully transitioned into a complete control artist. He mixed in a changeup more often, and he went from a guy who didn't walk many to a guy who walked virtually no one. He even finished with a winning record at 15–13. Again, though, Matlack was one of the best pitchers in the league and received no recognition for it because his team stunk. No one was taking the award from the 25–3 season that Ron Guidry, but a top three finish for Matlack may have been warranted.

---

10. nydailynews.com/sports/baseball/mets/2008/11/29/2008-11-29_where_are_they_
   now_exmet_jon_matlack_can.html (http://nydn.us/11MID)

In 1979, the heavy workload caught up to Matlack and he blew out his elbow. The injury would require Tommy John surgery. He returned to the team in 1980 as a capable workhorse, but he wasn't the dominant pitcher he had been. Of course, he was never really given the chance to return to form, either. The players went on strike in 1981 and Matlack served on the negotiating committee. There was speculation that Rangers ownership resented Matlack's role in the union, and after a mildly disappointing 1981 season his status with the team was unclear. Confused about his role, he turned to Rangers vice president Eddie Robinson, who informed him he was no longer penciled into the rotation. He also told him, "We're not thinking about trading you. On the other hand, nobody is bringing up your name."[11] Matlack stuck around for two more seasons and retired after being released by the Rangers in 1983.

Since then, Matlack has stayed active in the game. He spent a year playing in the Senior Professional Baseball Association in 1990, acquitting himself well with a 10–2 record. He also started coaching in 1987, first in the Padres organization and eventually with the White Sox. In 1996 he was named the Tigers' pitching coach but resigned with three weeks left in the season due to personal reasons. Ever since, he's served as the Tigers' minor league pitching coordinator.

In the end, almost all of Matlack's career value came during the stretch from 1972 to 1978. It wasn't a particularly long run, but over those seven seasons he finished seventh in shutouts, ninth in ERA+, 10th in Pitcher WAR, and 13th in strikeout rate. The names ahead of him on these lists include Tom Seaver, Jim Palmer, Bert Blyleven, Steve Carlton, Nolan Ryan, Gaylord Perry, and Ferguson Jenkins. Matlack certainly did not have the career length to warrant Hall of Fame consideration, but he was in Hall of Fame company during his peak years. It does make you wonder how differently Matlack would be remembered if modern voting mentalities were in place in the 1970s. Maybe he wouldn't have any additional hardware, but Matlack did have the misfortune of running up against some very unique seasons in baseball history—Carlton's 1972, Marshall's 1974, Guidry's 1978—and the voters' tendencies haven't changed that much, at least not yet. It does seem likely that he would have had more top five finishes, though.

But it's the enduring memory that would be different. Matlack is

11. sportsillustrated.cnn.com/vault/article/magazine/MAG1125392/index.htm
(http://bit.ly/hQhfIS)

eighth among all Mets in WAR, ahead of more spoken names like Keith Hernandez, Sid Fernandez, Howard Johnson, Mike Piazza, Jose Reyes, Al Leiter, Gary Carter, and Mookie Wilson. That doesn't mean he's the eighth-best Met of all time, nor does it mean he was better than all those ranked behind him. But it certainly puts him in the argument, an argument few fans make these days. The reason for that is simple: perception. Nobody thought of him as an elite player in the 1970s, despite him playing at an elite level for several years. And perception is passed down from generation to generation, until the memory just slowly fades away.

So Matlack's name slips from memory. He's remembered as a number-three starter, notable solely for not being Tom Seaver or Jerry Koosman. In a strange way, he has long since ceased to be Jon Matlack, his identity inextricably tied to the men who overshadowed him.

CHAPTER TWENTY

THE 2006 METS, THEN AND NOW

WILL LEITCH

Of the last decade, no New York Mets team made an impact like the 2006 Mets. That team blasted through the NL East with 97 wins, breezed past the Los Angeles Dodgers in the NLDS, and looked well on its way to the World Series. Then So Taguchi and Scott Spezio and Yadier Molina and Adam Wainwright happened.

Greg Prince, one of the bloggers at Faith and Fear in Flushing, has a famous theory he calls "The Legacy of Yadier Molina." In that NLCS, the Mets—fielding their most exciting, most dominant team since the days of Gooden and Strawberry—lost in the most heartbreaking fashion imaginable to the aging, 83-win St. Louis Cardinals, thanks mostly to a ninth-inning home run by the Cardinals' catcher off the since-exiled Aaron Heilman. The reason it hurt so much was that was the definitive Mets team: young, fun, energetic, loopy. The Mets were supposed to be sleek and streamlined.

David Wright was the all-American, the Mets version of a young Mantle—smiling, chiseled, shining. Carlos Beltran had overcome his own Mets drama, staving off a previous season of boos to look like the all-around superstar the Mets thought they were getting in the first place. Carlos Delgado was the quixotic, fascinating slugger, the political activist who spoke out against President Bush and the Iraq War and, before coming to New York, famously refused to stand for "God Bless America." And standing as the symbol of it all was shortstop Jose Reyes, a hyperactive 23-year-old wunderkind whose pure joy at playing the game of baseball was exceeded only by the joy of those watching him slide headfirst into third after knocking one into the Shea Stadium gap.

Then, Molina's homer. With that loss, Prince wrote, "the Mets dug themselves into a hole from which they've never climbed out. It's always October 19, 2006. Ownership and general management has proceeded as if this is forever a World Series club in every sense but that of accomplishment." Omar Minaya acted like his team was perpetually one piece away, while other pieces, the ones he wasn't looking at, slowly eroded.

We sense you nodding your head along.

This offseason, the Mets finally cleaned house, firing Minaya and Jerry Manuel, bringing in new blood and, at last, putting that 2006 season behind them. Sandy Alderson and his crew are being patient and looking at the past few years dispassionately. They no longer see the Mets like they were in 2006... just... one... pitch... away. They're starting over.

That doesn't mean we should forget that 2006 team, though. Let's take a look back at each player on that team, what they were then, and where they are now.

As you'll see, a lot can change in five years.

❖   ❖   ❖

BRIAN BANNISTER

Then: Became first ever Brooklyn Cyclones pitcher to make the big leagues with the Mets. Was traded after the season to Kansas City for Ambiorix Burgos.

Now: Pitching in Japan. An avid photographer, he had a gallery show of his Royals teammates showing for weeks in Kansas City.

HEATH BELL

Then: The third year of an endless shuffle between Shea and Norfolk. He ultimately spent eight largely fruitless years in the Mets' organization.

Now: Closer for the Padres. Led the National League with 42 saves and was named to the 2010 All-Star team.

CARLOS BELTRAN

Then: Tied Mets single-season record with 41 homers and also stole 18 bases. Notched a .981 OPS, the best of his career. Struck out against Adam Wainwright to end the NLCS.

Now: Still with Mets. His arthritic right knee has cost him much of his athleticism and power. In the final year of his seven-year, $119 million contract.

CHAD BRADFORD

Then: Submarining right-hander who threw five scoreless innings in the NLCS.

Now: Out of baseball. Currently coaching high school baseball in Mississippi. Is being portrayed by actor Casey Bond in the upcoming *Moneyball* movie.

RAMON CASTRO

Then: Backup catcher who lost a chance to start when the Mets traded for Lo Duca. Missed large swaths of the season with injuries.

Now: Backup catcher for the Chicago White Sox. Caught Mark Buehrle's perfect game in 2009, just one of 20 men in baseball history to have done so.

ENDY CHAVEZ

Then: Defensive-minded outfielder who hit .306 that season, a career high. Leapt over the Shea Stadium left-field wall to bring back a sure Scott Rolen homer, ensuring his immortal place in Mets lore.

Now: Out of baseball. Tore his anterior cruciate ligament in a game for the Mariners in July 2009 and never played in the majors again.

CARLOS DELGADO

Then: After coming over in an offseason trade from the Marlins for Mike Jacobs, Yusmeiro Petit, and Grant Psomas, he smashed 38 homers. Was the team's best player that postseason, including three homers against the Cardinals.

Now: Out of baseball but hoping to get back in. Finished his four years with the Mets with a hip ailment. Briefly signed with the Red Sox at the end of the 2010 season but never made the majors. Is attempting a comeback this season but has not been signed by any team.

VICTOR DIAZ

Then: Traded to Texas for catcher Mike Nickeas in August.

Now: Out of baseball. Was once projected by a WFAN radio personality to have a better career than David Wright or Jose Reyes.

MIKE DIFELICE

Then: Occasional backup catcher. Batted .080.

Now: Out of baseball. Manager of the Mets' Rookie-ball team in Kingsport.

PEDRO FELICIANO

Then: LOOGY specialist signed from the Fukuoka Softbank Hawks in Japan before the season.

Now: Reliever for the New York Yankees. Led the majors in appearances for the Mets in 2008, 2009, and 2010. He's currently second in all-time pitching appearances for the Mets in franchise history, behind John Franco.

CLIFF FLOYD

Then: As usual, battled injuries all season. Pinch-hit in the ninth inning of NLCS Game 7 and struck out in his last at-bat as a Met.

Now: Out of baseball. Played 10 games as a Padre in 2009 before retiring. Now an analyst for Fox Sports Florida.

BARTOLOME FORTUNATO

Then: The wonderfully named Fortunato came over in the Zambrano-Kazmir trade. He pitched three innings in 2006 and gave up nine runs. He still somehow ended the year with a 1–0 record.

Now: Out of baseball. Pitching for Bridgeport Bluefish of the Atlantic League.

JULIO FRANCO

Then: Signed a two-year contract with the Mets before the season even though he was 47 years old. Became the oldest man in baseball history ever to pinch run. Went 0-for-2 in the NLCS.

Now: Out of major league baseball, finally. Spent a total of 31 years in professional baseball.

TOM GLAVINE

Then: Had his best season as a Met, going 15–7 with a 3.82 ERA. Pitched wonderfully in the Game 1 of the NLDS—inspiring Albert Pujols's infamous "he wasn't that good" quote—but lost Game 5.

Now: Out of baseball. He'll be in the Hall of Fame soon, but it won't be for what he did as a Met. Will never be forgiven for the final game of 2007, when he notched only one out in a game the Mets needed to win for a postseason spot. Did earn his 300th win with the Mets, though.

GEREMI GONZALEZ

Then: Started three games and managed no decisions despite a 7.71 ERA. Was traded to Milwaukee midseason.

Now: Tragically died after being struck by lightning in 2008 at the age of 33.

SHAWN GREEN

Then: The 2006 team's biggest disappointment. Hit .240 after the All-Star break and never approached his highs in with the Dodgers. Did bat .304 in the NLCS.

Now: Out of baseball. Retired after the Mets declined his option for the 2008 season.

AARON HEILMAN

Then: Frustrated by not being named a starter, he was still solid in relief. Then he gave up the homer to Yadier Molina in Game 7. Amazingly, pitched two more years for the Mets after that.

Now: Reliever for Arizona. Still frustrated he's not a starter.

ANDERSON HERNANDEZ

Then: A speedster defensive specialist who couldn't hit, he most famously pinch-ran for Paul Lo Duca in the ninth inning of NLCS Game 7 as the potential winning run.

Now: Houston Astros reserve infielder. He'll be fighting for a roster spot this spring.

ORLANDO HERNANDEZ

Then: Traded to the Mets by Arizona early in the year, he had 20 starts and pitched so well he was handed the Game 1 NLDS start. Tore a calf muscle running pregame sprints, though, and was left off the postseason roster.

Now: Out of baseball. 82 years old.

ROBERTO HERNANDEZ

Then: Came over in the Xavier Nady-Oliver Perez trade. Made three appearances in the NLCS and didn't give up a run.

Now: Out of baseball. Pitched in more than 1,000 games over his 16-year career and made the All-Star game twice.

PHILIP HUMBER

Then: One-time hot prospect—the third pick of the 2004 draft—pitched two scoreless innings in September.

Now: Reliever with the Chicago White Sox. Fighting for a roster spot. Best known to Mets fans for his costly loss in the pennant chase in September 2007.

JORGE JULIO

Then: Appeared in 27 games and even earned a save. Was traded to Arizona in May for Orlando Hernandez.

Now: Out of baseball. Pitching for Bridgeport Bluefish of the Atlantic League.

RICKY LEDEE

Then: Claimed on waivers in August. Batted 36 times and had three hits, one a homer.

Now: Out of baseball. One of only three men to play for all four current and former NYC franchises, the Mets, Yankees, Giants, and Dodgers. Jose Vizcaino and Darryl Strawberry are the others.

JOSE LIMA

Then: Started four games and was hammered in all four of them. Ended season with a 9.87 ERA. Never pitched in the majors again.

Now: Tragically died of a heart attack in 2010 at the age of 37.

PAUL LO DUCA

Then: Hit .318 but with only 24 walks in 551 plate appearances. Considered one of the team's "emotional leaders."

Now: Out of baseball. Was accused in the Mitchell Report of writing a bounced check for HGH. Now working as an analyst for a horse racing TV network.

JOHN MAINE

Then: Brilliantly outdueled Chris Carpenter to win NLCS Game 6 and force a Game 7. Had a 2.63 ERA in three postseason starts.

Now: Non-tendered by Mets at the end of the 2010 season, he was still looking for work, perhaps with Philadelphia, at press time.

ELI MARRERO

Then: Came over in Kaz Matsui trade but was released by the Mets two months later.

Now: Out of baseball. Perhaps most noteworthy to Mets fans as one of the two players (along with J.D. Drew) the Cardinals traded to get Adam Wainwright.

PEDRO MARTINEZ

Then: Slipped in the dugout while changing his shirt in May and wasn't the same the rest of the year. Didn't pitch after September because of a torn rotator cuff and a torn calf muscle.

Now: Out of baseball. But you never know with Pedro.

KAZ MATSUI

Then: Hit a home run in his first at-bat for the third consecutive season. No longer playing shortstop at this point, and heavily booed by the Shea faithful, he was traded to Colorado for Eli Marrero in June.

Now: Back in Japan. Had a terrific season for Colorado in 2007, helping them reach the World Series. Sidelined by an anal fissure after signing with the Astros in 2008 and was never the same.

LASTINGS MILLEDGE

Then: The future. Only 21 years old, made his major league debut in May and hit his first major league homer in July, a game-tying blast off the Giants' Armando Benitez in the bottom of the 10th inning. As he returned to his position, he high-fived some Shea Stadium fans, angering manager Willie Randolph. In September, veteran closer Billy Wagner put a sign on his locker saying, "Know Your Place, Rook." Was not on the postseason roster.

Now: Traded by the Mets after the 2007 season to Washington for Ryan Church and Brian Schneider, then later sent to Pittsburgh. Signed a minor league deal with the White Sox in February. Still only 25 years old.

XAVIER NADY

Then: Desperate for pitching after injuries to Pedro Martinez and Duaner Sanchez, the Mets traded Nady, their starting right fielder, to Pittsburgh in July for Oliver Perez and Roberto Hernandez.

Now: A reserve outfielder for the Arizona Diamondbacks. Won a World Series ring in 2009 with the Yankees despite his season ending after seven games due to injury.

DARREN OLIVER

Then: LOOGY specialist. A godsend in NLCS Game 3, throwing six scoreless innings after Steve Trachsel left. Almost named to start Game 7, but lost out to Oliver Perez.

Now: Reliever for Texas Rangers. Has pitched in 19 postseason games since 2006, including every postseason since, for the Angels and the Rangers.

HENRY OWENS

Then: Threw four innings and gave up four earned runs. Was traded to Florida after the season.

Now: Out of baseball. Was suspended 50 games for a PED offense after the 2008 season but has never returned to the majors to serve it.

MIKE PELFREY

Then: Big Pelf started four games in July and August and won two of them, at the age of 22.

Now: Expected Mets opening day 2011 starter. Won 15 games last year, with a 3.66 ERA

OLIVER PEREZ

Then: A panic trade late in the season, he was lousy for the Mets, notching a 6.38 ERA in seven starts. Then, shockingly, he pitched his best game as a Met in NLCS Game 7, nearly sending the Mets to the World Series.

Now: Still a Met. Sorry. Just one more year and $12 million to go, folks.

JOSE REYES

Then: Hit .300, the only time he's yet done so in a full season, led the league in stolen bases and triples, made his first All-Star team, and finished seventh in MVP voting. He also hit 19 homers and drove in 81 runs, both career highs. His .841 OPS was also the best of his career.

Now: Still a Met. Has struggled with injuries but was reasonably healthy last year, at least in the second half. Never became the superstar many predicted, but he's still only 27. He's a free agent after this year.

ROYCE RING

Then: One-time big prospect was on the big league club for only three weeks.

Now: Reliever for Seattle Mariners. Fighting for job in spring training. Pitched five games for the Yankees in 2010.

DUANER SANCHEZ

Then: Young pitcher who was terrific until a taxicab accident in July—caused by a drunk driver—separated his shoulder and ended his season.

Now: Out of baseball. He was never the same after the accident and now pitches for the Sussex Skyhawks in the Atlantic League.

ALAY SOLER

Then: Sent back to the minors after being rocked by the Yankees in an interleague game.

Now: Out of baseball. Never made the majors again after that game.

KELLY STINNETT

Then: Yet another backup catcher. Had one hit.

Now: Out of baseball.

STEVE TRACHSEL

Then: Earned 15 wins with the Mets, but few fans. Left NLCS Game 3 in the second inning and never pitched for the Mets again.

Now: Out of baseball. Still taking an hour between pitches, though.

MICHAEL TUCKER

Then: Promoted by the Mets as outfield insurance when Cliff Floyd went on the DL. Had two hits in five at-bats against the Cardinals.

Now: Out of baseball. Last seen playing for the Southern Maryland Blue Crabs in the Atlantic League.

JOSE VALENTIN

Then: Played the majority of games at second base. Led off the ninth inning of NLCS Game 7 with a single but was stranded on third base.

Now: Out of baseball. Fouled a ball off his tibia in May 2007 and never played again.

BILLY WAGNER

Then: Another of the team's emotional leaders, he earned 40 saves with a 2.24 ERA. Gave up a crushing homer to So Taguchi in NLCS Game 2, though.

Now: Out of baseball. Retired after another outstanding season with the Atlanta Braves in 2010. Still not a fan of Lastings Milledge.

DAVE WILLIAMS

Then: Somehow started five games for the Mets in August and September. It didn't go well, with a 5.59 ERA, though he did go 3–1.

Now: Out of baseball. Pitched for the Mets twice in 2007 to the tune of a 22.50 ERA. That was all for him.

CHRIS WOODWARD

Then: One-time utility wunderkind was injured much of the year. Hit .216.

Now: Seattle Mariners minor leaguer. With three different teams, he still hasn't hit better than .216 since playing with the Mets.

DAVID WRIGHT

Then: Hit 26 homers and co-led the team with 116 RBI, including a team-record 74 at the All-Star break. In August, signed a six-year contract extension worth $56.5 million. Struggled mightily in the NLCS, hitting just .160.

Now: Still a Met. Had the best season of his career in 2007 but suffered an odd, seemingly Citi Field-related power outage in 2009. Rebounded to hit 29 homers last year. Like the team, he still has not had a chance for postseason redemption in the intervening years.

Victor Zambrano

Then: Not Scott Kazmir. Had Tommy John surgery in May. All told, though, wasn't that horrible with the Mets in 2005.

Now: Out of baseball.

❖   ❖   ❖

They may have broken our hearts, but they're still the most important Mets team in 10 years, and should not be forgotten.

These Mets were brash but respectful, fresh but experienced, playful but focused. This was the team that was going to end Mets fans' suffering. It had to be them. At the very least, they were the start of something. Not the end.

But maybe, after all, the future wasn't what everyone thought it would be.

CHAPTER TWENTY-ONE

'ROUND MIDNIGHT

MATTHEW CALLAN

A s I watched Game 5 of the 2000 World Series for the first time
in 10 years, one moment stuck out more than any other. Once
the final out was recorded, and the Yankees celebrated on the field as
the Mets fixed thousand-mile stares on them, there was no prerecorded
music, nothing blaring over the PA system that had so terrorized the
FOX crew all series. At that moment, Shea Stadium's organist took over,
choosing a wistful tune to play: Thelonious Monk's "'Round Midnight".

It might have seemed an odd choice at the time, or maybe oppres-
sively literal—the last out was recorded almost exactly at the stroke of
midnight—but in retrospect it was appropriate. The clock had struck 12
for the 2000 Mets—not just for their season, but their reputation.

It is an article of faith among many Mets fans that the 1999 team,
despite not winning the NL pennant, was vastly superior to the 2000
one. The stated reasons are almost universally emotional. The 1999 team
had a certain something that the 2000 team did not. Arguing against fan
reactions like these is like trying to box a ghost. And having studied both
teams closely over the past few years, I'm not sure I want to argue against
them. Colored by the passage of time, the power of nostalgia, and What
We Know Now-isms, I simply like the 1999 team better.

I have a soft spot in my heart (and head) for the 1999 Mets, because
that was the team which drew me back to baseball after spending most
of high school and college ignoring sports. Apparently, I was not the
only one. When I examined the season at length, game-by-game, for
"The 1999 Project" at my own website, I received loads of feedback from
people who fell in love with this team as much as I had. Invariably and
without any prompting, they would also profess to loving the 1999 Mets
more than the 2000 Mets.

But the question then becomes, why? Why does a team that made it
deeper into the playoffs get the short end of our memory stick?

The first reason is related to the folkways of Mets fans. Every fanbase
has its mythos, the thing it believes deeply about its team and itself. The
Cubs are Lovable Losers. The Steelers are Blue Collar. The Flyers are

The Broad Street Bullies. Details that fit into such definitions are celebrated. Everything else is secondary to the mythos.

The Mets' myth is one of miracles. They are the team of improbability. When they win, they win in unimaginable ways that would be cut from a B-movie script. They overcome impossible odds, pull victory from the jaws of defeat, make heroes of men formerly unknown. When they lose, they do so in heart-wrenching, punch-in-the-gut fashion. There is no in-between.

How true is any of this? As true as any other myth. It says more about the believer than it does about reality. The important thing is that, by these criteria, 1999 is the quintessential Mets season. The team had a largely anonymous pitching staff, an outfield of interchangeable parts—one of which was a future Hall of Famer enjoying his penultimate productive season—and two former strike replacement players.

There were plenty of superstars on the 1999 Mets, too, Mike Piazza being the prime example. But the stars often take a backseat in our memories of that season, since it is more fitting for the Mets myth that we focus on the unlikely and unglitzy aspects of the team. Though their offense was better than most people remember—fifth in the NL in runs scored while playing their home games at spacious Shea, league leaders in both OBP and OPS+—they were most celebrated not for their bats but their gloves, an often-neglected, unglamorous aspect of the game.

That summer, *Sports Illustrated* put Robin Ventura, John Olerud, Edgardo Alfonzo, and Rey Ordonez on its cover and asked, "The Best Infield Ever?" Even the phrasing as a question fit perfectly into the team's identity, as if *SI* could barely believe it themselves: Can these people possibly make up the best infield ever? Are you kidding me? Really?

Throughout 1999, the Mets made noise about overtaking the mighty Braves in the NL East. They went into a late-September series in Atlanta only one game behind in the standings, but a sweep at the hands of the Braves, with each loss coming in crushing fashion, destroyed any dream of first place. It began a seven-game losing streak that also dropped the Mets out of the lead in the Wild-Card race.

At the tail end of the seven-game slide, the Mets lost two of three at Shea to the Braves and stood two games out of the playoff picture, surpassed by the Reds. The Mets resurrected themselves with a sweep of the lowly Pirates—and some help from the even-lowlier Brewers, who took two of three from Cincinnati—taking the last game in a walk-off when a wild pitch allowed Melvin Mora to score the winning run in the bottom of the ninth. They then travelled to Cincinnati for a one-game playoff to determine the NL Wild Card, a game they won thanks to a complete-game shutout by Al Leiter.

For an encore, they immediately went to Arizona for the Division Series to face Randy Johnson—who struck out a mind-boggling 364 batters that year—and proceeded to hang seven runs on him. They lost slugger Mike Piazza for the series with a thumb injury, then saw his backup, former pizza-delivery manager Todd Pratt, win the clincher with a walk-off home run that *just* eluded the glove of center fielder Steve Finley.

And then the Mets had to take on the Braves yet again in the NLCS. They dropped the first three games, playing a brand of anemic, mistake-filled baseball they'd avoided all season. Then, suddenly, it seemed as if they had the Braves right where they wanted them. Game 4 was a Mets win after the team came back against the reprehensible John Rocker. Game 5 dragged on and on into the night, the Mets' bullpen holding on until the top of the 15th, when the Braves finally scored a run against Octavio Dotel. Naturally, as if preordained by the myth, the Mets rose from the grave in the bottom half, loading the bases, walking in the tying run, and winning on what would forever become known as the Grand Slam Single.

Back in Atlanta for Game 6, ace Al Leiter, pitching on short rest and a bum knee, was knocked out of the game in the first, not recording an out before the Braves scored five runs. Slowly, the Mets crawled their way back into the game and tied it on an opposite-field homer by Piazza—still recovering from his thumb injury and a concussion suffered earlier in the series—off of John Smoltz in the seventh.

The Mets went ahead for the first time in the eighth, and dreams of a Game 7 looked like they might come true. But Atlanta tied it in the bottom half. In the 10th, the Mets went ahead again, but, again, the Braves tied it in their half of the inning. The Mets luck finally ran out, for the game and the season, when trade-deadline acquisition Kenny Rogers walked in the winning run in the bottom of the 11th.

If you're a Mets fan, you probably know all of this already. I'm recounting it only because I can barely believe any of it myself. And I have yet to mention any of the Bobby Valentine-related drama that occurred that season. His infamous Dugout Disguise Incident, when he snuck back into the dugout after an ejection by using a pair of fake glasses and a Groucho Marx-style painted mustache, is only the tip of the iceberg.

The 1999 team's insane highs and insane lows seem, in retrospect, almost admirable, as if their wings melted from flying too close to the sun. I've always thought 2000 suffers in the collective fan memory because it came so soon after 1999, a season with which few others can compete. But when I reviewed the 2000 season on a game-by-game basis, I found it wasn't the drama-free walk in the park that my memory believed it was.

The 2000 season began with two games in Japan, the second won on a Benny Agbayani grand slam, a homer that probably saved his major league career. John Rocker made his return to Queens after an off-season interview in which he slammed New York in his inimitably ignorant fashion, necessitating the presence of several hundred of New York's Finest. During the series, the Mets enjoyed a cathartic 10-run rally against the Braves on Fireworks Night. They also put up their biggest Subway Series win to date with a 12–2 drubbing of the Yankees in the Bronx. After a torrid month of August, they flirted with first place before another September swoon forced them to enter the playoffs via the Wild Card.

The playoffs began in typical Mets fashion. After losing to the Giants in Game 1 of the Division Series, they won three games in a row, all nail-biting classics. Game 2 saw the Mets overcome a ninth-inning Armando Benitez meltdown, surge ahead in the top of the 10th, and win it when John Franco struck out Barry Bonds looking. Back at Shea, they won Game 3 by rallying against the formerly untouchable Robb Nen, then capped it off with a walk-off homer by Agbayani in the bottom of the 13th. They clinched the series the next afternoon thanks to heroics from another unlikely source, the soft-tossing Bobby Jones, who somehow pitched a complete-game, one-hit shutout.

But compared to 1999, some found their path to the playoffs wanting. Many sportswriters took the Mets to task for "settling" for the Wild Card—still a relatively new innovation—considering it only slightly better than a participation trophy. Dave Anderson of *The New York Times* griped, "The Wild Card is baseball's consolation prize. You don't celebrate a consolation prize. You just accept it." Mets GM Steve Phillips went so far as to say the team would not celebrate on the field when they clinched. Despite another September swoon, the Mets won that consolation prize easily, thus avoiding a reprisal of the near-death experiences from the year before.

Then came the NLCS against the Cardinals. Despite a positive outcome and the appearance of some of the loudest, most raucous crowds in Shea Stadium history—they literally made the ballpark rock—it was an ugly affair. Only one game was close (Game 2) and even that was marked by fielding errors and the skin-crawling implosion of Rick Ankiel. Though every Mets fan feared facing the Braves again, their absence removed much of the drama—and certainly the revenge factor—from the series. Thanks largely to the pitching of Mike Hampton and the out-of-nowhere emergence of Timo Perez, the Mets made short work of St. Louis in five games.

That brings us to the World Series and the second reason why the 2000 team is not as well remembered: their opponent.

The 2000 Mets became little more than a conduit through which the Yankees could fulfill the mythos of their fanbase—that the 2000 Yankees were a continuation of the dynastic teams of 1998 and 1999. The Mets also allowed Roger Clemens to redeem himself to Yankees fans and thrust himself into the pantheon of True Yankees, a place he stayed until his post-retirement public downfall.

When a team loses a championship title, at least in a one-team town, the local coverage is usually sympathetic, complete with scattered sentiments of "Oh, well, we'll get 'em next time!" The 2000 Mets were never afforded such a luxury. They would be compared unfavorably to the Yankees for the next few months and perhaps forever. Their fans, surrounded by partisans of The Enemy, would never have a chance to salve their wounds. Instead, they would have to hear from everyone—including fellow sufferers—how their favorite team had failed.

The narrative that emerged—the only one that could—is that the Mets simply did not belong on the same stage as the Yankees. That they should have been grateful to share the field with this latest Yankee Dynasty. "In the end, the Mets were not the Subway Series' Little Engine That Could," Murray Chass wrote in the type of assessment that would soon be repeated ad nauseam by many of his compatriots. "They couldn't because the Yankees were the Super Chiefs... Torre's team became champions again, and Valentine's turned into pumpkins."[1]

Some of this talk was prompted by the Mets' play in the World Series. Game 1, for example, featured several key mistakes and blown opportunities by the Mets which may have cost them the game. But just a month earlier, most writers were singing a different tune.

---

1. nytimes.com/2000/10/27/sports/on-baseball-the-winners-and-still-champions. html (http://nyti.ms/giTJFl)

Throughout 2000, the Yankees looked nothing like the two-time defending world champions. Injuries, age, and malaise caused them to sleepwalk through the regular season, as they captured the division virtually in spite of themselves with just 87 wins. The collective New York sports press raked the Yankees over the coals for losing the swagger and luster of their recent past, for looking like they couldn't be bothered to care about what happened between the lines from April to September.

After the division "clincher," during which the Yankees were pummeled by the Orioles—the Red Sox eliminated themselves with a loss to the Rays—Chass's *Times* Jack Curry wrote of the eventual world champs,

> *The Yankees have been complacent, a team plodding toward the postseason while the regular season unfolds and they unravel. Did anyone ever speculate that Joe Torre would want to switch places with Bobby Valentine in late September? Yesterday afternoon, Torre would have.*[2]

Clemens took the brunt of the criticism. The Yankees traded for him prior to the 1999 season, dealing away the enormously popular (and popularly enormous) David Wells to Toronto. Thanks to this, The Rocket had two strikes against him before he even threw a pitch for the Yankees, and his spotty record—particularly in the 1999 postseason—did not help matters. He was not horrible by any means. He simply wasn't the otherworldly player the fans had expected him to be.

Worst of all, the Mets pummeled him in each of his first three starts in pinstripes. After the Mets torched him for eight runs on June 9—including a grand slam by Piazza—he was booed off the mound by the Yankee Stadium crowd. The tabloids compared him unfavorably to the Mets' catcher, who thrived in the same spotlight that wilted the pitcher. After Joe Torre chalked up Clemens's Subway Series struggles to "the pressure of living up to yourself," Mike Lupica of *The Daily News* opined, "Piazza has done just fine with it, hasn't he?"[3]

The next time Clemens faced Piazza—during the Bronx leg of a two-stadium doubleheader—he beaned the catcher in the head with a 92-mph fastball. Piazza suffered a concussion and was forced to miss the

2. nytimes.com/2000/09/30/sports/sports-of-the-times-real-yankees-need-to-stand-and-deliver.html (http://nyti.ms/fbHy9y)

3. nydailynews.com/archives/sports/2000/06/10/2000-06-10_real_apple_star_s_drive_take.html (http://nydn.us/eXJlzW)

All-Star Game. Few outside the Yankees' clubhouse thought it was unintentional, but those within it bristled at being questioned about the incident. Derek Jeter was asked after the game if the controversy had truly ended, since the two teams would presumably not play each other again that season. The future captain played dumb and simply said, "Why wouldn't it be over?"[4]

As it turned out, they would face each other again, on the biggest stage baseball has to offer. A dream matchup between the Mets and Yankees drove the collective sports press crazy with hype, speculation, and nostalgia for Subway Series of yore. The Yankees wanted none of it. Compared to the Mets—who were quite chatty with the press, sometimes to their detriment—the Yankees were as tight-lipped as humanly possible. When they deigned to address reporters' queries, they acted aggrieved and annoyed at every line of questioning, particularly the Clemens-Piazza subject.

More than anyone else, Clemens bristled at the questions, as if he were the one who had been beaned. After a mediocre Division Series against Oakland, he'd finally pitched a playoff gem for the Yankees with a complete-game, one-hit shutout against Seattle in Game 4 of the ALCS. In a familiar refrain, Mariners shortstop Alex Rodriguez complained about nearly getting hit in the head by one of The Rocket's fastballs. "I guess his control was a bit off," he said sarcastically after the game.[5] At the time, this was generally considered sour grapes.

Clemens thought he'd finally proved himself on a big stage and was angered by the questions about Piazza's success against him. And though he admitted no wrongdoing for hitting Piazza, he publicly expressed displeasure for being painted as the villain of that incident. During the World Series, FOX analyst Tim McCarver recalled an interview he did with Clemens just after the beaning incident. "I don't care if Mike Piazza respected me or not," Clemens said in a voice McCarver described as "devoid of emotion." Clemens continued, "I'm not out there to get a hitter's respect."

That became undeniably clear in Game 2 of the World Series. In his first at-bat against Clemens since getting beaned, Piazza broke his bat on a foul ball, the bulk of the lumber skidding toward the mound. As

---

4. nydailynews.com/archives/sports/2000/07/09/2000-07-09_on_track_for_subway_sweep_su.html (http://nydn.us/g9TQMP)

5. sportsillustrated.cnn.com/baseball/mlb/2000/postseason/news/2000/10/14/lockerroom_mariners_game4 (http://bit.ly/ikq3Nj)

Piazza jogged up the first base line to run out the foul, Clemens picked up the fat end of the bat and heaved it into the catcher's path, splinters flying everywhere.

Benches emptied and harsh words were exchanged, but no further violence was committed. Clemens protested then—and forever after—that he mistook the bat for the ball, despite the million or so reasons why this is laughably transparent. Amazingly, Clemens was allowed to stay on the mound. Given tacit approval for his outburst, he dominated the Mets, striking out nine and limiting them to three hits over eight shutout innings.

Clemens's act was heinous and inexplicable, but in terms of games-manship, it was brilliant. It put the Mets in a no-win situation. Retaliate and they would lose some of their best players for who knows how many games while also looking like a bunch of animals. Not retaliating meant looking impassive, uncaring, and weak.

The Mets chose the latter, and before the game had even ended, people questioned their drive, their passion, even their manhood. During the FOX broadcast, analyst Bob Brenly wondered why Piazza "hadn't charged the mound more forcefully." To this day, despite Clemens's public fall from grace after a host of PED-related accusations which began with the Mitchell Report, it still doesn't take long to find people who will tell you that his bat-throwing act was a sign of his—and the Yankees'—fortitude and the Mets' "failure" to respond a sign of the exact opposite.

Torre said as much in the post-game press conference when he threatened to walk out after reporters were incredulous that he believed Clemens's excuse of mistaking the shattered bat for the ball. He chalked up Clemens's act to drive and fire. "If some guys take that competitiveness and put another tag on it, then I can't help it. These guys have a need to win."[6] Clemens himself griped about how the bat-chucking episode overshadowed his performance. "I can't believe this. We win Game 2 in the World Series, and all they ask about is this shit," he whined, as if he had been an innocent bystander and not the instigator.[7]

In his excellent article on Clemens's perjury indictment, Joe Posnanski watched the bat-chucking incident again and noticed that the pitch-

6. nydailynews.com/archives/sports/2000/10/24/2000-10-24_can_t_root_for_damn_yankees.html (http://nydn.us/dT4QB0)
7. sportsillustrated.cnn.com/baseball/mlb/2000/world_series/news/2000/10/22/pearlman_game2ws/ (http://bit.ly/iff6TT)

er made no effort at an apology.[8] As Piazza screamed at him, Clemens ignored the man he almost assaulted and instead plead his case to the home-plate umpire. His main interest was not to atone, but to get over. Piazza had become a mere footnote to The Rocket's quest, and the Mets no more than a speed bump on the road to a Yankees championship.

When George Steinbrenner complimented the Mets and their fans for their good behavior during the Series—"We were treated so well, and our people could walk around by themselves with no problems."[9]— it came across as a veiled insult, as if the visiting team should have been treated more roughly. *The Daily News* celebrated Yankee Stadium's aptly named Bleacher Creatures every day for engaging in behavior more befitting caged animals.[10] Mets fans hadn't done anything like that during the World Series. The story then went that they, like the team they rooted for, must also have lacked the heart of a champion.

After the Series, the Mets were offered a chance by Mayor Giuliani to participate in a massive parade honoring both teams. They were smart enough to decline. "It should be the Yankees' day of celebration for winning the World Series," GM Steve Phillips explained. "They deserve the stage to themselves."[11] One can only imagine the howls of derision that would have followed the Mets if they'd accepted the Mayor's offer, allowing themselves to be presented to the public like treasures from Gaul carried forth by Caesar's armies.

In the accelerated pace of the 21st century and the highlight-driven, ESPN-style sports world, entire seasons—and sometimes entire eras—need to be distilled to bite-sized pieces. For those purposes, the 2000 Mets are mentioned only as side note in the monolithic depiction of the 1998–2000 Yankees. This does a disservice to the 2000 Yankees, who are actually more compelling in light of their regular-season struggles.

But more than anything else, the 2000 Mets had to be diminished in our collective memory because they were the sacrificial lamb that enabled Roger Clemens to become a True Yankee. After the 2000 World Series, few fans or writers questioned his pinstriped bona fides. He now

8. joeposnanski.si.com/2010/08/19/the-indictment-of-roger-clemens-2 (http://bit.ly/cSSmOl)
9. nytimes.com/2000/10/27/sports/sports-of-the-times-a-not-so-hostile-take-over-at-shea.html (http://nyti.ms/fy0TFp)
10. nydailynews.com/archives/news/2000/10/23/2000-10-23_not_hail_fellows_well-met.html (http://nydn.us/ifSpLy)
11. nydailynews.com/archives/news/2000/10/28/2000-10-28_amazin_s_to_skip_yankees___r.html (http://nydn.us/fmUzot)

fit perfectly into the Steinbrennerian ideal that proclaims winning to be its own excuse. Anyone who questioned his tactics was a sore loser who questioned Excellence itself.

Clemens milked a Brett Favre-style retirement tour for all it was worth in 2003, drawing cheers and tears as each subsequent start at Yankee Stadium looked as if it would be the last of his career. Despite changing his mind and pitching for the Astros shortly thereafter, he was able to make a dramatic return to the Bronx in 2007 in which he was welcomed with open arms. Later that year, Clemens received an elegiac *Yankeeography* from the YES Network, thus equating him with greats like Mickey Mantle and Yogi Berra.

Of course, Clemens has now had his fall from grace. Does that mean the 2000 Mets deserve a rehabilitation? If so, they haven't received it. In 2010, the Mets invited some members of the 2000 team to Citi Field during the interleague Subway Series to celebrate the 10th anniversary of winning the pennant. Many people—even Mets fans—laughed at the idea. Why would they bother to celebrate a team of failures?

Since sports are zero-sum games with only one winner, essentially all teams that don't capture a championship are failures. That seems to be a horrible way to look at baseball. And life. At the end of the day, sports are entertainment. A team's job is not to achieve success on our behalf, no matter how many fans act otherwise. It is to engage us, interest us. Pull at our heart strings. If a favorite movie doesn't win the Oscar for Best Picture, does that mean it "failed?"

Baseball seasons are like productions. Some are undeniable triumphs. Others flawed but courageous. Some truly are failures. But 1999 and 2000 do not fall into this category. They're like ambitious films with some amazing performances and memorable scenes. As a whole, maybe they don't "work," but they remain worth watching, worth admiring.

I still have a prejudice in favor of 1999 over 2000, but I firmly believe both seasons were successes. My heart goes out to anyone who thinks otherwise.

CHAPTER TWENTY-TWO

GLAVOTAGE

JAMES KANNENGIESER

"I can't stand it, I know you planned it." —Beastie Boys, "Sabotage"

In the early evening of September 30, 2007, Tom Glavine spoke with reporters about the disastrous results of Game 162. Said Glavine: "I'm not devastated. I'm disappointed. Devastation is for much greater things in life."[1] For the thousands of Mets fans who had endured the 9–2 drubbing at the hands of the Marlins, few things in life were of greater import. For a short time, at least. Glavine was disappointed. Mets fans were destroyed.

That final game of the 2007 collapse is still a sore subject for Mets fans, but that hasn't stopped the Amazin' Avenue community from theorizing what really happened to Glavine that day. Were the Marlins fired up from the previous game's festivities (recall the Jose Reyes-Miguel Olivo dust-up at third base)? Maybe, but so were the desperate Mets. Did 41-year-old Glavine simply run out of gas? Also possible, but 44-year-old Jamie Moyer tossed a gem down I-95 that day to help the Phillies beat the Nationals and clinch the NL East title. Random variation and bad luck are other reasonable explanations. But there is a more sinister conspiracy theory which explains Glavine's meltdown and also some of his Mets career: *glavotage*, a mash-up of "Glavine" and "sabotage."

Creation of the Glavotage Theory was a group effort by members of the Amazin' Avenue community. It evolved somewhat naturally and eventually a proper definition came about:

The act of sending a player to a rival team with the express purpose of destroying said team from within.

❖   ❖   ❖

---

1. nbcsports.msnbc.com/id/21067818

Glavine spent five seasons with the Mets. He signed a four-year, $42.5 million contract prior to the 2003 season, then later agreed to a one-year, $10.5 million deal which kept him in Queens through 2007. A dreadful debut—a 9–3 pounding on Opening Day 2003—and even worse finale bookended a seemingly respectable run in Flushing. He compiled a 3.97 ERA, won his 300th career game in 2007, and did well for himself and his team in the 2006 postseason.

Still, there was something fishy about the career-Brave's tenure with the Mets.

Entered into circumstantial evidence as Exhibit A for the Glavotage Case is Glavine's performance against the Braves as a Met. For his career, he tossed at least 100 innings against 15 different teams. Against those teams, he posted the worst numbers against the Braves in the following statistics:

- ERA, 5.15
- WHIP, 1.51
- Strikeout rate, 3.5 strikeouts per nine innings
- K/BB ratio, 1.00
- Home run rate, 1.50 home runs allowed per 9 innings
- Winning percentage, .267

Against non-Braves opponents, Glavine enjoyed a terrific 3.82 ERA. Against the Braves, he transformed into Alay Soler. Glavine spent much of his career owning the Mets, to the tune of a 2.82 ERA and a long-bemoaned 7-inning shutout in Game 3 of the 1999 NLCS. Hopes that he could bring his rival-domination skills to the Mets were dashed time after time.

Exhibit B is the aforementioned Game 162 from 2007.

Exhibit C consists of unsubstantiated chatter, a staple of any conspiracy theory worth its salt. Glavotage proponents assert that Glavine had a hand in many of the Mets' key problems which began in 2003. Examples:

- Urging Jim Duquette to trade Scott Kazmir for Victor Zambrano.
- Hinting to Omar Minaya that Marlon Anderson and Julio Franco needed to be locked up to multi-year deals.

- Expressing to Mets talent evaluators that Heath Bell was too hittable, despite his gaudy peripherals

- Telling Mets scouts and player-development officials that college relievers are the next big thing.

- Pointing out to Billy Wagner that rookies should know their place.

- Introducing the Wilpons to Bernie Madoff.

Such insidious actions slowly devastated the Mets, although none could be directly pinned on Glavine. Sort of like Nurse Ratched subtly demoralizing the patients in *One Flew Over The Cuckoo's Nest*. The quiet and unassuming appearance of professional competence masked a systematic dismantling of the promising Mets organization.

The Braves were reportedly unwilling to offer Glavine any more than a two-year contract when he became a free agent in 2002. This is generally given as the main reason for his departure to New York. The conspiracy theorists posit that this was simply a cover for the nefarious Glavotage Plan. Glavine was an aging—but not ancient—36 years old at the time. He was the epitome of health, rarely missing a start during his career. Why would the Braves let one of their all-time greats go to a division rival when he was still an effective pitcher? Specifics of the conspiracy have yet to be confirmed, but in the name of imagination, I'll give it a shot:

> *Glavotage was conceived by highly successful Atlanta Braves GM John Schuerholz during the 2002–2003 offseason. The Braves won the NL East for the 11th consecutive season in 2002, finishing with a stellar 101–59 record in a mediocre division. Chipper and Andruw Jones were performing at Hall of Fame levels, while Greg Maddux, Glavine, and John Smoltz continued to anchor a dominant pitching staff. Youngsters Kelly Johnson and Wilson Betemit were well-regarded prospects in the organization, both on the cusp of contributing. All signs pointed to continued success for the Bravos. But Schuerholz worried.*

> *The Hall of Fame-caliber pitching triumvirate was aging. Outfielder Gary Sheffield and catcher Javy Lopez would likely*

leave via free agency in short order. On top of all that, the NL East was filled with teams on the rise. Phenoms Josh Beckett and Miguel Cabrera were ready to hit the big leagues, improving an already-talented young Marlins team. The Phillies boasted a pair of top pitching prospects in Brett Myers and Gavin Floyd. Outfielder Marlon Byrd and infielders Chase Utley and Ryan Howard also bolstered a strong Phillies farm system. Jose Reyes, Scott Kazmir, Aaron Heilman, and a then-unheralded David Wright had the Mets, and their mighty checkbook, looking primed for a decade of dominance.

Schuerholz realized he could no longer focus solely on improving his team. He needed to find a way to subvert his rivals. Billy Beane and the Oakland A's had Moneyball; Schuerholz had Glavotage. Glavine was tasked to sign with the Mets and perform the following responsibilities:

1. Tank games against the Braves.

2. Choke in any do-or-die spots.

3. Covertly undermine the organization from top to bottom.

These were to be done while pitching well enough overall to remain in the Mets' rotation. Upon successful completion of the mission, Glavine would have a lifetime job waiting for him in the Braves' organization, either as a player or executive. He agreed, and easily checked tasks No. 1 and No. 3 off the list.

He had too much pride to blow his starts in the 2006 playoffs, much to the chagrin of Schuerholz. But Game 162 of 2007 offered the ultimate opportunity to atone, and Glavine came through. The Mets went into a tailspin after that game, as their on-field and off-field embarrassments piled up in subsequent years. Glavotage accomplished.

Glavine then signed a one-year contract with the Braves prior to the 2008 season and eventually became a special assistant to Schuerholz, now the Braves' team president.

A lesser-known but mildly successful part of Schuerholz's secret rival-destroying plan was the trade of Kevin Millwood to the Phillies during the 2002–2003 offseason. The Braves received 26-year-old replacement-level catcher Johnny Estrada *in return for Millwood, a two-time 18-game winner. It seemed one-sided, but sabotage was the motivation. Let's call this portion of the Glavotage Plan "Operation Killwood". Millwood completed task No. 1 of the plan—he successfully mailed in his starts against the Braves as a Phillie. In six starts spanning 30.2 innings, he went 0–6 with a 9.10 ERA and 1.00 K/ BB ratio. Even worse than Glavine's performance against the Braves! Unfortunately for Schuerholz, Millwood failed at tasks No. 2 and No. 3. He eventually departed for Cleveland via free agency and ruined any chance at lifetime Braves employment. And the Phillies have dominated the NL East since 2007.*

In reality, there is no hard evidence to back up this cockamamie conspiracy theory. It's less plausible than the Keith Hernandez–Roger McDowell spitting incident in that infamous episode of *Seinfeld*. Glavine had a decent, if a bit awkward, run with the Mets. And to his credit, he has since clarified his "I'm not devastated" declaration. Here he is speaking to *USA Today* in April, 2008:

"If people interpreted that as me not caring, then I'm sorry about that because that wasn't my intent, because I did care about it. I was upset about it. Like I've said many times, it's bothered me more than any game I've ever pitched."[2]

Stuff happens—even Hall of Fame-caliber pitchers have off-days. One of Glavine's worst happened to come at a terrible time, when the reeling Mets needed their starter to at least give them a chance. This is his legacy for many Mets fans. Others choose to focus on the stability he brought to the rotation while wearing the orange and blue. A smaller group sticks with the Glavotage Theory, continuing to be leery of the calculating Braves organization and recognizing Glavine as a pawn in a larger plot. And to any member of the Mets' new front office who counts himself among the conspiracy theorists: Why can't a Mets version of Glavotage be undertaken in the future? Johan Santana will almost certainly be a free agent after the 2013 season and will be 35 years old entering 2014. Maybe the Braves will be in the market for an aging-but-still-effective lefty starting pitcher.

"Santana Subversion", anyone?

---

2. usatoday.com/sports/baseball/2008-04-25-1014599312_x.htm (http://usat.ly/g3o8MG)

Statistics Glossary

About Our Statistics

A s we prepared our player profile section, we realized that we would need to include some statistics. While we could have simply included a write-up on each player, we wanted to provide readers with as much information as possible, and the best way to do that adequately was with carefully selected statistics. We don't want to just tell you what we think about the players on the Mets' roster. We want to empower you to formulate informed opinions.

After deciding that we needed them, we faced another dilemma: Which stats should we include? We feel that the most basic statistics, the ones most people already know, just don't convey enough information. Pitcher wins and losses? They tell you how the team performed when a pitcher started, not how the pitcher performed.

Instead, you'll find more qualitative information in our stat tables. Mike Pelfrey might throw a sinker, but how much of a ground ball pitcher is he? How terrible is Oliver Perez? How many wins does Angel Pagan really add to the ball club? The statistics we included help answer these questions. If you know the terms we use, great. If you don't, we've included this glossary for you. Some of them are basic. Others, not so much. The goal at Amazin' Avenue isn't to alienate anyone, it's to provide people with the knowledge to be an informed fan of the game we all love.

Batting Statistics

G: Games played

PA: Plate appearances. The number of times a player came to the plate.

R: Runs scored

HR: Home runs

RBI: Runs batted in

BB%: Hitter's walk rate. The percentage of a batter's plate appearances that result in a walk. A direct measure of patience.

K%: Hitter's strikeout rate. The percentage of a batter's plate appearances that result in a strikeout. While strikeouts themselves are only slightly more damaging than any other kind of out, they, in conjunction with walk rate, provide you with an idea of how disciplined a hitter is. This is especially helpful when evaluating young players and prospects.

AVG: Batting average. Plain ol' hits divided by at-bats. The NL average was .255 in 2010.

OBP: On-base percentage. This is how often a player reaches base safely based on his number of plate appearances. Put another way, it's how often the player does not make an out. A player who never makes an out will have a 1.000 OBP. The average NL OBP was .324 in 2010.

SLG: Slugging percentage. The average number of bases a player gains per at-bat. A player who homers in every at-bat will have a 4.000 SLG. The NL average was .399 in 2010.

BABIP: Batting average on balls in play, or the percentage of balls put into the field of play—plate appearances minus walks, hit-by-pitches, strikeouts, and home runs—that turn into hits. While a high BABIP is more indicative of a skill for a hitter than for a pitcher, a season in which a hitter drastically over- or underperforms his career norm may indicate a fluke season. An average BABIP is around .300.

wOBA: Weighted on-base average, a statistic developed by Tom Tango, is a comprehensive metric that takes all aspects of hitting and weights each one proportionate to its run value (i.e., its correlation to run scoring). Think of it as a superior alternative to on-base plus slugging (OPS), which often makes one-dimensional sluggers look more productive than they are. It attempts to combine on-base and slugging percentages while adjusting for the difference in scale between the two—player slugging percentages are almost always higher than on-base percentages despite on-base ability leading to more runs. wOBA then puts the whole result on a scale roughly equivalent to on-base percentage. An average wOBA is .330. Terrible is .300 or lower. Great is .400 or higher. For instance, Josh Hamilton had a .447 wOBA in 2010 while Cesar Izturis was way down at .248. One caveat: The numbers are neither park-adjusted nor league-adjusted.

SB: Stolen bases

SB%: Stolen base success rate, or stolen bases divided by attempts. A stolen base, for the most part, only advances a baserunner one base. A caught stealing is twice as harmful as the stolen base is beneficial: It removes a baserunner, but it also adds an out, substantially reducing a team's chances of scoring. Therefore, we like to see baserunners be successful twice as often as they're caught, and that's just to break even. Baserunners caught more often than that are doing more harm than good. An effective baserunner is successful at least 75% of the time.

WAR: Wins above replacement. This represents the sum of a player's contributions on the field—batting, defense, and a positional adjustment—and compares it to what a readily available replacement—say, a Triple-A player—would provide. It presents the result in a win total since wins are the fundamental currency of baseball. Don't get too caught up in what "replacement" represents. It's just meant to give the number a scale by which to compare players. An average player will add about 1.5 wins of value in a full season. A very good one, 4.0 wins or more. Evan Longoria provided 7.7 WAR in 2010; Pedro Feliz, -2.3 WAR.

Pitching Statistics

G: Games pitched

IP: Innings pitched

H: Hits allowed

BB: Walks allowed

K: Strikeouts

BB/9: Walk rate. The number of walks a pitcher allows per nine innings of work. The NL average was 3.3 in 2010.

K/9: Strikeout rate. The number of strikeouts a pitcher averages per nine innings of work. The NL average was 7.4 in 2010.

HR: Home runs allowed. The average NL pitcher gives up about 1.0 per nine innings, though this will fluctuate depending on the home park where the pitcher does most of his pitching.

ERA: Earned run average. The number of earned runs a pitcher gives up per nine innings pitched. While a somewhat useful measure, it is important to note that it also incorporates the quality of the defense behind the pitcher. If a pitcher is working with an outstanding defense, his ERA will be lower. The NL ERA was 4.02 in 2010.

FIP: Fielding-independent pitching. Because most pitchers have very little control over how often balls in play are converted into outs, it's not always easy to evaluate pitchers fairly. Most traditional attempts actually evaluate how the whole defense performs, not just the pitcher—ERA, for example. One way of dealing with this dilemma is to simply remove balls in play from the equation. This is what FIP does. It evaluates a pitcher's ability to get strikeouts, limit non-intentional walks, and prevent home runs. In other words, it isolates the three things pitchers have the most direct control over and presents the result in an ERA-style number for easy understanding. A pitcher with a lower FIP than an ERA may be due to improve and the converse is also true.

BABIP: Batting average on balls in play. The percentage of balls batted into the field of play—all plate appearances that do not result in a walk, strikeout, hit batter, or home run—that become hits. Pitchers have limited control over balls that enter the field of play. As a result, most (but not all) pitchers have a BABIP in the neighborhood of .300. If a pitcher is significantly below that mark, he can reasonably be expected to face a decline the next season unless he's backed by a tremendous defense. Ground ball pitchers also often have lower BABIP numbers. Pitchers with an extremely high BABIP were probably unlucky and can be expected to improve.

LOB%: Left-on-base percentage. This is the percentage of baserunners a pitcher allows that do not score. Generally speaking, good pitchers, especially those who get a fair share of strikeouts, strand a high percentage of runners. The major league average is roughly 70% for starters and 72% for relievers, though better pitchers will consistently exceed that number. If a pitcher leaves more batters on base than his established performance level would indicate, it would make sense to assume he got a little lucky. Likewise, a pitcher who finds more than his usual share of baserunners scoring might just be experiencing a little bad luck.

LD%: Line drive rate. The percentage of batted balls categorized as line drives. About 75% of line drives become hits, so pitchers with high line drive rates can be expected to have higher BABIPs. The average is 18.9%.

GB%: Ground ball rate. The percentage of batted balls allowed that are hit on the ground. Pitchers do have control over their ground ball rates, and a grounder can't go over the fence for a home run, making high ground ball rates advantageous to pitchers. The average ground ball rate is 43.2%.

302

WAR: Wins above replacement. The pitcher equivalent to batter WAR, this version sticks to pitching—there are no fielding or hitting components at all. It uses runs allowed as its foundation and then adjusts for league and park contexts. It computes the number of runs the pitcher saved with no help from his teammates, figures out what an easily available replacement would have done in the same playing time, and presents the difference in an easy-to-understand win total. Like with hitters, the average is around 1.5 WAR and a very good player will accumulate 4 or more. Roy Halladay put up a mark of 6.9 in 2010, and Oliver Perez clocked in at -1.5. Relievers typically put up much lower numbers due to lower inning counts and saves are not given extra credit. Joakim Soria's 3.8 was the best among relievers last year.

ZiPS Projections Explained

ZiPS is a projection system written by Dan Szymborski to project performance in individual baseball players. We have included ZiPS numbers as 2011 data in the statistics table included with player profiles.

The ZiPS name comes from sZymborski Projection System. This system has its basis in the Defense-Independent Pitching Statistics (DIPS) that Voros McCracken developed in 1999. ZiPS was originally designed just for projecting pitchers, but the realization came that forecasting pitchers without doing the same for hitters would be insufficient. Since it was the first attempt at a non-Voros projection system while still utilizing some of the discoveries in DIPS theory, it was decided to name it ZiPS with a lowercase *i* as a way of paying homage to DIPS and the long-gone TV show *CHiPs*.

DIPS is applied to pitcher projections by attempting to predict future Batting Average on Balls In Play (BABIP) based on a number of factors. At its base, ZiPS includes the knowledge, championed by Voros, that there is a very strong regression to the mean for this aspect of pitching. Along with that is information about each pitcher's tendencies to pitch above his team, his natural BABIP tendencies based on information like handedness, whether or not the pitcher is a knuckleballer, and his groundball-to-flyball ratio.

Players in the 24–28 age range have four years of statistics used in a weighted format (8, 5, 4, 3). Players outside that age range have their projections based on a three-year weighted statistic.

Along with that weighting system, the ZiPS formula includes growth and decline curves based on a number of player types constructed from similar characteristics found in large groups. For pitchers, this might be strikeout rate. Batters might be categorized based on their Speed Score,[1] BABIP, handedness, or other attributes.

The playing-time calculation is based solely on recent playing time. ZiPS, as a consequence, only projects injuries to the extent that injuries were reflected in previous playing time. The same is true for how platoon splits impact projections.

While some players may have non-statistical attributes which they contribute to their team, like leadership or an ability to perform well despite nagging injuries, ZiPS is only designed to do what computers do best: run numbers. If someone believes there's a truly compelling reason to ignore a player's projection because of one of the unmeasured factors, it's suggested they follow their gut reaction and only use a computer projection as an initial objective evaluation, not a final prediction.

The net result of all these elements can be seen in a player's projections. It's important to remember that the statistics shown are based on a player reaching the estimated playing time in the majors. For a player with a projection of .230/.270/.400 in the majors, his comparable line might be .260/.320/.450 if he plays in Triple-A, or .290/.360/.500 in Double-A, depending on other factors like the league scoring levels and park factors.

Overall league offense levels, similar to how individual player projections are handled, are based on weighting recent seasons. Doing it this way enables ZiPS to present a player's statistics in formats we are all familiar reading, like projecting a guy to hit .270/.330/.450 rather than saying he should have a batting average 1% better than league average, an on-base percentage 3% below league average, etc.

The value in any projection system lies in its accuracy (or inaccuracy, as is probably the case with most projection systems). ZiPS, freely available since it was published before the 2003 season, is about as accurate as any commercially available projection system. For a quick review of projection-system performance in one season, a list of results for 2006 are available online.[2]

---

1. baseballthinkfactory.org/btf/scholars/ruane/articles/speed_scores.htm
   (http://bit.ly/fjf9OO)
2. baseballthinkfactory.org/files/newsstand/discussion/2006_projection_results
   (http://bit.ly/evFxSG)

ACKNOWLEDGMENTS

ERIC SIMON

Writing, editing, and assembling a collaborative project like the *Amazin' Avenue Annual* on a budget of roughly zero dollars is not nearly as easy as you'd think—or, if you've produced a book like that yourself, exactly as difficult as you think. There are many people whose generosity of time and spirit were poured into this book and to whom very little was promised in return. There are far more people to thank than space or memory will allow, but the following were principally responsible for making sure we had something instead of nothing.

To the impeccably talented crew at Amazin' Avenue, whose love of the team and the craft shine through on every page. You are my friends and my colleagues and this book belongs to you.

To the many wonderful authors who contributed chapters this year, this book would hardly be as colorful, enlightening, or wide-ranging in perspective without your efforts. You are enviably insightful and always engaging, and we are better off for your involvement.

To Sean Forman of Baseball-Reference.com and David Appelman of Fangraphs.com for allowing us the use of their wonderful baseball statistics. Also to Dan Szymborski of BaseballThinkFactory.org, who rearranged his ZiPS projection schedule to accommodate our deadline.

To Eric Lent, Lauren Fisher, and Suzanne Lupovici for their legal counsel on matters of which I have neither the first clue nor the last.

To John Costello and Dan Shtob for their angel investments in this project, specifically to ensure that David Wright's properly chiseled mug could appear on the cover.

To Andrew Yankech at ACTA Sports, who boldly broke with the tradition of general interest baseball publications in order to distribute this humble team-specific offering.

To Dave Studenmund, for his advice about bookmaking and all of his work at The Hardball Times.

To Carolyn Simon, my little sister, who took last year's book and a rudimentary understanding of baseball in order to craft a truly indispensable style guide which we referenced throughout the writing and editing processed.

To Alex Nelson, a great friend who has plenty of bylines throughout the book but is recognized here for his tireless editing and sagely advice along the way. He stepped in to read and edit copy when I could no longer bear the thought of it, and all of this after supposedly retiring from blogging.

To Brad Lappin, without whom this book would have turned out quite badly; that is, if it turned out at all. My biggest fear—though simultaneously my great hope—is that someone finally recognizes his talents and rewards them in ways with which we can't possibly hope to compete (i.e., pay him). He has been supportive when we needed it, always ready with a thoughtful suggestion about content, a shrewd marketing idea, or even something we might consider for next year's annual. Too, he has never shied from offering criticism when the situation demanded it of him. This book bears his fingerprints on every page and it is no exaggeration to say that there would be no *Amazin' Avenue Annual* were it not for Brad. He is a genius and a friend.

Finally, to Kimberly Simon, always my love and occasionally my editor, for bemoaning the countless hours I spent working on this book only to become its most tireless champion once it was finished.

ABOUT THE AUTHORS

Eric Simon is a software developer from northern New Jersey and has run Amazin' Avenue since its inception in 2005. His parents had Mets season tickets in 1987 and 1988 and now here we are. When he's not working full-time or watching/writing/thinking about the Mets, he manages the baseball blogs for SB Nation. The rest of his time is spent with his wife, Kim, and their two dogs, Oscar and Riley.

Alex Nelson is a Long Island-based title examiner and freelance writer. A lifelong Mets fan, he was a writer and editor at the Mets Geek blog from 2006 to 2009 before joining Amazin' Avenue.

Sam Page is a New York University student from Nashville, TN. He has written at Amazin' Avenue since December 2008.

James Kannengieser writes for Amazin' Avenue and previously contributed to Mets Geek. He is a CPA from Long Island and is still haunted by the memory of December 15, 1999—the day John Olerud left the Mets to sign with the Mariners.

Rob Castellano is a graduate student and lifelong Mets fan from Putnam County, NY, who joined Amazin' Avenue in early 2010. Aside from getting to 15–20 Mets games a summer, Rob enjoys watching way too much minor league baseball and spending time with his fiancée, Brittany, and their sweet-yet-misunderstood dog, Shea.

Eno Sarris has lived in twelve cities in four countries (at last count), but his love of baseball has endured. He writes for FanGraphs, Bloomberg Sports, RotoWorld, and Amazin' Avenue. He also manages RotoHardball on SB Nation. Fried pickles and David Wright make him smile.

Matthew Callan can be found griping on a daily basis at Scratchbomb. com. You may have seen his writing at *McSweeneys*, the *New York Press*, and *Best American Non-Required Reading*; if so, please return it to him. He is working on a novel as well as a book about the 1999–2000 Mets.

Chris McShane is a Mets fan living in the Bronx who writes for Amazin' Avenue and attends many more Mets game than any sane person should. He likes his beer ice cold and the weather just the opposite.

❖   ❖   ❖

Tommy Bennett writes for Baseball Prospectus and lives in New York. His work has appeared at ESPN.com, Beyond the Box Score, and in several baseball books.

Ted Berg works as the senior editorial producer for SNY.tv, where he writes the popular "TedQuarters" blog. He loves Taco Bell, funk music, and television.

Justin Bopp is a Network Operations Analyst in Kansas City, Missouri, and manages Beyond the Box Score, where he writes, edits, and produces crack sabergraphics for a growing audience. His work has appeared at ESPN.com, MLBTradeRumors.com, and kotaku.com. Despite being a life-long Royals fan, he still loves baseball.

Grant Brisbee is the author of McCovey Chronicles, the San Francisco Giants representative on the SB Nation network. His hobbies include watching the 2010 NLDS, the 2010 NLCS, and the 2010 World Series over and over and over.

Ken Davidoff is the national baseball writer for *Newsday* and has been covering Major League Baseball since 1996. He is currently the president of the Baseball Writers Association of America. A graduate of the University of Michigan, Ken can be seen regularly on *Fox Sports Extra* on Fox 5 in New York.

Jason Fry is the cowriter of Faith and Fear in Flushing. He came of age as a Mets fan in 1976, when his favorite player was Mike Phillips, and now lives in Brooklyn, NY.

Will Leitch is a contributing editor at *New York Magazine* and the founding editor of Deadspin. He is the author of four books: *Life As A Loser* (2003), *Catch* (2005), *God Save The Fan* (2008), and *Are We Winning?* (2010). He lives in Brooklyn.

Satchel Price currently writes as a columnist for SB Nation's Beyond the Box Score. He's also a freshman at American University who desperately hopes to see a contending Nationals team before he graduates.

Greg Prince is the cowriter of Faith and Fear in Flushing, watching the Mets and living to tell about it since 1969. He resides on Long Island but still calls Shea Stadium home.

Joe Posnanski is a Senior Writer at *Sports Illustrated*. He was sports columnist at *The Kansas City Star* from 1996–2009, during which time he was twice named the best sports columnist in America by The Associated Press Sports Editors. He has written three books: *The Machine: The Story of the 1975 Cincinnati Reds*, *The Good Stuff*, and *The Soul of Baseball: A Road Trip Through Buck O'Neil's America*, which won the prestigious Casey Award as the best baseball book of 2007.

Josh Smolow knows that he could never throw a 73-mph fastball. He writes for Beyond the Box Score and The Hardball Times and does occasional work for Amazin' Avenue and MetsMinorLeagueBlog.com. His favorite colors are clearly blue and orange.

Jeff Sullivan writes about the Mariners at LookoutLanding.com and general baseball at SBNation.com/MLB. He can be found in Oregon bars.

INDEX

D

G

M

Y

Z